GORDON STRACHAN

GORDON STRACHAN

A Biography

Leo Moynihan

To my Mum and Dad – thank you so much

First published in Great Britain in 2004 by
Virgin Books Ltd
Thames Wharf Studios
Rainville Road
London
W6 9HA

A catalogue record for this book is available from the British Library.

ISBN 1 85227 205 8

Typeset by Phoenix Photosetting, Chatham, Kent
Printed and bound in Great Britain by
CPD Wales

CONTENTS

ACKNOWLEDGEMENTS VII

FOREWORD BY HOWARD WILKINSON IX

1 FLASH GORDON! 1
2 BLINDED BY A PASSION 6
3 DISCOVERY 21
4 NOT A DANDY DON 32
5 THE NORTH STAR 42
6 NOT BAD FOR A FISHING VILLAGE 72
7 LITTLE AND LARGE 96
8 A UNITED FRONT 116
9 NO REGRETS 130
10 A CHEEKY WEE BASTARD 151
11 THE KEYS TO A RUSTY ROLLS-ROYCE 163
12 MARCHING ON TOGETHER 179
13 BANANAS, PORRIDGE AND SEAWEED 190
14 GOODBYE TO ALL THAT 197
15 LEARNING THE SLIPPERY SLOPES 205
16 SAINTS ALIVE 230
BIBLIOGRAPHY 239
INDEX 241

ACKNOWLEDGEMENTS

I'd like to thank everyone at Virgin Books, especially Vanessa Daubney for giving me the opportunity to write this book, for all her support, patience, for lunch and for not gloating (too much) about her beloved Arsenal.

A special thanks to Justyn Barnes and Sam Pilger for the tip-off, their advice, material and contacts. Cheers, guys. Ken MacAskill for his invaluable help regarding Strachan's schooldays and for the loan of so many great cuttings and pictures, Patrick Barclay for his advice and books, Howard Wilkinson for his time and Foreword, and to Kevin, Lisa and Ruby Taylor, without whose generosity and hospitality I would have been just a homeless Englishman in Edinburgh struggling with the language. I really appreciate it.

I'd also like to thank the following for their enthusiasm, time, knowledge and help in making the writing of this book such an enjoyable experience for me:

Roy Aitken, Arthur Albiston, Matt Allen, Sue Amaradivakara, Ron Atkinson, Jon Bradley, Alan Brazil, Craig Brown, David Burrows, Alec Caldwell, Jamie Cook, John Dickson, Dick Donnelly, Dion Dublin, Dave Forbes at Dundee, Bobby Ford, Roddy Forsythe, Glenn Gibbons, Tommy Gemmell, Chris Haynes, John Hewitt, Ken Hughes, Johnny Giles, Paul Grace, Steve Guise, Joe Jordan, Stuart Kennedy, Archie Knox, Mark Lawrenson, Mick Lawson, James Lawton, Rupert Lowe, Louis Massarella, Kurt McGrath, Eamonn McCabe, Allan McDougall, Mark McGhee, Hugh McIlvanney, Alex McLeish, Billy McNeil, Audrey Mill at Rangers, Alex Miller, Willie Miller, Andy Mitten, Ken Montgomery, Kevin Moran, Candy Moynihan, Rosie Moynihan, Antti Niemi, Steve Ogrizovic, Struan Roger, Andy Roxburgh, Dave Sadler, Ron Scott, Hugh Sleight, Mat Snow, Frank Stapleton, Ravinder Takher, Andy Turner, Claire Walton at Aston Villa, Gordon Wallace, John Wark, Irvine Welsh, Rob Wightman, Tom Wilkinson and Jeremy Wilson.

Finally, a big thank you to my two flatmates, Mark and Rob, for putting up with all the cuttings, books and general mess over the last six months, the Steeles and Admiral Football Clubs for helping take my mind off work, Viren Soma for all the lunches, and last but nowhere near least my eighteen-month-old niece, Layla, for smiling inanely every time anyone said the words 'GORDON STRACHAN'.

Leo Moynihan
June 2004

FOREWORD

There's an old English saying, 'Good things come in small parcels,' and an old Yorkshire saying, 'Tha gets nowt for nowt.' In Gordon's case, both were highly appropriate. Signing him was not easy. He had already spoken to his old pal 'Big Ron' and he seemed certain to go to Sheffield Wednesday. That would cost me an extra £25,000. Very soon after I told Alex Ferguson of our interest, he was back on the phone, telling me Sheffield Wednesday had offered £25,000 more and he'd reluctantly have to ask me to match it. Or at least that's what he said.

Seriously, he was worth every penny. From the moment we met in Leeds United's chief executive's house, I knew he was my sort of player, my sort of person. I explained my dream for Leeds: promotion, then the championship in five years, Europe, youth development, everything. I convinced him that leaving Manchester United did not have to be the beginning of the end; instead it could just be a new beginning.

From the day he joined us, he never short-changed the club or me. My beliefs became his; his values matched mine. He led by example and, when example was not enough, there was always a few well-chosen words: 'King Tongue' could silence anyone. As a player, his contribution to Leeds United's success during his prime there ranks with the greats of the Revie era.

As a manager, he has only just begun, but he has the qualities to go right to the top, if he wants to, that is. In saying that, please don't misunderstand me, I'm not expressing doubts about his commitment, there's no one more committed. But more than just commitment, Gordon truly cares. Players of his stature are constantly in demand, visits to hospitals, openings, good causes and such. Gordon was top of the league when it came to that, but his duty didn't end there. His self-imposed list of extra duties was twice as long as anyone else's, performed quietly, no publicity, no photographs and no interviews.

I remember one youngster who was terminally ill. I'd pop in to see him on Saturday mornings before home games, only to find that Gordon had been there before me, plus perhaps once or twice in the week. That caring extends equally to his friends and family and that means more than football to him. If the cost to them was too great, I think he'd reluctantly refuse to pay that price.

He now needs a top club and if I were a top club's chairman I'd have no hesitation, as he can go on to be a top manager. He has well served his apprenticeship, and my belief is we will see him back very soon. Rod Stewart's team may have to do without its star player!

As a player, he won everything the domestic game has to offer, and he has his rightful place in the history books of Scottish and English soccer. He can now go on to match that as a manager. After all foreign managers have proven how good they can be. I say foreign, because I for one have never understood a single word he says.

Howard Wilkinson

1. FLASH GORDON!

GORDON AFTER ANOTHER FINE PERFORMANCE BY HIS STRIKER JAMES BEATTIE: *I would like to thank James's parents for what they did 25 years ago.*

A monster of a car moves towards the training-ground gates. You know the type: the off-road vehicles favoured on the road by mums doing the school run, and by professional footballers in need of their space. His is a Porsche, a brand like its driver better known for its compact build and wonderful performance. The gates slowly open and the car moves out for the last time. A scattering of autograph hunters are joined today by cameras and microphones. His window slides down as if about to reveal a Mafia Don and everyone at the club is thanked. He's off. 'But, Gordon,' asks one reporter hoping for one last Strachanism, 'why today?'

'It's Friday.' He smiles. 'It's the end of the week.' With that the giant car pulls away into the distance.

Those reporters are strangely going to miss him, and while he can do without them for a little while he will miss the players, to whom he has just had to say goodbye. After training he told the men who had helped him raise the profile of this modest south-coast club that that would be his last session with them. He would see each of them individually to say thank you. 'I was one of the first in,' says his Finnish goalkeeper Antti Niemi, the tough-guy football image betrayed by the clear sentiment in his voice. 'It was emotional. I thanked him for all he'd done. He gave me my chance in the Premiership and I will always be grateful. I hope he knows how much that meant to me.'

So why now? To so many in the game it had seemed that Strachan had found the perfect vehicle. Under Strachan, Southampton had become an entertaining yet resolute team; they possessed one of the newest and most impressive stadiums in the Premiership; they had reached the FA Cup Final, played in Europe and had a number of internationals on the books. It was time, though, to move on. Throughout his successful and charismatic time in the game, Strachan had been like a shark, desperate to keep moving. He has been capable of the unexpected, both with a ball at his feet and with his career choices, and now, well, it seemed he had sold us all another dummy.

He signed for Southampton in October 2001, and on agreeing a two-and-a-half-year contract had promised his wife Lesley that he would take a break. It had got tough during his previous job at Coventry and the short break between jobs was hardly ideal. Strachan was too tempted by the role offered to him by Southampton's chairman Rupert Lowe, too engrossed in a game that had been his livelihood for over thirty years. The problem was he knew that that very same engrossment can also change a man and he was adamant that if that ever happened it was time to take a step back.

That's what he'd done. But there must be an ulterior motive. There must have been a row with Mr Lowe (Strachan once described himself and Lowe as 'the odd couple'); there must have been a better job offer and this was his way of slyly getting out of the club. After all, this is football and this was a season where lies, deceit and wrongdoing had left their soiled footprints all over the game's fragile reputation. While football's celebrities chose to buy bed linen rather than take compulsory drug tests, sit in foreign prison cells rather than play on pitches, and brought the word 'roasting' to football's strange new vocabulary book, a man keeping a promise to his wife was hardly conceivable.

A man putting his family first? That raised eyebrows, but Strachan was sticking to it. Since donning a manager's tracksuit and enduring the stress that comes with the profession, it was clear Strachan would be immersed in the job at hand. It was hard for the role of manager not to change him; always feisty, always first with a quick one-liner, Strachan was now also carrying the weight of a club on those slender but sturdy shoulders. At Coventry he had lost a game on their way ultimately to relegation. The family was expecting visitors on the Sunday but he couldn't get the defeat out of his head. 'A walk will help,' he told Lesley. 'I'll go for a little walk to ensure I'm reasonable company.' Three hours later, Lesley received a phone call from her weary husband. 'I'm seventeen miles away, can you pick me up?'

Things hadn't changed at Southampton and, while he also cited the need for a hip replacement, it was the chance to have a break that was so appealing. 'I'm not saying I'm walking away from football,' he told the press in January 2004 once the news had broken. 'But there are other things I would like to do, though I am not arrogant to think I can take a break and then get straight back into football.'

The season had started with Southampton riding the crest of a wave that had taken the club past the Solent and on to the rich waters of European football. Despite not progressing beyond the first round, the club's fans were hailing their manager as the best since Lawrie McMenemy a whole generation before. Strachan though was aware of his pending decision and, sitting on a plane returning from a game on the Continent, he quietly told his chairman the news. He would be leaving at the end of the season. 'It was a blow,' says Lowe calmly, like an experienced farmer resolved to losing his prize bull. 'Of course it was but that was the contract he had signed so that was that.'

Lowe of course tried to stall any final decision: Strachan could have time to think about it and improved financial packages would be offered, but his mind was made up. This was not about money. The two men agreed that the matter should stay between them, not easy in the modern world, but while it did the team's form could continue to prosper and, with the aid of a 2–1 win at Liverpool, they even ventured as high as fourth before Christmas. Lofty heights had been climbed and the expedition's leader was now an admired man, but as one of the most respected young managers in the country would he plant his flag in Southampton's soil and commit his future to them? Southampton's public and local press had become agitated by a lack of progress concerning their manager's contract and called for the club to sort it out quickly. Theirs was now a stable football club and they wanted it to stay that way.

It wouldn't. A little over a week into the New Year, the *Daily Express* ran the story, 'STRACHAN TO QUIT SAINTS.' It was a huge blow, to the fans, the chairman and to Strachan, who felt let down by the leak. It was going to make life very hard. 'Whilst it was a private matter between Gordon and me, the situation was tenable,' claims Lowe. 'But, once it became common knowledge, it became very difficult for the club. There was pressure on us all, me, Gordon, the players and life was made very difficult. It was a retrograde step that really didn't suit anyone.'

Lowe was right about the players. The club's form had been patchy going into January (a 0–0 draw with Leicester had the opponents' manager Micky Adams admitting he 'was glad he got in free') and it got worse as they managed to win only one of their following five games after the story had gone public. It seemed that the harmony that had secured so many positives over the past year or so was beginning to splutter under the weight of rumour, counter-rumour and speculation. 'Things weren't going well at all,' admits Niemi. 'We had been as surprised as anyone with his announcement and whilst we are professionals and want to play well in every game, whatever the circumstances, Gordon I think was becoming aware that the news had affected some of the lads. That worried him.'

It had become too much. The day after the story broke, reports of Strachan's decision appeared next to possible applicants for the job. Mark Hughes and Micky Adams were immediate 'favourites', and everyone pondered if Strachan would be joining struggling Leeds or Tottenham, or heading home to Celtic or Hibernian. One name stood out amongst the print like succulent fish and chips. Glenn Hoddle, the man who had left Southampton over two years earlier and who had now been sacked at Tottenham, was a candidate. A rumour that sent ripples of dissent around the club's supporters, still squeamish from Hoddle's initial abandonment.

In early February, Strachan and Lowe met and decided that now was the right time for the manager to depart and to let his chairman search for a new man. Lowe likened his role at the club to that of Captain Kirk on the *Starship Enterprise*, but now, without his canny Scottie, who on earth was going to continue to beam the club up to new heights? He was keen on Hoddle, there was no doubt about it, but the reaction from hurting fans was clear. 'Glenn wanted the job,' claims Lowe. 'The way he had left though made it impossible for him to return. I must say that some were pro his return but many were anti it. What you can forget is that people in football have very deep feelings and our fans demonstrated that. If Glenn had come back the club would have been split.'

What was unanimous at the club was the depth of gratitude and admiration that Strachan took with him. Fans inundated the club's website with good wishes and appreciative messages. This wasn't a manager jumping ship. This was a manager proudly and honestly resting his sea-weary legs. Southampton's captain and long-term defender Jason Dodd gratefully said, 'Gordon has had a massive effect on all the players. We cannot underestimate what he has done.' While James Beattie, now the club's star man, said, 'The gaffer has turned around the way in which the club [and he] is perceived.'

While the players pined after him, he couldn't easily forget them. Football raced far too prominently through his veins for that. On leaving that February, Lesley and he took a well-earned holiday to a favourite destination in Florida. As they lay by the pool soaking up the rays – or, in Strachan's pale case, deflecting them – he couldn't keep his mind from swaying across the Atlantic to St Mary's where Southampton were entertaining Everton, their first home game since he had left. Strachan's mobile informed him of the score: 1–0 to Everton, 2–0 at half-time; 2–1, Strachan was fidgeting now; 3–1, it didn't look good; 3–2 and, in the last minute, 3–3. Strachan let out a cheer that made it patently clear to his American companions that their guest was having a nice day.

It wasn't to be the only break that Strachan enjoyed. His was to be a sabbatical, the kind of break usually enjoyed by students trying to find themselves between jobs, and maybe that's exactly what it was. The Strachans visited Milan (although it may have been to study the football as well as the shops), and fulfilled an ambition of travelling around Australia together, unnoticed and unharassed. To those who know Strachan well, though, their instinct is that the game is never far from his mind.

'He's already asked me to arrange if he can go and watch big clubs working,' Andy Roxburgh, UEFA's Technical Director, told me not long after Strachan's decision to leave Southampton. 'It's a working sabbatical. He has been to see top coaches work and that's because he is learning the game. He's very open and always has been to knowledge, which is great. If you want to live with the Wengers of this world, you have to be up to date and take in the wider world. You must adapt ideas and make them fresh. Strachan is like that, a student of the game.'

His players, too, having worked with and been inspired by his enthusiasm, are sure they will soon be up against the man they used to call boss. 'His plan is to have a whole year off,' says Niemi affectionately. 'I would bet my house though that he will take a job very soon. I cannot see him being without football for much longer.' There will be plenty who hope so. 'He is an extremely charismatic individual,' purrs Rupert Lowe. 'He is great fun and has that wicked sense of humour that you can't help but love. Charismatic and unique is how I'd describe him. Football is better with him in it rather than out.'

2. BLINDED BY A PASSION

REPORTER: *You must be delighted with that result?*
GORDON: *You're spot on! You can read me like a book.*

The ball zips across the school's playground like a perfectly skimmed pebble over the ocean. From one end to another, the action flows and, without much regard for shape, formation or any other of the game's annoying little idiosyncrasies, the boys revel in the barely organised chaos that shapes this and every break-time.

A small, red-haired boy moves purposefully from the school building towards the action. Dressed in uniform, pens regimentally placed in his blazer pocket, the boy keeps his head down, avoiding the scary-looking older boys trying to charm a cheeky cigarette off the scarier-looking girls. His short steps pick up as he reaches his goal. 'Where've ya been, Gordie?' cries one player desperate for reinforcements. 'We're getting done 9–3, wee man, get ya arse in here, pal!'

The boy is straight into the action. He takes a pass perfectly and in one smooth action knocks the ball to the far post for his jubilant classmate to pull a goal back. On this concrete arena the boy is king; wee Gordie is a giant. The boy is everywhere, his enthusiasm effervescent and his skill there for all to see. He heckles boys to whom – in the complex world of playground politics – he shouldn't even be talking. Here he has their respect; here he has authority.

An opponent wriggles free and sets off towards goal. Blissfully unaware of the boy stalking him like a small fox, he shapes to shoot. Without breaking his stride the boy stretches, slides and takes the ball from his adversary's feet. The ball is won, but no one notices a pen from the boy's blazer slip out and fly towards his freckly face. The praise ringing in his ears is replaced by a sharp and piercing pain in his eye. Then there is darkness. The school stops as an ambulance hurls itself onto its grounds. 'Gordon's lost an eye,' screams a boy. 'He'll never play for Hibs now!'

Two weeks later a fifteen-year-old Gordon Strachan, whose vision as a professional footballer lit up overflowing stadiums from Motherwell to Mexico City, sits in hospital, his right eye heavily bandaged, wondering if he will ever properly see again. The pen had plunged straight into the socket, damaging the optic nerve and now was the moment of truth. He had recently signed for his boyhood heroes Hibernian, and this could jeopardise his dreams, his passion. All he could think of was Lex Shields. A boy younger than him at school and also a fine player. Hibs had been keen to take on Lex but cooled their interest when discovering he had a glass eye. Was he to suffer the same fate?

The boy, for all his spirit, sits frozen. His parents are with him, gripping his hands as the bandage is slowly removed. Darkness is slowly replaced by blurs, which in turn are replaced by colour and form. The pen had come within a thousandth of an inch of permanently blinding the right eye, but the boy and his parents, momentarily overjoyed with restored vision, soon realise it is a half vision that would remain with him throughout his career. For Gordon Strachan the player, if he were to close his left eye, would be able to see only the top half of the object he was looking at. The future though was the furthest thing from the boy's mind. He was all right; the bandages were off and he would soon be back on that football pitch. That was the most important thing.

Gordon David Strachan was born on 9 February 1957, the first child of Jim and Catherine, a young couple from Edinburgh. The world was changing, its boundaries constantly broadening. The space age began as the Soviet Union launched Sputnik 1, the first artificial satellite; nine black schoolchildren attempted to attend an all-white Arkansas high school, sparking mass riots; and Edinburgh's Duke had the title Prince bestowed upon him by his wife. For a young couple and their child in north Edinburgh, however, the world was a much smaller place.

Jim, Catherine and Gordon had moved into 4/4 Muirhouse Grove, a new council block on Edinburgh's Muirhouse district. Built up in the late 1950s, Muirhouse was a typical Scottish housing scheme. Young working families moved in and settled in a community where morale was high. Among those families living near the Strachans was that of the author Irvine Welsh, today still a resident of Scotland's capital. Welsh, who went on to bring the area and nearby Leith to life in his novel *Trainspotting*, recalls a vibrant place to grow up. 'It was a happy time,' he says. 'It sounds like a cliché but kids would go out late and play, you know jumpers for goalposts and forty-a-side matches.

Throughout the sixties, the spirit was good. It was a real community, with people wanting to make the best of where they lived and make it better. Things turned though in the late seventies and eighties. Thatcher arrived as did mass unemployment and an influx of cheap Pakistani heroin. The place took a bit of a hammering and became a kind of ghetto, branded the drug and AIDS capital of Europe.'

For Strachan as a boy though, his life was simple and routine. Food was always on the table, yet a little more modest as the week wore on. Eating well over the weekend, the quality of the menu would subside with the week before soup and something from the chippy on a Friday.

Catherine worked in the local whisky distillery, but it was Scotland's other great passion that was bestowed upon Strachan by his father, a keen amateur footballer who had had trials with Raith Rovers before earning a living as a scaffolder. Football was ingrained in the community, and, despite not having siblings until the age of eight and the arrival of his sister Laura, Strachan had countless playmates always willing to kick a ball about, build bonfires or bunk onto the nearby Silverknowes public golf course.

It was football though that held Strachan's attention over anything else. His dad had seen to that by whisking his five-year-old boy off to Easter Road, home of Edinburgh's Hibernian Football Club. Hibernian had been formed by Irish Catholic immigrants in 1845, but for the Strachans theirs was a simple love of the club over any religious tendencies. Anyway, it was a proud club to support. Hibs had a rich history in Scottish football, had taken part in the inaugural season of the European Champions Cup and had competed heartily with their Glasgow rivals over the decades. Hibernian's attacking flair had gripped the Scottish game after the war, and Strachan was unfortunate to have been born too late to see their renowned front line, dubbed 'the famous five'. While most children were brought up on Enid Blyton's stories, Strachan, via his enthusiastic father, was weaned on tales whose protagonists Willie Ormond, Bobby Johnstone, Gordon Smith, Eddie Turnball (who would soon become more acquainted with the Strachans) and Lawrie Reilly worked their heroics on the way to bringing three Scottish titles to the capital in the late forties and early fifties.

Those halcyon days might have waned slightly at Easter Road but for the five-year-old Strachan, the atmosphere, smells and banter had him hooked. On that first afternoon it had nearly all gone wrong as his son's eye was immediately caught by the opposition. That first game at Easter Road was prophetically against Aberdeen, and it was their tricky right-sided ball player Charlie Cooke, later of Dundee and Chelsea, who had Strachan – as well as his new team's defenders – well and truly mesmerised. Strachan would soon more than emulate Cooke's feats on Aberdeen's right wing but for all of his tricks it was Hibernian who ultimately cast a spell over the boy.

Strachan moved on to Silverknowes primary school, not far from the Muirhouse estate, and immediately began to shine on the playground with a ball at his feet. It was the mid-sixties and, although the most popular activity for a while at Silverknowes was re-enacting the cinematic hit *Zulu* on the playground with lines of kids playing Michael Caine against the tribal enemy, it was at football that Strachan clearly enjoyed seeing the whites of his opponents' eyes. Mrs Webster's class – of which Strachan was one – would take on Mrs Pemberton's set, and although declaring a severe lack of knowledge when it came to association football his teacher must have had a sixth sense about her young student and requested he pick the team, thus giving him his first managerial role at the tender age of nine.

Standing out for more than his flame-coloured hair, Strachan was playing with boys two years his senior. The school team was run by the janitor Mr Day who would take his eager troops to their matches on the number 16 or 27 bus. With Strachan's precocious talents on board, however, they hardly needed a master tactician in charge. Allan McDougall, a close childhood friend of Strachan and school teammate, recalls their ground-breaking style of play and lets out a mischievous laugh. 'All we had to do was give it to Gordon. He would literally run rings around the other kids and end up scoring or giving me a simple tap-in.'

Grabbing the limelight at Silverknowes, Strachan was noticed by an opposing manager: Tom Aitken, who was also a janitor at the nearby Groathill School. Aitken ran a boys' amateur football club called Edinburgh Thistle, whose catchment area included Strachan's little world in Muirhouse, and Strachan was immediately invited to join. Playing for Craigroysten secondary school while still at primary school, as well as the respected Thistle, earned him almost celebratory status among the boys on his and surrounding estates.

It was a tag that came in handy once his days at the large and potentially frightening Craigroysten secondary school began. A tough place to learn in a tough area, it could be daunting and for many it was, but Strachan had the advantage of being recognised by most. 'That's wee Gordie. Did ya see his goal on Saturday? He'll be bangin' 'em in at the Hibees soon.'

By the early seventies Muirhouse and the surrounding estates of Pilton and Drylaw were becoming less desirable places to live. John Dickson, a team-mate of Strachan at Edinburgh Thistle, grew up in neighbouring Pilton, and, despite also enjoying a young footballer's immunity from aggro, he was under no doubt that trouble lingered around every street corner: 'The likes of Gordon and myself were known footballers so we could walk around the estate with a bit more freedom than others. Our faces were well known as we were doing well for our local teams. It was becoming a rough place to live. We were very lucky in many respects as we grew up and got out before the drugs took control, but even back then there was always trouble and some nasty fights.'

Strachan has attributed his legendary fitness to his constant running to the shops and back as a boy to get groceries for his mum to avoid the hassle. Light hearted as ever, Strachan's words were tinged with a reality regarding a nasty element to the hordes of youths standing around his estate at night. The most unsavoury group came from nearby Drylaw. Young Mental Drylaw, or YMD as they liked to be known, would often infiltrate Muirhouse looking for trouble. 'They were a mad gang,' recalls Dickson. 'A real crazy firm. They were wild and could have held their own on any estate you care to mention. They were vicious and wild and were known for carrying knives.'

The boys were taught menacing ways in which to punch (in self-defence of course) an assailant, with your house keys protruding through each finger for maximum damage. Strachan, though, kept his nose clean and continued to be excused from rival bouts. The extent of his brushes with the long arm of the law would amount to no more than kicking a ball about on the estate's roundabouts. 'People were either good fighters, proper hard cases or they could play football,' says Irvine Welsh. 'You would be labelled by these two skills, or perhaps having the gift of the gab, but that was how you could get some sort of status.'

Strachan was content. His milk round was a source of some pocket money and fitness. Muirhouse had expanded and among the small blocks such as that inhabited by the Strachans sprouted new high-rise towers. Temperamental lifts saw Strachan often carting pints of milk up and down 23 floors to make sure the Muirhouse residents had their tea just the way they liked it. Sean Connery, also a one-time milkman from Edinburgh, by now had become James Bond and would have been proud of his young compatriot's efforts.

Strachan's competitive nature was being nurtured with games of golf (at which he also began to show a strong talent), snooker (if he and his friends could find a hall) and Subbuteo. The table-football game enjoyed by so many young boys was a firm favourite. 'Gordon loved playing and collecting teams,' recalls Allan McDougall. 'We would regularly put on tournaments which turned out to be very well-organised and competitive affairs. It's a shame that none of those young entrepreneurs went on to run the Scottish Football Association.'

His boundless energy, though, meant he liked nothing more than to be outside, dribbling a football or lifting a sneaky little seven iron onto the green but he knew how to relax and as a child loved Elvis. The Beatles may have been all the rage in more fashionable Liverpool and London, but in 4/4 Muirhouse Grove the King reigned supreme and to this day, while the posters have presumably come off the bedroom walls, Elvis lives on in the Strachan household.

He continued to support Hibs with a passion, and hordes of boys from the estates, if not cadging a lift off a passing fan, would get the 16 bus (worryingly painted in the burgundy and white of arch city rivals Hearts) past the Granton district of Edinburgh, along Newhaven and up Leith Walk to Easter Road. For the other passengers it was far from a peaceful journey as the Hibs boys made their presence well and truly felt with their incessant singing, often incurring the wrath of the driver who would threaten them with a long walk. It would take more than an irate bus driver to dampen their spirits, and the boys would alight at Balfour's Bar, just down the road from their beloved stadium. Inside, Strachan's attention was fixated by his heroes: Pat Stanton (who would eventually coach Strachan at Aberdeen), Willie Wilson in goal, Joe Davies, Eric Stevenson, Bobby Duncan, Alec Cropley and Peter Cormack, who went on to win honours under Bill Shankly at Liverpool.

They would eventually all have to take a back seat as Strachan's Saturdays were given over to playing rather than watching football. He could get to Easter Road for the occasional mid-week match, but it was participating that was all-important. The morning game would be for

Craigroysten. Ken MacAskill, an English teacher at the school, however bleary eyed from the night before, picked the team and drove them to away games. Although he never taught Strachan, MacAskill came to know him well as his star player, and his enthusiasm as we chat in a pub not far from his pupil's old stomping ground underlines his pride in playing a small part in a local hero's career. 'When he started playing for us, the call from the opposing touchline would be "stick two players on the wee red-haired feller", and other managers would come over to me afterwards and ask, "Where the hell did you find him?" That changed though and soon opponents were shouting, "Mark wee Strachan. Don't give him any room!"'

Being denied space and often double marked on the school playing fields was, to a talented but fledgling footballer, a blessing. It became clear that Strachan, rather than being nullified, had the footballing wherewithal to use his status to the team's advantage. Playing at old-fashioned inside-right for Craigroysten, he would drift out to the wing, taking his pursuers with him, all the while creating space for his grateful team-mates to exploit. His clear thinking and excellence belied his age, while his confidence belied his size. 'A lot was said about his height,' recalls MacAskill, 'but only by those who hadn't seen him play that much. It became obvious that with the ball his stature didn't matter. Anyway, he may have been small, but he was by no means slight, and like a future Scotland team-mate of his, Kenny Dalglish, he used his weight very well. He had a tremendous low centre of gravity and used it to perfection.'

Strachan's ability as a young footballer had given him the confidence that a small boy might otherwise lack. Being able to bark orders at bigger and older boys every Saturday put inches on him, and he was soon giving team-talks in the dressing room. John Dickson and his other team-mates at Thistle were left with no doubt about his temperament: 'He was a fiery character that's for sure. He was never a good loser but while he hated losing he never had tantrums, even at a young age. He would have a go at his team-mates but in a constructive way. Remember he was a wee kid and the vast majority of us were bigger than him. But that made no difference to Gordon. If he felt he was right, he would tell you in no uncertain terms.'

Self-assured but not cocky, his persona around a football pitch was taking shape. 'He had a prickly nature,' says MacAskill, laughing. 'That may have come from a bit of a Napoleon complex that some smaller guys have. They have to try that bit harder to get where they want and in that respect Gordon was no exception. Don't get me wrong, he was a natural athlete, but very, very competitive. From a young age when the team would be getting a hiding Gordon would never give up. He would have tears in his eyes but would keep going, always chasing lost causes. For all that, his will to win was eclipsed by his enjoyment for the game. There was huge enjoyment on the football field from Gordon. He loved it so much and would visibly shine and glow with a ball at his feet.'

Crowds – by school football standards – were impressive; far from one man and his dog. It could be argued that the majority of the men there on a Saturday morning were waiting impatiently for the local Doo'cot pub to open and serve them all a much-needed hair of the dog, but one fixture always had the school crowds flocking: Craigroysten versus Ainslie Park. Ainslie Park was a school only streets away from Strachan's and there was no love lost when it came to competing on the football pitch. John Dickson attended Ainslie Park and was himself a decent player tipped to go far. Playing at left-back put him in direct opposition to Strachan and he relished the days they turned over the Craigroysten boys: 'Being close to him meant it was always nice when we beat them. It was that competitive streak in Gordon. I played with him at Thistle and he hated losing out on bragging rights for a few months. He would sometimes blame our pitch, which he hated playing on. It was called Seagull Hill and was admittedly on a huge slope. We were playing one year and my school were attacking but the ball broke to the left and Gordon was on to it. He galloped up the hill, took on the last defender, rounded the keeper and knocked it towards goal.

'At this point I was on the eighteen-yard line with no right to prevent the goal but, due to the hill, Gordon's effort slowed up just enough to allow me to slide in and make the clearance. If looks could kill, I wouldn't be talking to you today. He gave me the deadliest of stares; he just couldn't believe he hadn't scored. He had high standards.'

Dickson's big claim to fame is that Strachan, challenging for an aerial ball, caught his mouth with the back of his head, splitting his lip and killing his two front teeth. He still has the scar and the crowns. 'I never did send him the bill.'

Into his teenage years and the game was becoming serious. Edinburgh Thistle were doing well in the local area and reaching national finals. Here Strachan came across plenty of names that would later cross his path as a pro. The Scottish Juvenile Under-16 Cup was ideal for future star-gazing, and Strachan would have to learn early about losing cup finals, coming runner-up twice. The first defeat came at the hands of an impressive club from Dundee called St Colomba's who beat their challengers from the capital 5–1. Losing to the likes of Greame Payne, David Narey and John Holt, who all made names for themselves at Dundee United, and John McPhail, a future team-mate of Strachan's at Dundee, was no shame. The other final was lost by the narrower score line of 2–1 to a Dunfermline club. Strachan's job of making progress down the right side in that final was hindered by a sixteen-year-old left back named Douglas Rougvie. He was huge and Strachan, only fifteen and barely reaching Rougvie's waist, had no joy that day, but would soon come to rely on his opponent's large frame during their days at Aberdeen.

Thistle's Tom Aitken had taken Strachan under his wing. A scholar of the game and a true gentleman, Aitken was just what he needed. Strachan was well known for his backchat, and teachers, friends and referees would all be on the receiving end. A history teacher at Craigroysten went by the name of Mr Gillette, sported a huge beard and had to put up with Strachan's remarks on the obvious connection between the two. Harmless stuff, but Aitken saw his behaviour as an unnecessary distraction and came down hard on his somewhat audacious prodigy in order that all that talent would be realised.

By the age of fourteen, Strachan, as well as playing for his school and club, was turning out for the Edinburgh Schools Select side that included a sweeper called Arthur Albiston from Edinburgh school Forresters. Albiston would eventually play with Strachan at Manchester United and room with him at the 1986 World Cup in Mexico. For now they had smaller fish to fry and took on Fife in the Scottish Schools Cup first round. An Edinburgh paper was quick to point out which Edinburgh player might just steal the show. 'Gordon Strachan of Craigroysten ... could very well be the ace in the Edinburgh pack. A strong, forceful type, he holds a big chance of winning a Scottish cap this season.'

They were right but first there was Fife to deal with and hope quickly turned into disappointment as they were knocked out 3–2 by a spirited side led by a young Allan Evans who would go on to win Scotland caps alongside Strachan, as well as the English

Championship and European Cup with Aston Villa. 'It was crazy,' recalls Albiston. 'We were very disappointed not to have won as we were a team picked from a far bigger catchment area and had some great players. Five of us, including Gordon of course, went on to play for the Scottish under-15s that year, but that day we slipped up.'

Despite that setback, the Edinburgh side showed their mettle in the yearly clash with their schoolboy counterparts from Glasgow who boasted an impressive array of young talent including Alex O'Hara who went on to play for Rangers. The game, played at Hearts' Tyncastle, was won 5–0 by Edinburgh, and Strachan, who scored the fifth goal from the penalty spot, was on his way to international recognition. Strachan was aching to represent his country but thought he had blown it after a moment of impudence playing for his school.

Just a school game maybe, but Strachan was still everywhere, showing the determination to win that had got him to the verge of pulling on the Scotland jersey he so craved. The referee cared little for the Craigroysten star's reputation, awarding decision after decision against him. Referees today will vouch for Strachan's acidic tongue and it was clearly getting some practice at this young age as he turned on the man in black. Red cards in those days and at this level were rare but he was soon given his marching orders. The reality of what had happened so soon before the Scotland squad was announced sank in as Strachan sat distraught and alone in the dressing room. 'They'll never pick me now,' he said, his lip quivering as he was driven home by MacAskill. 'They'll nae want me now.'

Inconsolable he ran straight to his room, refusing to listen to his teacher and his dad's assurances that all would be fine; that the selectors wouldn't hold it against him. This time his elders were right and soon he was turning out against England at Ibrox in Glasgow. The game finished 1–1; a young Raymond Wilkins cancelling out Albiston's penalty. That game was followed by an away trip to take on the West Germans at Saarbrucken in front of 40,000 fans. The match finished in a magnificent 4–4 draw, and the experience of having a blazer fitted, posing for newspapers and boarding planes might have been daunting, especially for a young boy who had never been as far as Butlins in Ayr and who even into adulthood had never seen the military tattoo his home town is famous for. Not so, says Albiston. 'Gordon took it all in his stride. Even as a child it was a case of what you see is what you get. He was a confident lad and that was reflected in not only his play but also how he carried himself within the squad. He had great confidence in his own ability.'

It was a confidence shared by most of his peers and his family. His father was a great supporter, attending games and offering advice. His mother, proud of her son's ability and the effort he was putting into his talent, was nevertheless cautious about its tendency to eclipse everything else, most notably his schoolwork. Playing the level of football he was playing of course meant that a number of club scouts and representatives were contacting his parents and showing interest in signing him on Schoolboy Forms. Decisions had to be made. Should Strachan leave school outright and put faith in his talents with a ball or should he stay on at Craigroysten and gain his qualifications? It wasn't as if Strachan was a poor student. He'd done well in his studies, his competitive nature propelling him to keep his work up to scratch, and was even sent from the top stream of his year to sit an entrance examination for the nearby and renowned Trinity School. Jim Strachan knew though that his son had his mind set on the game of football and revelled in his son's progress. For Catherine the uncertain world of professional football was far less appealing.

Every night she'd be at her son. 'What if you don't make it in football?' she'd scold. 'You'll have nothing else to fall back on.' Her words though were in vain, and with the amount of interest being shown by clubs the young Strachan had every right to feel that the talent that he had been nurturing from such a young age would blossom into his dream career. His association to Edinburgh Thistle had attracted many admiring eyes. Glasgow's Old Firm had sent scouts, and for a while Rangers showed a lot of interest. Their scout, sporting an expensive mackintosh and an even dearer cigar, ran the rule over Strachan and other boys at Thistle a number of times but the Protestant club's interest waned when they could not be guaranteed that Strachan was not Catholic. The Strachans were not religious people, but here being a fan of the Catholic Hibernian side may well have denied him the chance to join one of Scotland's giants. No matter, Manchester City, Coventry City and Nottingham Forest from England were sniffing about Muirhouse but it was an offer closer to home and to his heart that had the teenager jumping about his living room.

Hibs of course were the ideal, and Strachan's heroes were showing a real interest in his game. It became known that Strachan, for so long *the* player in the area, might soon be signing for the mighty Hibs. 'We used to taunt our rival mates who supported Hearts,' says Welsh laughing, who had witnessed first hand how much his young neighbour stood out, even in those forty-a-side games. 'We'd say, "We've got a young kid called Gordon Strachan and he is going to be bloody brilliant man." We weren't joking either, he really was that good.'

Edinburgh Thistle had been formed by an Archie Buchanan, once a player at Easter Road, and he still had ties with the club and their scouting system. They liked what they saw and approached Strachan to train and sign forms with them. It was a dream come true and for a Hibs fanatic like Strachan a simple case of 'where do I sign?' The club had recently gained a new chairman, Tom Hart, who wanted a new manager and happened to be a good friend of Eddie Turnball. Turnball had been an integral part of the club's glory years and the inside-right in that 'Famous Five' front line. He had recently done a great job as boss at Aberdeen, winning the Scottish Cup in 1970, but his heart too lay with Hibs and he immediately took over the vacant position at Easter Road.

Turnball went over the forms that they were offering the local boy and was not happy. A great footballing man and coach, Turnball was not averse to speaking his mind and voiced his apprehension with Strachan's father. Already slightly apprehensive about Strachan's height, the new boss took issue with the expenses being offered to young Strachan and resented the amount of money being laid out on bare essentials such as football boots. Jim was having none of it and fiercely argued his son's corner. It must have been a surreal situation for the Edinburgh scaffolder: here he was in the presence of one of Hibernian's greatest ever players, a personal hero, and he's having a slanging match over the price of the latest Adidas footwear. Jim stood firm, underlining the degree of support he would offer his son, but unfortunately so did Turnball. If he were going to be a pro, Strachan would have to look elsewhere than his beloved Hibernian Football Club. 'Just another case of Hibs shooting themselves in the foot,' laments Welsh, still bitter at never seeing Strachan donning the famous green and white of his local side.

Distraught at the thought of not joining Hibs as a player, Strachan was consoled by the continued interest from clubs all over Britain. Dundee Football Club had been alerted to Strachan shortly before the run-in with Turnball, and now they could make their move. Strachan had been playing a school match for Craigroysten in Dundee and was shining on the right. It wasn't long before a scout approached MacAskill, this time from the Dens Park club.

'Is that wee red-haired fellow available?' came the usual enquiry.

'No, he's about to sign for Hibs,' replied Strachan's teacher, oblivious to what lay ahead and that was that. So impressed, though, was the man from Dundee that he made sure the club kept tabs on that wee red-haired fellow's progress, and after the altercation at Easter Road the club moved in. Alex Somerville, representing Dundee Football Club, did the groundwork and Strachan and his parents liked what was on offer from a club who, while not a major force in Scottish football, were a club a young player could excel at. Somerville reported back to his club that all looked in order; he and the Strachans had a verbal agreement and soon one of the capital's brightest prospects would be signing on the dotted line. Their optimism, however, was ill founded: neither they nor Strachan had counted on the temptation of a certain Manchester United.

Days after Somerville's visit, Strachan was out playing football with his mates. There was a knock at the door at Muirhouse Grove that evening from a man calling on behalf of former European Champions Manchester United. Jim Strachan, not wanting to burn any bridges, took the man over to the Silverknowes golf club for a drink and to hear what a giant of world football had to offer his boy. Strachan returned to be dazzled by the news but tried hard to see through the glitz and the glamour of such a mouth-watering offer. At fourteen, Strachan was aware that many of his peers, enticed by the glamour of English football, were returning home without ever making their mark beyond Hadrian's Wall. These were hard life decisions for a fourteen-year-old to make and, even armed with the knowledge that other Scottish boys were failing in England, the offer from Manchester was hugely tempting. His fellow Edinburgh and Scotland team-mate Arthur Albiston had also been approached by Old Trafford and was very impressed by what he heard. 'It was all very professional. United sent flight tickets, sent someone to pick me up and put me up in a hotel for the time I was there on trial. It was amazing, and before I knew it I was a Manchester United player.'

The same temptations were laid in front of Strachan. Flights, a hotel and the promise of a certain George Best greeting him at the airport were all very alluring, but Strachan, for all the appeal of such an offer, had his doubts. He had no doubt of the opportunity in front of him but

– and with further testimony to his confidence in his own ability – concluded that he should try to learn and make the grade at a club like Dundee and when (rather than if) he was ready he could make the journey to England. The club, after all, had a good pedigree when it came to producing talent. Alan Gilzean and Ian Ure had both made their mark at Dens Park. Ure had been a lively centre-half who went on to play for Arsenal and Manchester United while Gilzean, having learned the art of goal scoring on the shores of the River Tay, set off to Tottenham and became Jimmy Greaves's favourite strike partner. So Strachan stood firm and duly contacted one of the biggest clubs in the world to say 'thanks, but no thanks'. Dundee could have hardly blamed their target for reneging on the deal: nothing had been signed and they had only the word of a fourteen-year-old, but in this case it was enough. Alex Somerville made his way back to the Strachans' home and this time he meant business, bringing first-team manager John Prentice and chief scout Tom Arnott along to prevent any last-minute hiccups. There were none, and Strachan was a schoolboy footballer at Dundee.

Strachan spent his formative months as a Dundee schoolboy splitting his time between Craigroysten and training with the club two or three times a week. In 1972, aged fifteen, he was old enough to leave his schooling behind and become a full-time member of the ground staff at the club's Dens Park stadium. The school was very proud of their star footballer's achievements. One teacher commented that 'the lad will regret not doing his O Levels' but for his friends, the school and for Muirhouse he was a teenager to be proud of, a boy who had got out of a hard place to grow up. 'It was a miracle that any of us made it,' says his old Thistle team-mate John Dickson. 'People go on today about the likes of Rio Ferdinand and Paul Gascoigne and the areas they came out of, but Gordon came much, much further. Edinburgh is generally regarded as Scotland's pretty city, but I'm here to tell you that where we grew up was and is as bad as anywhere you care to mention. I've always followed his career and the one thing I'd give him the most credit for is the way he always looked after our manager at Thistle Tom Aitken. Once Gordon made it, Tom never missed a Scottish game at Hampden Park as Gordon would always sort him out a ticket.'

There is a local expression in Edinburgh, 'I kent his faither', meaning I knew his father and alluding to how a successful individual can become isolated from where he grew up. Not so Strachan. 'He's been back a number of times to do presentations at the school, whereas it could have been so easy to walk away. For all he has won in the game, I think his best achievement was never forgetting where he came from.'

Dickson's words sum up the feelings of so many who grew up with Strachan and were witness to his infectious enthusiasm and energy. One ex-schoolmate, however, would say only, 'All I remember about the little runt is that he always had a runny nose and a ball at his feet.' Nose wiped but the ball still there, Strachan, now Muirhouse's big man, crossed the Forth and Tay Bridge to learn the trade that he hoped would make him a star.

3. DISCOVERY

REPORTER: *Where will Marion Pahars fit into the team line-up?*
GORDON: *Not telling you! It's a secret.*

Trains roll into Dundee off the impressive Tay Bridge and into the self-proclaimed Town of Discovery, so called after the vessel that took Captain Scott on his exploration of Antarctica at the beginning of the twentieth century. Built in Dundee's shipyards, *Discovery* left her home town in 1901 and made the hazardous journey via London to the South Pole but now sits proudly on the town's waterfront. For one fifteen-year-old making his way into Dundee every morning, the town was the starting point of his very own adventure that he hoped would take him to the top of the world rather than the very bottom. After waking each morning at six o'clock, Strachan left his parents' home in Muirhouse and made his way through the estate to catch the bus for Edinburgh's Waverley Station. The men, themselves off to work, gave a knowing nod as a show of their appreciation and pride for the estate's young footballer.

Gordon arrived at the club as a schoolboy who, however used to plaudits, was now working and playing with some of the country's top footballers. Trophies were hardly cascading into the Dens Park trophy cabinet, but the club was seen as being on an equal footing with the likes of Hibs, Hearts and Aberdeen, all of whom were chasing the Old Firm's coat tails. Gordon was now spending time with players he had seen at Easter Road and on the television: Gordon Wallace, that prolific little goal scorer who, in 1968, had become the first non-Old Firm player to win the Scottish Football Writers' Player of the Year, having helped himself to 30 goals that season; John Duncan, who would soon move to Tottenham Hotspur; Jocky Scott, Davie Johnstone – these were all fine pros, and Gordon quickly realised this was not the time or the place to bark orders at the big boys. Not yet anyway.

It was the hour-long train journey into Dundee each day that would bring Gordon's character to the fore. Far from a lonely or tedious commute into work, Strachan was joined by up to 14 members of the Dens Park playing staff who hailed from and lived in

Edinburgh. The train took the travelling footballers past Murrayfield rugby stadium, out of the capital and across the Forth River on to Dundee, but this was not the time to sit back and enjoy the epic landscape of Scotland's east coast. The camaraderie and the banter suited the lad from Muirhouse down to the ground. Senior players such as the big centre-half George Stewart, Bobby Robinson, Bobby Ford and Ian Anderson held court on the train, but it was Alec Caldwell, a young pro at Dundee, who became his close friend and soon his partner in crime. Caldwell enthuses over those journeys and noticed that Gordon, now a full-time member of Dundee's ground staff, was beginning to give as good as he got. 'Where Gordon was from in Edinburgh dictated that, if you're not capable of giving the chat back, you'd end up the butt of everyone's jokes and he'd obviously learned to give it. He grew in confidence and always had an answer. Anyway he had no time to be shy, especially by the way he played football. He was always shouting for the ball, always making himself available.'

The guard on the morning train, an avid Hearts fan, had a milky coffee and a bacon roll waiting for each player (his reward a constant supply of tickets for Dundee–Hearts games) to offer much needed fuel, not necessarily for the morning's training but for the game of cards that would see them there. 'The card games were dangerous,' admits Caldwell. 'I got involved early on but lost my entire wardrobe and decided it was not for me. It was part and parcel of the game and players such as big George Stewart loved to train hard but also loved a pint and a game of cards. It's probably changed a bit now, but that's how we passed the time. Stewart used his experience to take cash off us poor young guys.' Gordon was slower on the uptake and large chunks of his initial £15-a-week wage would end up in the wily centre-half's wallet.

Cards were hardly his forte but Strachan's football, developed on the Muirhouse estate and now groomed by a new manager and coaching staff, was coming along nicely. John Prentice, the manager who had made the trip to Edinburgh to meet the Strachans, had left the club only months after securing Strachan's signature. An ex-Scotland manager, albeit for a matter of months in the mid-sixties, had built a decent team but, only months after signing young Strachan, had become disillusioned with the game. Dwindling crowds and the financial insecurities surrounding Scottish football meant he walked away from the game to help run his in-laws' bagpipe-making business in

Canada. He was replaced by former Rangers boss Davie White. White had been dismissed by the Ibrox club, becoming the only manager to leave without winning honours, but set about his role at Dundee with immediate vigour. For Strachan it was a time to listen, learn and clean boots. After training, with the senior players on the train back home, Strachan and the other youngsters were left to their duties. As well as polishing the team's boots, kits had to be sorted and chores around the ground carried out as efficiently or perhaps inefficiently as possible. 'Our main role was to get on the groundsman's nerves,' says Caldwell, laughing. 'Gordon was always finding ways of getting out of the mundane stuff about the place. He would fool about and do just enough to get by. It wasn't the nicest of stuff to be doing and like most teenagers when it came to a bit of hard work we looked to skive.' Not keen on the smell of boot polish and paint, Strachan soon realised that there was only one real way out. 'Hey, Alec, c'mon, let's get ourselves in the first team quick, we'll no have to do a thing then, pal!'

Behind his jokes lay the serious desire to get ahead. Strachan was shining in the reserves and gaining much attention, and Caldwell for one was duly impressed. 'We had a great reserve team with the likes of Tom Henry, our great mate George Mackie and myself, but it was Gordon who stood out. He was always after the ball, taking the knocks and dominating games. We were all just off the first team but wee Gordon was knocking on its door the loudest.' Aged sixteen, Strachan won Scotland's Reserve Team Player of the Year, and in 1973 Dundee also won the League Cup with a Gordon Wallace goal beating Celtic. The town was ecstatic at a well-deserved piece of silverware but for the ever-improving Strachan it meant his working life in the stiffs had to go on.

By now Strachan had moved out of his parents' home in Edinburgh and into digs in Dundee. Training, working at the ground and getting home so late were taking their toll, and when the club suggested that he and Caldwell save the club some money on expenses and find somewhere in town to live they jumped at the chance. Young men, living alone for the first time with no one there to watch over them, professional athletes or not, are going to enjoy themselves – and that's exactly what Strachan and his mates did. They eventually found rooms in the Broughton Ferry area of Dundee and without much time for staying put in their rooms would go out and, well, act like teenagers. For Strachan it was a wild period in his life, where lifetime friendships and relationships were formed. 'They were great days and we were always up to something or other,' reflects Caldwell. The boys, a Laurel-and-Hardy-like double act, were the life and soul, and keen to dish out stick to their esteemed colleagues. 'Gordon Wallace or Ian Phillip would pick us up to go to training. We'd sit in the back and rip shreds out of each car. "C'mon, we could get out and push faster than this car's going. Put your foot down." Ian Phillip, a real gentleman, once turned up, the proud owner of a brand new Volkswagen Beetle. Half-way to training we broke down. So proud was Ian that he'd forgot to check that his new car had a full tank and we'd run out of petrol. The two of us in the back were in stitches. "We'll get the bus from here, pal." We were young men living alone, myself, George Mackie and Gordon; we had no one staring over us and we were excited. I suppose we acted our age and loved a joke and a dig at each other. Even when we get together now the jokes don't stop.'

Here were a group of young, exciting prospects, who knew they were in Dundee to learn a trade but who, despite the best efforts of their caring landladies, were loath to sit in their digs getting bored. Earning £15 a week plus an extra £75 win bonus, Strachan joked he didn't know what to do with such riches other than give chunks of it to the town's many pub landlords. Caldwell along with team-mate George Mackie were Strachan's usual drinking partners, but both could handle it that bit better than their smaller pal. 'We'd go into town after training and have a few beers, and that was usually all it took Gordon before he was pissed!' says Caldwell, laughing. Word of these frequent visits to bars got back to a concerned Davie White and the revellers were hauled into his office, to receive a ticking off like a couple of naughty schoolboys. There was no major problem – boys will be boys – but Strachan was aware that despite the good press he was receiving he had better take stock or end up back in Muirhouse.

That was not to say that he and his mates completely gave up painting the town red. But it was now Saturday night, after a match, that was the time to party. Think John Travolta in the opening sequence to the classic seventies film *Saturday Night Fever*. Shirts unbuttoned, razor-sharp creases ironed into the bell-bottom trousers and platform shoes immaculately polished, the boys would make their way out into the calling night. Any comparisons with Travolta must stop there I'm afraid. 'We'd try all the dancing but when it came to the ladies we weren't the luckiest right enough.' Caldwell laughs. 'Two ginger laddies stood no chance! Gordon loved his platforms as they put on the inches but the problem was everyone wore them so everyone was still that wee bit bigger than him. Having said that, I can't talk. I was more likely to fall off my platforms than pick up in them.'

Undeterred, Gordon soon unleashed his charms on the dance floor and in doing so wooed local girl Lesley Scott. Happy to have met someone smaller than himself, he was in for a surprise when she revealed she had taken her platforms off to dance and when back on she was soon looking down on her new beau. Size wouldn't matter though: romance blossomed and Strachan had himself a girlfriend. To be fair, he was becoming quite a catch. Not only was he on the cusp of that first-team place, he was also out of digs and sharing a flat with Caldwell. Strachan's appearances had been merely as a substitute and a run-out in the old Drybrough Cup, a competition held at the beginning of each season to reward the highest goal-scorers from the previous campaign but 28 July 1973 saw the sixteen-year-old Strachan get on in a 1–0 home win over Raith Rovers. The next two seasons saw only a couple of outings including a trip to Easter Road to face Hibs, where no doubt he was a little less raucous on the bus there than he used to be with his Muirhouse mates.

It was in the summer of 1975, settled in a flat with Caldwell and in a relationship with Lesley, that Strachan made a solid claim for first-team action. Dundee had laid a new pitch at Dens Park over the summer and invited Arsenal up from London for a pre-season friendly to christen the surface. Arsenal were a top side, sporting a number of high-profile internationals, such as Pat Rice, Sammy Nelson and a young Liam Brady, as well as an ex-Hibs player and boyhood hero of Strachan, Alec Cropley. The biggest draw of the afternoon, however, was the England captain and World Cup winner Alan Ball. If Strachan was going to make his mark on the team, this was the day to do it and he had already taken strides in his quest to get noticed. Alan Ball at the time was endorsing a new pair of white football boots. White boots, purple boots, boots with the name of a player's pet Chihuahua etched across them – they are all the rage in the modern game but back then they were a novelty. Strachan was on to it and went out and purchased a pair. It was a cheeky act of intent as he ran out ready to take on the English captain at his own memorable game.

Ball's presence was all the incentive Strachan needed, and their tussle in the midfield was his big break. Tenacious in the tackle and creative with the ball, Strachan stamped his authority on the Arsenal man and the game. Dundee ran out 2–1 winners but more importantly to the Scottish press a new hero had arrived. The next day's *Sunday Post* was adamant that a star had been born and ran the headline: 'STRACHAN ROASTS ALAN BALL – DUNDEE FIND A NEW BILLY BREMNER.' Ron Scott, still on the paper and at the time writing under the name Bill McFarlane, gushed over the performance of Dundee's young prospect:

> *In eighteen-year-old Gordon Strachan, Dundee undoubtedly had the man of the match. When he was substituted twelve minutes from the end, England skipper Alan Ball led the thunderous standing ovation given to the Edinburgh teenager. Because, for all the seventy-eight minutes he played directly against Ball in midfield, Strachan came well out on top and Ball, sportingly, was prepared to admit it. As well as being a good ball player, Strachan has tons of guts and dig in the tackle. A real Billy Bremner in the making, if ever I saw one.*

High praise indeed. Billy Bremner, although approaching the twilight of a glorious career, was every Scotsman's favourite midfielder, whose combative yet skilful game was the very epitome of how they thought the game should be played north of the border. Ball himself had noticed the young player's ability and, having applauded the youngster off when he was substituted late on, he approached his then manager Bertie Mee on the coach journey back to London. 'Boss,' he said in that unmistakable high-pitched tone, 'you have to buy that ginger-haired kid. He's going to be brilliant, take it from me.'

Mee didn't act upon his captain's advice and so Strachan remained at Dens Park. The 1975/76 season was the inaugural campaign for the Scottish Premier League, where the cream was now supposed to rise to the top, and for Strachan that's exactly what he hoped to do. Although not yet a regular, Strachan was beginning to make an impact, playing in 17 of his side's 36 Premier League games. The obvious self-belief that had so obviously manifested itself off the pitch was starting to appear where it mattered most, on it. 'Gordon had a swagger about him from an early age and became the cocky kid in the side,' reflects the team's top goal-scorer Gordon Wallace. 'He could be a wee bit greedy and, as I always said, he passed the ball once he was finished with it. Rather than releasing it when you were in a better position to score, he would hold it and lick it, and lick it and lick it. Then, with the world and his wife around him, he would pass it, but often the chance had gone. He was only a teenager, and was learning his trade but would still get a tongue lashing from Jocky Scott or myself. That didn't deter wee Gordon though and he would just mutter under his breath, "Away, you fucking great bastard." He had great belief in what he was doing and had the arrogance we all needed to make it.'

In and out of the first eleven, and with Davie White's side hauled into a relegation dogfight, it took another friendly against English opposition to underline his potential. Everton this time hosted the game mid-way through the season and had roared into a 3–0 lead at half-time. Strachan had witnessed the mauling from the bench but was now sent on to see what he could do. Again, the English side were bamboozled by his energy and skill, and again he stood head and shoulders (without the aid of his platforms) above the rest. The game finished 3–3 and for the first time the English press and the nation's managers saw what a gem Dundee had unearthed. A friendly maybe, but Strachan would have to be involved from now on. The relegation battle went on: St Johnstone were already down and it would be one of three from Dundee, their city rivals Dundee United and Aberdeen to join them in the new First Division.

It went to the wire and Dundee could only wait and hope that Dundee United lost their last game of the season. They had grounds to be optimistic as it was at Ibrox, but their tangerine neighbours got the unexpected draw they needed to gleefully send Dundee down. It was a huge blow for a club that like today's Scottish clubs was suffering severe financial distress. The reality of relegation meant that there was talk of the club going part-time and, for the first time in his short career, self-doubt crept into Strachan's mind. His sleep was disrupted by his mother's words before he left Craigroysten High School: 'You'll have nothing to fall back on' went over and over in his head. Strachan was now at last a fixture in the first team but it was a team playing First Division football and that he had not expected.

The club were far from solvent but the threat of part-time status evaporated and the new challenge of getting back to the Premier League soon became paramount. There was a change of manager as Davie White left, not merely under the cloud of relegation. His wife had contracted multiple sclerosis and White left football to care for her. Who would take over? Who could get the best out of a squad low on morale and leadership? The answer to that question lay closer than at first thought. Tommy Gemmell, an integral part of Celtic's European Cup-winning team of 1967 (he scored their equaliser that famous night), had joined the Dens Park playing staff in 1973 and had had a big effect on Strachan, who would listen in awe to the Lisbon Lion's stories of lifting the big old trophy and placing Scottish football on the continental map. Gemmell was a larger-than-life presence in the Dundee dressing room. His thick head of blond hair and his gleaming white smile invited comparisons with the Hollywood luminary Danny Kaye. A showman himself on and off the pitch, it was Gemmell who was entrusted with the job of getting the club's name back in lights.

'It was a strange situation as the board asked me my thoughts on a successor,' recalls the ever-cheerful Gemmell. 'I highly recommended my ex-Celtic team-mate Bertie Auld, whom I knew to be a good man, and he was called in for an interview. I fully expected him to get the job but to my surprise they came to me and said that Auld had himself advised that they give me the job. And that was that.' Gemmell was in the hot seat and proved to be the very antithesis of his thoughtful predecessor. Whereas Davie White was the wily tactician, Gemmell was one of the lads, enjoying a joke and a beer. Strachan adored him and under his tuition became more than just a first-team regular. 'When I joined the club in 1973, I went to Dens Park a couple of weeks before pre-season training,' reflects Gemmell, today a financial adviser in Glasgow. 'There were some of the youngsters having a game of five-a-side behind one of the goals and so I went over to join in. There was Gordon, just a wee boy really, but such ability, even then. He was always wanting the ball to his little feet, always busy and that never left him.'

For Gemmell, there was a job to do and he felt he had the set of players to do it. 'We were unlucky to go down, we really were. It was on goal average that we actually got relegated but we were no worse then Dundee United or Aberdeen, but while they got on with challenging the Old Firm over the next ten years we had to struggle out of the First Division. But that's just how football's cookie crumbles.' Scotland's First Division was never going to be an easy place to get out of, but Strachan continued to shine, so much so that Gemmell handed him the captaincy for much of the season. 'That seemed the right thing to do. He seemed to thrive on the responsibility and would never hide on the pitch, however things were going.' Only nineteen, Strachan was never entirely comfortable with the skipper's armband. He felt he was too young for the job and although he demonstrated plenty of verbal enthusiasm felt he lacked the natural leadership qualities of those who would later captain him. 'He was bloody loud on the pitch, but mainly when you didn't pass him the ball,' says Alec Caldwell with a laugh. 'Gemmell gave him the role as everything on the pitch seemed to go through Gordon and so it seemed natural that he get the position. It was a prestige thing really.'

Skipper, nights at the cinema with Lesley rather than the pub with the boys; Strachan was starting to live the life of a senior player yet things on the pitch weren't running so smoothly. The team was not blazing a trail through the lower league like many had expected, and the fans were losing patience. Strachan was not above stick from the Dens Park faithful and was soon questioning the direction that both the club and his own career were heading. To the young and eager player, Dundee seemed to be sitting back on its laurels and feeling sorry for itself. Gemmell was great fun but had achieved so much in the game as a player that he may have lacked the spirit and drive to get the club back in the Premier League. Gemmell would head home straight after training, turn up late for the team bus and would play the joker when the team needed a sergeant major. It wasn't that Strachan didn't respect his manager, far from it, but he felt a lack of drive had filtered down to the players. Training had become unprofessional, the smell of booze in the training-ground dressing-room was not uncommon and the club was suffering from what Strachan saw as their fatal mistake in not giving the manager's job to Jim McLean. Their ex-coach had worked under John Prentice but left to take over at Dundee United and would steer them to Premier League glory while their neighbours across the street faltered. In this atmosphere Strachan was becoming increasingly concerned with his future. He wanted to be playing at the top but envisioned a career playing at Brechin or Forfar.

Strachan had clearly set himself high standards off the pitch, but even he fell below them when Gemmell brought in former Celtic team-mate and Lisbon Lion Jimmy Johnstone. The impish, enigmatic Johnstone had been a star at Parkhead, and the sight of his 5ft 4in frame and flame-coloured hair skipping down the wing, his socks rolled round his ankles and a cheeky grin blazed across his face was iconic of the game in the 1960s. Gemmell brought him to Dens Park hoping that he'd inject some fresh impetus into the side, and, true enough, each time he received a pass a hush would descend over whatever stadium they were in.

As well as his ability on the ball, Johnstone arrived with quite a reputation for his exuberant behaviour. His most recent and most publicised misdemeanour had come in 1974 before a Home International with England at Hampden Park. The Scotland squad were staying in Largs on the west coast and Johnstone, after a few drams too many, took it upon himself to get into a rowing boat with only one oar and set out for sea. Singing away and oblivious to his dangerous course out towards the Atlantic, it wasn't long before he had to be rescued by the coastguard. It summed up the man that two days later he turned on the style and helped his country to a 2–0 win over the auld enemy.

The 1977/78 season had again started slowly at Dens Park and Strachan was getting over a painful operation to remove his big toenails, which had become infected. Johnstone too was 'injured' and perhaps seeing a bit of himself in the young, fiery Strachan took him under his wing. It was a place Strachan would not want to be for long. One day, his team-mates at training, Johnstone asked his young protégé to come for lunch and more than a simple Dundee mince roll was on Johnstone's menu. How could any football fan turn down lunch with a national hero? But a bite to eat accompanied by a bottle of wine at the Queen's Hotel turned into three or four bottles and the question 'Where to next?' Strachan's place was the answer, where they drank more before stumbling outside to have a kick-about with some local kids. A European Cup winner and a future Scotland captain hurling themselves around the pavement must have had the curtains twitching down the street. The inebriated twosome soon set off for more refreshments, this time to Errol, the village Johnstone was staying in just outside Dundee. What hadn't registered in their pickled heads was that it was also the village in which Tommy Gemmell lived and owned a business.

'Jimmy was staying in my hotel,' Gemmell recalls, somewhat despairingly. 'They stupidly came back but went to the pub over the road from mine and got more and more pissed. It's only a small village, of course, and soon news that my two star players were legless over the road filtered back to me.' Gemmell made his way only to be confronted by a decidedly vacant-looking Gordon Strachan. 'Where the hell do you think you're going?' asked the Dundee manager.

'Where am I going?' replied Strachan, his head down and oblivious to whom he was talking to. 'I don't even know where I am.' Before he could finish his sentence, the penny had dropped: Strachan was face to face with Gemmell and far from his good books. Drunken tears rolling in his eyes, he could only mumble, 'Please, boss, sorry, boss, can you get me a taxi, boss?'

Gemmell took one look at the state of his young midfield prospect, one look at Jimmy Johnstone sitting upright at the bar, sinking another, and gently whispered to Strachan, 'Wee man, I told you to keep away from that little bastard.'

Gemmell got Strachan home and allowed him to sleep it off. The manager, an extrovert himself, knew exactly what went on in the game and was lenient with the offending pair. Johnstone didn't last too long at the club – too many late arrivals at his boss's hotel saw to that – but Gemmell was also concerned about Strachan's role in a side finding it increasingly arduous to express themselves in the First Division where creativity was swamped before it could prosper. 'It was a hard, hard division and Gordon was getting kicked a lot,' reflects Gemmell. 'It was tough and I was beginning to use him sparingly. Gordon was never happy being dropped, but as a playmaker he was getting kicked out of games. If we had played the total football that he wanted we'd never have got out of that division. We had to rough it up a bit and that meant leaving the wee man out.' Things had to change and, for Strachan, very soon they would.

4. NOT A DANDY DON

REPORTER: *There's no negative vibes or negative feelings here?*
GORDON: *Apart from yourself, we're all quite positive round here. I'm going to whack you over the head with a big stick, down, negative man, down.*

The summer of 1977. *Star Wars* had taken young cinema-goers to a galaxy far, far away while the Sex Pistols were doing their best to whip the nation's youth into a frenzy, sending the Queen's Silver Jubilee celebrations and the establishment into a state of apoplexy. For Strachan, such callow distractions were to be ignored. He was now twenty years old; it was time to move his football and his life on. After all, he was no longer making these choices alone. Lesley Scott had done Strachan the honour of becoming his wife that summer at Strathmartin Church in Dundee. Going into another season in the new First Division, he would have to decide on his future a family man.

The wedding had been a memorable day with George Mackie carrying out best-man duties while Alec Caldwell took on the role of usher. The bride's party had good reason for trepidation when it came to that trio and weddings. George Mackie had been married only recently and it was Strachan then who was best man. The groom and friends went out to toast his last night as – to put it in footballing terms – a free agent. But, as ever, one pint turned into too many and the groom was far from feeling his best as he waited upon his betrothed at church. With his complexion matching the white of his bride's dress Mackie was soon disrupting his vows to run out of the church and release the previous night's excesses. 'We'd all had too much,' reflects Caldwell somewhat understatedly. 'The worst of it, and George won't thank me for telling you, was that he also threw up his two front teeth. If you look at all George's wedding photos he's not smiling in any of them.' No doubt neither was his bride.

Strachan's big day went off without any such disruptions but his football at Dundee was less than smooth. The 1977/78 season was only weeks old but Strachan could not shake off the feeling that he had to get away. He had to move on and somehow better himself. Arsenal, the first team to witness his array of talents, were reportedly showing an interest, Celtic too, but it was the move south to the English game that would again prove tempting. Strachan had resisted once before by rejecting the move to Old Trafford but the bright lights of the capital had a way of blinding a young player's better judgement. They had before and would again and, despite there being no firm offer, the English game was again worth thinking about. 'He thought about it all right,' reflects Caldwell. 'We discussed it together a lot but my advice to him was hold on. He could go down to England in good time. I reminded him of Peter Marinello who, in 1970, had joined Arsenal from Hibs for a massive £100,000 but who duly disappeared under that price and pressure. Down there Gordon would be a small fish in a big pond and that is hard. He should stay, learn more in the Scottish Premier League and then he could move.'

It was advice that Strachan heeded but that couldn't take away the urge to get out of Dens Park. He had become disillusioned with the lackadaisical atmosphere at Dens Park. He had learned a lot from coaches such as Hugh Robertson and senior pros such as George Stewart and Gordon Wallace, and for that he was grateful, but having been utilised as a man marker in one game that autumn he knew that it was time to break free from the First Division and Dundee.

Tommy Gemmell had received a number of enquiries but – despite the feeling that his young midfielder was not fully up to the hard knocks of life outside the top flight – was in no rush to sell him. One phone call to the manager would soon change that. 'The chairman got on to the phone to me one Monday morning. "We need £50,000 by Friday," he said, "or the banks are closing the gates." Look at Scottish football today, all the clubs have the same problem, too many outgoings and it was the same then. We were in trouble. My old pal at Celtic, Billy McNeill, had recently become manager at Aberdeen and had phoned me a couple of times to ask about wee Gordon but I had said he wasn't for sale, but now I had to raise the cash.'

A deal would have to be struck but Gemmell couldn't lose a player like Strachan and just see the cash be lost in a raging sea of debt, so he thrashed out a settlement that saw Aberdeen's Jim Shirra plus £50,000 make their way down the coast to Dundee. Shirra was a physical player and in Gemmell's eyes perfect for the job at hand. The deal was done but still came as a shock to Dundee's fans and press. Dick

Donnelly, as a commentator on Radio Tay, has followed Dundee for years. He was shocked one morning as he stopped to offer the young player a lift at the side of the road. 'Do ya want a lift wee, man?' asked Donnelly, opening the door for Strachan.

'Aye, Dick, can you take me to the station, I'm away to sign for Aberdeen.'

Donnelly was stunned. 'You're joking!' 'Dick,' answered a weary Strachan, 'if I'm honest I can't take any more of this.'

The contract was thrashed out, taking Strachan's wages to £85 plus a signing-on fee that he would later regret for being too low. No matter now, though – Strachan was at a club going places and it was here that he would enjoy unprecedented success.

Aberdeen's Pittodrie Stadium is on the one hand an unassuming place. A compact, less than intimidating atmosphere next to a public links golf-course, it should offer no real threat. However, flanked by an eerie, yet beautiful old cemetery and with the dark clouds rolling off a disgruntled North Sea, it can seem a far more foreboding venue. The club though had not exactly instilled this sense of fear into its foes from the West Coast's Old Firm and sat comfortably in that second tier of teams competing for trophies. The championship had been won way back in 1955 but they were now nowhere near consistent enough to challenge Rangers and Celtic for the title. Ally MacLeod at least had lifted the Dons from the slump of 1976 when they had so nearly gone down, but at Strachan and Dundee's expense missed out on that embarrassment on the last day of the season. Like a fresh breeze, MacLeod had brought his unique sense of optimism to Pittodrie as well as players willing and able to shine in the red of Aberdeen. Dom Sullivan would prove a useful servant having joined from Clyde, while the part-time Stuart Kennedy, a shipyard worker from Falkirk, arrived for a paltry £25,000 and would go on to shine at right-back right up to the superb victory in Europe seven years later.

The town of Aberdeen had changed drastically since the discovery of oil in 1970 and the economic boom that followed swelled the city's population and morale. Similarly in 1977, optimism surrounding the football club gushed like black gold when MacLeod's side won the League Cup. Rangers were demolished 5–1 at Hampden in the semi-final while Celtic were dismissed 2–1 in a tense final. The Old Firm were not impenetrable and any team wanting to take on the challenge of breaking their stranglehold on the Scottish game would have to truly believe that. Consistency in the league was the key and, despite all his good work, MacLeod could not find that in his first and only full season at the helm.

He had gone on and on to the national press that he had found his dream job in the North East. Silverware and adulation could be followed by true and sustained success. This was a club he felt could dominate and, while he was correct, it would have to be done without him. Dream job or not, when the Scottish Football Association – impressed by his work at Aberdeen – came asking in the spring of 1977 for him to lead his country through the last two qualifying games and on to the 1978 World Cup in Argentina, it was too much to turn down. The job of getting there had been half done after all. Willie Ormond had led the Scots to the brink of qualification but had left to take over a struggling Hearts side. Under MacLeod the Scots went through, having knocked Wales out of a play-off at Anfield, and his unceasing sense of optimism was immediately transferred to the Tartan Army amid ultimately tenuous predictions of World Cup glory.

No one at Aberdeen begrudged MacLeod his decision but someone would have to be chosen successfully to carry on his good work. Aberdeen needed a good, honest man and the board were keen for it to be a young manager willing to take an improving club forward. Pittodrie had plans to become the first all-seated stadium in Britain but had had its reputation slightly tarnished with a betting scandal towards the end of that season. Aberdeen had been beaten by Strachan's Dundee in a Scottish Cup tie but the local paper, the *Press and Journal*, had received an anonymous tip-off that three Aberdeen players had each placed £500 on Dundee to win at 8–1. A national paper was to run the story but after an investigation and a lack of evidence the story fizzled out. No matter, the club needed not only a talented young manager to lead the side but also someone with a reputation to restore the club's good name.

Alex Stuart was a young Aberdonian manager working at Ayr United and Alex Ferguson was building a decent young side at St Mirren, but it was Billy McNeill, enjoying his first managerial role at Clyde, who most interested the Aberdeen board. His name was synonymous with glory in the Scottish game. The captain of the Lisbon Lions, his experience and education under the great Jock Stein would surely hold him in good stead as he embarked on life in the dug-out. 'It was sad to see the infectious MacLeod leave but getting McNeill in was fantastic,' recalls Stuart Kennedy, a mainstay in the Aberdeen back four and pushing successfully for a place in Scotland's World Cup squad that summer. 'The thing about McNeill was his chest came into a room five yards before Billy. We all knew him; we all knew what he had achieved at Celtic as a player and that lifted us all.'

McNeill inherited a solid side and was eager to lead a generation of players brought up on his achievements to victory. Willie Miller, Joe Harper and Bobby Clarke were by now renowned Scottish pros and the backbone of the Aberdeen side. His first game, a 3–1 victory over Rangers, had the fans drooling. For a man forever swathed in the green and white of Celtic, but now sporting a bright red shirt under his jacket, it was the perfect start. At the final whistle Jock Wallace, the Rangers manager, menacingly walked towards the new Aberdeen boss. 'You beat the Huns hey,' he sneered. 'I bet you think you're fucking clever now.'

He did and for McNeill there were no doubts: he had arrived at a club with great potential, so it was now up to him to fill in the pieces, and he immediately went to work. Steve Archibald, a former car mechanic, followed McNeill from Clyde in a deal worth £20,000 (brilliant business when you consider the money they would get for him only three years later); Steve Ritchie came from Hereford; and Ian Scanlon, a fine left-sided ball player, arrived from Notts County.

McNeill is sitting patiently in a Glasgow hotel waiting to chat about his fond memories at Aberdeen. His glasses sit on the edge of his nose as a young waiter, not even born when his customer lifted the European Cup in Lisbon, brings us a couple of coffees with a knowing glint in his eye. Legends never fade. From the off, it is evident that McNeill thoroughly enjoyed his time at Aberdeen and, before the caffeine has a chance to kick in, the mention of Strachan and Pittodrie gets his pulse racing. 'I loved being there. My wife and I took to the place and its people immediately. It was a very calming atmosphere, a one-club town, which helped of course, and Ally had left a solid base to build upon and we got off to a decent start.' But why Strachan?

'I hadn't seen Gordon play before I arrived at Aberdeen, but one day, having had our game postponed, I went to see Dundee and was immediately struck by what a good player he was. He had everything I liked.' McNeill becomes animated, his arms assisting his words as he thinks back to Strachan's raw talents. 'He was busy, always involved with lots of class and natural aggression. I said to myself, brilliant, this kid is worth looking at again. Let's go for him.' Not let down, McNeill's mind was almost made up but he, like most managers, sought a second opinion to put his mind at rest. 'Dundee had a League Cup tie against Queen of the South who were managed by my pal from Celtic, Mike Jackson. I asked him to keep an eye on Gordon for me and called him back immediately after the game. Mike's team had thrashed Dundee 6–0, which was a huge shock, and I couldn't stop him talking about his team. "Mike, Mike, what about the lad, Strachan?" I asked. "Big man, Dundee were hopeless, absolutely bloody hopeless; but that wee bastard, he kept showing for the ball, kept working and never lay down. He was the only player they had." "That'll do me."'

McNeill, thanks largely to a Dundee bank, had his man and without delay was ecstatically telling the press to expect great things from the new boy from Edinburgh. 'This may not be the biggest signing Aberdeen have ever made but, in my opinion, it could well become the best. After all, Gordon is only twenty and the club can expect at least another ten years from him. It's a great signing for the future and I'm sure the Pittodrie fans will come to realise his great ability.' Strachan was put straight into the side playing at Dundee United on Guy Fawkes' Day 1977. Aberdeen won 1–0 but the fireworks that McNeill hoped would follow his signing were slow to catch alight.

Strachan had skipped into his first training session the Monday after his debut full of his usual enthusiasm. Gone were the stagnant sessions at Dundee; the feelings of boredom had disappeared as he got kitted out and ready to show his new team-mates what he could do. Unfortunately for Strachan, almost the very first thing he did do was go over on his ankle trying to tackle a young trialist. Taken straight to hospital for a check-up, it was far from the ideal way to impress new employers. McNeill was desperate to have his new side take shape, and with Strachan just as eager to make his home debut the following Saturday, he received injections in the damaged ankle and took to his new stage. With the new signing not fully fit and struggling to cope with Premier League football again, the local fans were far from asking for an encore. A couple of nondescript performances later and the critics were waiting in the wings. Strachan did manage to score in a 4–0 win at home to Motherwell, but a week later, and still feeling the initial injury to his ankle, he was scythed down by St Mirren's burly left-back Alex Beckett and was out of the game for a month. Immobile, unimpressive and homeless. It was hardly the best start to a new life.

The latter problem regarding his home life had been getting him down, as he had been living out of a suitcase at a hotel in Aberdeen. For the first two months after his arrival, Lesley had stayed in Dundee to wrap up her work, but, having joined him, living in an en-suite double was hardly an idyllic beginning to married life. They had no complaints about where they were situated: the Ashley House Hotel run by Ruth and Charlie Rettie was a homely place that housed many of the new faces at the club. Ally McLeod had stayed there, as had Billy McNeill and his family, as well as new signings Steve Archibald and Ian Scanlon. To this day the Retties remain firm friends of the Strachans but, after five months, finding their own home remained a priority.

Strachan had more time on his hands for house hunting than he might have liked. Having recovered from his injuries, he found it hard to break into an Aberdeen team putting together a very decent run of form. John McMaster, a talented left-sided player, had replaced the Leeds United-bound Arthur Graham and he and Dom Sullivan were providing the width. Strachan, with Archibald cup tied, could only get a look-in for Scottish Cup fixtures. His stop-start life began to take its toll. Stuart Kennedy, Strachan's room-mate at the club, could understand his frustrations. 'The niggling injuries to start with had had an effect and coupled with his living situation and the usual process of having to find his feet under a new manager took their toll. He wasn't depressed, he very rarely was, but it played on his mind. You must remember that Gordon was a technical player and the demands on him straight away from the fans and the manager were difficult. It's OK if you go hell for leather like a defender who can show the fans he's giving 100 per cent. For a skilful wee player like Gordon you have to impress right away and he found that hard.'

Strachan would come in from training hopeful of a place in the starting eleven. 'I think I did OK this week, don't you, Alec?' he'd ask his young team-mate Alex McLeish.

'Aye, wee man, you did good.'

'I reckon I might be in tomorrow.'

But before the team could go up on the board, reserve-team manager Teddy Scott was telling him he'd make him captain for the reserves the following day. Each time it was a blow. While his team-mates blazed a trail through the league beating both Celtic and Rangers, Strachan was forced to make do with the less glamorous surroundings of Peterhead and beyond. Teddy Scott was and remains a stalwart at Aberdeen Football Club. A very decent local man, before his recent retirement Scott had been a loyal servant to the club and served as player, coach, cleaner, tea-boy and shoulder to cry on for half a century. His attentive and sympathetic manner kept Strachan's spirits up even if the fans were far less supportive. The Pittodrie terraces had been less than generous with their allotted honeymoon period and had lost patience with the player their new manager had predicted would become their best ever. To be fair Strachan understood their feelings. He could hear the jeers and even the laughter coming from the terraces and was down, doubts again crept into his mind about his future in his game, his mortgage and his new wife. He had great faith in his ability but was flabbergasted at just how bad his form had got.

Approaching the end of the season Strachan was on the bench for a league match at Pittodrie against Partick Thistle. Strachan got on but further inept touches and passes were doing him no favours as far as the Aberdeen fans were concerned. It must have been a hearty relief to see a familiar face, as his best man and old friend George Mackie, now at Thistle, got stripped off and joined the action. 'It's OK, wee man, I've come on to help you out,' said Mackie, laughing. 'Just run up to me and I'll fall down.' What are best friends for, but before Mackie had a chance to carry out his selfless act it was Gordon who was on his arse, looking up at the Aberdeen sky, the whistles and jeers of his fans ringing in his ears.

For McNeill and his assistant John Clark their midfielder's form was an obvious worry. Clark had arrived after Strachan had signed and voiced his concerns to McNeill who he thought had made a mistake. McNeill tried everything in a manager's repertoire. The arm around the shoulder, the public dressing-down, but in hindsight knew that he had done the right thing bringing him to Aberdeen. 'I was aware it was getting him down but I knew his talent would come to the fore. Coming from Dundee to a club on the up had proved hard and I felt he needed toughening up. Sometimes I'd go over board, I know that now, but I was a young manager. We'd have our pre-match meals at the Retties' hotel where Gordon was staying. Gordon was sitting there eating his meal with the lads and his wife. "What the fuck is your wife doing in here?" I shouted. It was too much but I was trying anything to get a reaction. As for the fans, the Aberdeen supporters could be a parochial bunch at times. When John McMaster came in he wore Arthur Graham's number 11 shirt. The fans were immediately on his back comparing him to their departed hero. I had noticed it and gave John the number 4 jersey and his game picked up. It can be psychological.'

Strachan needed that break, but what with the side doing so well he would have to be patient. While far from the most popular player with the punters, his team-mates had immediately taken to his cheeky humour and ability to take a joke as well as dish one out. Willie Miller, by now captain of the side, recalls fondly Strachan's tentative steps into the dressing room and into that coiffeuring nightmare that was the 1970s bubble perm: 'Gordon was a little reserved maybe at first but not for long and soon that humour we all know today was apparent. In our dressing room he had to be able to take a bit of stick as well, especially when he got his perm. Most of us had one in those days and believe it or not they were the height of fashion. It was a style thing but the perm needed all your love and attention. Gordon though thought it was the easy option, something you could have done and forget about. Each morning he'd just get out of bed and come to training, so there he was in the dressing room, one side of his hair flattened where he had slept on it and the other this bouncy perm. We would all be grooming ourselves with our long combs seeing to our perms but for him there was no tender loving care, that's for sure.'

The players may have been drastically underachieving when it came to *haute couture* but their form on the pitch had made them model pros as far as their manager was concerned. 'We didn't lose a game from October until the climax of the season,' recalls McNeill. 'It was an aggressive side, full of characters. The aggression came from a will to win that they all identified with. They had their own personalities, but all could be bad tempered and strong willed and that was essential. The individuals were good but it was the team as a whole, that's what clicked.' The team had taken Jock Wallace's Rangers all the way to the last game of the season, and, while Aberdeen remained unbeaten after a 1–1 draw with Hibernian, it was not enough to stop the title winging its way to Ibrox. McNeill's men had been very unfortunate: they had beaten their Glasgow rivals three times that season in Premier action and so were to be excused going into the Scottish Cup final against them feeling more than a little confident.

Strachan, so often a gooseberry while his side flirted with Premier League glory, hoped the Cup would offer him a chance to taste the big occasion, to be part of something special and win over some fans along the way. Epitomising his first campaign at the club, Strachan was left out. Not even a substitute and far from happy. 'I picked a team at the time to win the game,' asserts McNeill. 'We had beaten Rangers 3–0 and bloody murdered them only three weeks previously and so I wanted more of the same. I thought Strachan was only a kid and the occasion would get to him. He took it badly, but who wouldn't? I wouldn't want anyone who wouldn't be down. Looking back I think I made a mistake: my players shit themselves to be honest and the 2–1 defeat flattered us.'

It was a harsh way to end the season, but for Strachan he was glad that it was all over. Far from wanting to attend a post-final reception he got off to bed early hoping his fortunes would change come the summer and come the new season. He and Lesley had finally moved into a new home in the smart Bridge of Don region in Aberdeen's suburbs and he hoped that that security would soon be transferred onto the pitch. He waved a far from fond farewell to the season and, despite the nagging feeling that he had let his new manager down, saw the next campaign as his chance to show exactly what he could do. His trepidation towards the club's fans was eased the following day as 20,000 people cheered their losing heroes home. 'For fuck sake, we lost,' says McNeill now, laughing, but for Strachan their optimism mirrored his own. As the manager addressed the fans, apologising for their lack of silverware and promising more effort for the following campaign, a small diminutive figure took it all in. It had been a tough year, but maybe, just maybe ...

5. THE NORTH STAR

REPORTER: *Welcome to Southampton Football Club. Do you think you're the right man to turn things around?*
GORDON: *No, I think they should have got George Graham because I am useless.*

If Strachan was relishing the challenge a new season brings, he soon wouldn't be alone. The whole club would have to get used to the sound of a new drum whose incessant banging would keep all the neighbours, both in Scotland and beyond, wide awake. Billy McNeill, like his predecessor Ally MacLeod, had been content and thriving on improving Aberdeen Football Club. His team, playing attractive football and boasting a fine array of talent, had pushed Rangers hard and, despite the Glaswegians winning the domestic Treble, it was McNeill who was awarded the Scottish Manager of the Year award in recognition of his achievements at what was still a modest set-up.

It seemed that the Dons had the man of the moment but yet again they were dealt a cruel hand. Just as Scotland had been the only job that MacLeod would have considered leaving them for, McNeill was soon confronted with a job offer from his beloved Parkhead. His mentor Jock Stein had not fully recovered from a bad car crash three years earlier and, having been offered a somewhat demeaning position in the club's commercial department, was to be offered the honour of managing his country, albeit via a very brief spell as boss of Leeds United.

Things had not been going well at Celtic and their domination since winning nine consecutive Championships between 1966 and 1974 had diminished. As well as Stein departing, the talismanic Kenny Dalglish had left for Scouse shores and the club had endured watching Rangers sweeping the domestic board while they suffered the indignity of finishing a paltry fifth. Jock Wallace had suddenly resigned from his post at Rangers and the ever-turning managerial merry-go-round of Scottish football soon gathered a momentum of its own. The Ibrox side had immediately promoted their time-honoured skipper John Greig and, as if keeping up with the Joneses, Celtic turned to their most successful captain and that meant bad news for Aberdeen. 'I was at the Manager of the Year awards,' recalls McNeill. 'They were held in Glasgow and big Jock [Stein] pulled me to one side and asked, "Do you want to come back to Celtic?" I didn't take it in, and Jock, not used to having to ask twice, wasn't about to beg. "Well, do you want to manage Celtic or not?" It had been Jock who had recommended me to Aberdeen and now he was enticing me away. I was shell-shocked.'

Celtic, not any other club. This was Celtic, the club he had led to European glory, the club he had captained and adored. It was too much. How could he say no? 'My wife Liz tried to talk me out of it,' says McNeill, laughing. 'We had settled in Aberdeen. It was a lovely place to live and work and my wife hated the idea of moving back to Glasgow, but what could I say? How could I turn down Jock and Celtic?'

There was only ever going to be one answer. Dick Donald, Aberdeen's highly respected chairman, received a telephone call on Friday, 26 May 1978. It was official: Celtic were to offer the job of manager to Billy McNeill, who would of course accept. Things though could have been very different for McNeill and Aberdeen.

'The situation at Aberdeen was perfect,' says McNeill, a tinge of melancholy filling his otherwise happy Glaswegian voice. 'It was all set up and crying out for success. When I look back on it, and despite the success I enjoyed at Celtic, I really think that I should have stayed. It was a fantastically well-organised club; there were only three directors, which is great for a manager, and the group of players I had were very strong. I suppose the pull on the heartstrings from Celtic Park was too strong. My head said no, but my heart said yes, yes! One thing I do regret is never working with Gordon Strachan, I mean the real Gordon Strachan. What a player he became, a true great. Right up there with Kenny Dalglish and Denis Law.'

It was a cruel blow to the hard-working Aberdeen board. The club that summer were celebrating their 75th anniversary but, before anyone blew out any candles, they would again be looking in the classifieds for available managers. For the players as well as the board it was a time of uncertainty. For Strachan, though far from happy to see the back of McNeill, he couldn't help but feel this was even more of a chance to wipe the slate clean. While some of his team-mates might fear a new man and his methods, Strachan felt he could thrive on proving himself. In truth, the burden of feeling that he had let down

McNeill had been lifted from his slight shoulders. Here was the second chance he craved and he looked on with interest to see who he would soon be calling 'boss'.

Dick Donald and his board had three men in mind. Bertie Auld and Tommy McLean were mentioned but this time it was the name Alex Ferguson that stood out from the crowd. They had show an interest in the young Govan man after MacLeod left, but now, with that merry-go-round going at full pelt, the time was perfect to make their move. In the same week that McNeill made his prodigal return to the capital, Ferguson had been sacked from his job at St Mirren. He had done a splendid job at Love Street, taking a young side into the Premier League, but having fallen out with their chairman Willie Todd he was dismissed. Ferguson was far from happy and would undergo a messy tribunal but was delighted that the chance had arisen to talk to the men from the north-east. Dick Donald sold himself and the club with his usual charm, and the announcement was made in time for Ferguson to soak in the history of his new club during their anniversary celebrations. The Ferguson era, that would eventually become known as 'The Glory Years', had begun. There was no doubt that under MacLeod and McNeill the club had got its pistons rolling, but Ferguson's desire would heat the flames and send the club full steam ahead through a period of success that will never again be surpassed at Pittodrie.

Ferguson came into pre-season training joking that with Aberdeen's recent track record he hoped to still be there come the following summer. At 35 he was not much older than the senior players at the club and it was apparent that egos might soon be dented. 'It was a much more uncertain time when Billy left than when he arrived,' admits Willie Miller. 'We all knew Billy; we all knew what he had achieved playing the game and his reputation preceded him. Even the other managers mentioned, Bertie Auld and Tom McLean, were well known but, as for this new man, well, his playing days had been far from prestigious and here he was determined to show who was boss.'

Indeed he was, but Ferguson's approach to the job coupled with some of the players' resentment to being told what to do by a man not much older than most of them caused rifts and made for awkward beginnings to Ferguson's reign. 'Alex was very volatile and it was a strange time,' says Miller. 'He's a fiery character and there was no diplomacy. He was in charge, what he said went and not a lot of thought went into what he said to people and let's say feathers were ruffled. He meant to make his mark and that's exactly what he did.'

In his autobiography, *Managing My Life*, Ferguson acknowledges that he may have been a little too heavy-handed in his approach to the club and its players: 'I made my life more trying than it need have been. I had not yet fully absorbed the lesson that it is usually unnecessary to seek direct confrontation and I was often too impetuous in my attempts to instil discipline.'

Ferguson's methods were not alienating just a minority and constant comparisons to what he had worked with at St Mirren didn't help his initial cause. 'He had brought up a good crop of young players at Love Street,' admits Stuart Kennedy, a former team-mate of Ferguson's from his time at Falkirk and now an established right-back for club and country. 'Tony Fitzpatrick, Billy Stark, Frank McGarvey, Les Richardson, Frank McDougall, Peter Weir and Dougie Bell; they made up a good side but Ferguson got off to the wrong foot because he kept on mentioning them in training. Joe Harper would be compared to Frank McGarvey and Gordon to Tony Fitzpatrick. That was bad enough but we'd beaten them every time we'd played them the previous season so it rubbed a lot of people up the wrong way. You have to remember that footballers are the biggest spit-the-dummy merchants in the world and didn't need to be unfavourably compared to anyone.'

The players resented his comparisons, that was clear, but in time the new manager would come to appreciate (slowly) what he had and make the adjustments to the squad that he saw necessary. The contentious Joe Harper more than anyone represented the old guard. To this day Harper is the club's record goal-scorer and dubbed 'King Joe' by his fans, but he more than anyone represented a threat to a new man who wouldn't stand for a clique of old pros not pulling their weight within *his* squad. Harper couldn't be expelled from matters completely, that would have been no way to sell himself to the paying public, but soon his ideas for a new strike force would take shape.

He had taken pre-season training not knowing much about his small, red-headed midfielder other than he had failed to deliver his potential. When going over the squad with his new manager, Dick Donald had asked whether Ferguson wanted to cash in on 'little Strachan'. The manager would not be so hasty. He had seen enough of the young player to suggest that the talent was there but more importantly so was the application. Strachan had proved himself fit, had impressed with his ball skills and his attitude to the new manager reflected how keen he was to impress and start afresh. He would be staying.

Ferguson saw him as the long-term player on the right side of Aberdeen's midfield but recognised the fact that his passing would have to improve if he was to be as penetrative as need be. Strachan and Ferguson would be, over the years, at loggerheads regarding Strachan's deployment and the term 'winger' did not sit easily with a player who saw himself as much more than someone restricted to hugging the touchline. For now, though, Strachan's game was improving and his presence in the team a regular occurrence. 'Gordon was settled now,' says Miller. 'He had his wife, his home, he even had a dog, and as that corresponded with the arrival of a new manager he had the fresh impetus to move on. He proved himself to Ferguson and pushed himself to the forefront of the manager's new team.'

Ferguson's choice of assistant manager had further increased Strachan's rosy demeanour. Ferguson had been keen on Walter Smith who was doing such a good job under Jim McLean at Dundee United. The shrewd McLean though was no mug. He wasn't going to let a man of Smith's credentials go, and with him at his side would bring outstanding success to Dundee United during the eighties. These would be halcyon days for the smaller clubs in Scotland, and Aberdeen and Dundee United became labelled 'The New Firm', in recognition of their achievements. For Ferguson, he would have to wait over twenty years to gain Smith's services, appointing him assistant at Old Trafford in early 2004, but for now would turn his attentions to a man who had played a big part in Strachan's upbringing in the game.

Pat Stanton was recently retired from football. A midfield player of genuine quality, Stanton had been capped sixteen times while at Hibernian and had been a long-time hero of the young Strachan. Now, not only would he be working every day on the training ground with an idol, Strachan would also have an ally from Edinburgh. If you weren't a local, the majority of people at Aberdeen hailed from the West Coast. Stanton could reminisce about Leith, the Castle, the Playhouse and the Festival – things that Strachan may have missed out on while he was growing up there but, still, they represented home. Ferguson, Stanton and of course Teddy Scott were in place, and soon so too would be the team. It would take time, and the first eighteen months were far from easy.

Ferguson had, perhaps unwisely, taken St Mirren to an industrial tribunal citing wrongful dismissal. The club had produced a numbered list of reasons for sacking Ferguson, ranging from misuse of expenses, swearing at a secretary and advising a bookmaker that his team were likely to win the following Saturday. It was an unprecedented case, which Ferguson eventually lost, and it remained a cloud over his head until the Christmas of 1978. The tribunal had decreed that the acceptance of £25-a-week expenses and a loose profanity at a club secretary were enough to find in favour of St Mirren. It was clear that Ferguson had simply been too demonstrative and opinionated for the chairman Willie Todd and, if his lawyer had had his way, pig-headed enough to take the matter to a court of law, but the case had sadly coincided with the deterioration of his father's health, who two months later passed away. Such an important influence on Ferguson, his last words to his son had been, 'Alex, it's just one of those things', and the matter was dropped.

The last game attended by Ferguson's father had been Aberdeen's League Cup semi-final victory over Hibernian at Dundee's Dens Park. Two clubs representing Strachan's footballing past would now propel him into a future full of honours as he prepared for his first big occasion in the red and white of Aberdeen. As it turned out, Strachan would play in two League Cup finals in a matter of months as the Scottish League changed the dates of the finals from spring to autumn. Neither were occasions to remember fondly. Aberdeen had seen off Hibernian to reach the 1979 League Cup final and would now pit their wits against Rangers. It was the sort of game that Ferguson would urge his troops to relish. If they were going to be successful, the Old Firm would have to be defeated, and not only on one-off occasions but consistently. The final at Hampden Park was a contentious affair. Strachan was clearly enjoying his first major occasion and always looked busy on the right. With clever runs and an intelligent range of passing, his natural game was causing all sorts of problems. A well-timed run into the box and beautifully weighted cross found Duncan Davidson unmarked at the back post. The midfielder did his best to waste the chance but Rangers' keeper Peter McCloy stoked the flames for all those who enjoy a laugh at Scottish goalkeepers and allowed the ball to roll over him and drop into his net.

Strachan wheeled away, arms aloft, a smile etched across his face while his knees bounced up to his proud chest. It was a magic moment for a young man who, only a year earlier, wondered if his football highs were going to be leading out the reserves to empty and prosaic stadiums. Here he was taking on the mighty Rangers in front of 60,000 fans. It was the stage on which he belonged, and now he needed the silverware to match but this wasn't to be the afternoon his vast collection of winners medals started taking shape. With Aberdeen 1–0 up and hoping for revenge for the previous season Scottish Cup final defeat, Doug Rougvie, the colossal full-back who had played against Strachan as a kid, was adjudged to have stamped on Rangers' Derek Johnstone. The referee, at first apparently oblivious to the challenge, seemed to be swayed by the ever vociferous Rangers support, and Rougvie, playing his first ever game at the national stadium, would bathe alone. Rougvie always protested his innocence and if Aberdeen felt aggrieved about that then there was soon more to come.

With their backs to the wall and ten minutes remaining, goalkeeper Bobby Clarke was injured challenging for the ball and, while the Dons' management team signalled frantically to get him attention, Rangers' Alex McDonald sizzled the ball past him and a replay looked the likely outcome. It was the least they deserved but, after the hullabaloo of Rougvie's sending off, the referee found seven minutes of injury time and Rangers' Colin Jackson, a born and bred Aberdonian, stole in where Rougvie would have marshalled and headed a cruel winner. Aberdeen had failed on the big occasion and it seemed while they were getting a hand on the Old Firm's fist they couldn't quite loosen the grip they had over the Scottish game.

Strachan though had raised a few eyebrows. A young footballer with intent, he was becoming earmarked as a man who could make a difference in a League desperate for new heroes. Glenn Gibbons, a respected Scottish journalist, had seen that spark from numerous press boxes and wanted to write a piece comparing Strachan with Dundee United's Greame Payne. Their equally slight frames, red hair and tricky wing-play promoted such analogies but Gibbons was soon straightened out when he called Payne's manager Jim McLean to chat about his idea. 'No, no, no,' came the reply from an adamant McLean. 'There's no comparison there, Glenn. Gordon has far more devil to his game and will go much further than wee Greame.'

The following season's final, this time held in December, was an even harsher blow. Aberdeen had done all the hard work getting to Hampden, beating both Rangers and Celtic on the way, and faced

McLean's Dundee United. Both teams were setting themselves for years of success but it was Aberdeen who looked the most likely and dominated the Hampden occasion. 'We hammered them in the first game,' says Kennedy, a tinge of frustration still creeping into his broad Stirlingshire tone. 'Somehow we drew nothing each and so had to play the replay at Dens Park in Dundee and literally over the road from United's home ground. That was frustrating, as we knew Dundee United had a phobia about playing at Hampden. They hated the place but the clubs decided that it was only fair on the travelling fans that the game, played on the Wednesday night, should be played closer to each team. I have always said that it would have been better to play at an empty Hampden and at least our fans would have a trophy. As it was, the replay was just another game to United who were a good team and they thrashed us 3–0 in what was the most atrocious weather conditions any of us had ever experienced.'

There could be no excuse. Strachan and Aberdeen were again losers, and while the fans had cheered home Billy McNeill's side after their Cup defeat in 1978 the streets were now empty. Second best was no longer a badge worn with pride. This time the players and staff were greeted at Pittodrie by a simple message, written boldly on its walls, 'YOU HAVE LET US DOWN AGAIN!' Nothing foul, nothing abusive, just a genuine plea from fans who felt that their side had much more to offer. It got to the players and soon they would respond and this time with feeling.

Strachan was a pivotal part of the side. As desperate as anyone to turn potential into something more tangible, his personal performances had been a real bonus for him, his side and his manager who saw his team gradually coming together. Mark McGhee joined from Newcastle United for £70,000 and that partnership he had had his heart set on was now a reality. After an injury at Celtic, Harper, the darling of Pittodrie's Beach End, was on his way. Jim Leighton, not yet a regular, was now pushing hard for Bobby Clarke's green jersey and, unbeknown to their rivals, the club were harbouring a fine crop of youngsters who would not have to wait long for their big chance. Alex McLeish had broken into the side and had begun laying foundations for a central defensive partnership with Willie Miller that would serve club and country for over a decade, while Neil Simpson, Neal Cooper, Eric Black and John Hewitt – who at the age of sixteen made his debut at home to St Mirren just three days after the League Cup final defeat to Dundee United – would soon play themselves into the side, the history books and the hearts of Dons fans everywhere.

Like his employers, Strachan too was putting an emphasis on a successful youth policy, becoming the proud father of a bouncing boy when Lesley had given birth to young Gavin in December 1978. Gavin, in years to come, would play football under his father at Coventry City and underlined his passion and athleticism for the game by arriving early on a Saturday while his father was away with Aberdeen. The Dons had an away fixture at Hearts in Strachan's native Edinburgh. The squad had travelled on the Friday night and stayed at the Post House Hotel in the smart Corstorphine area of the capital. Just around the corner was the zoo and being an animal lover Strachan went for a relaxing stroll around the grounds on the morning of the game. While admiring the polar bears, a handful of his team-mates came charging around the corner eager to find him. The ever-cheeky Strachan wondered what he had been found guilty of now as they got closer with an intent that suggested he would soon be closer to the bears than he might have liked. 'It's Lesley,' they cried. 'She's had to be rushed to hospital and has given birth to a boy!' It was momentous and heart-warming news, though, this being the seventies and paternal care not paramount in anyone's thoughts, Strachan played that afternoon in a 0–0 draw at Tyncastle.

A year later and a settled family man, Strachan's football career was about to leave behind the expectant world of potential and blossom into the class act it had not always promised to be. 'It was just around the time that I arrived that Gordon began to really fire,' says Mark McGhee about his old mate. 'Fergie saw something in him and tactically got it spot on. Without changing his position, he had Gordon playing further up the field. Rather than picking the ball up in his own half, Gordon was encouraged to be further forward and was receiving the ball in advanced positions and suddenly, rather than just being effective from deeper, he was creating a lot of opportunities. He could cross and pass the ball brilliant, but what he also did which I loved was take the ball for a wee run. That gave us all time to get forward, get a shape and into the box. He always helped the team develop their play, and that is invaluable.'

The weather that had marred their League Cup final defeat was a taster for what was a horrendous winter. Scotland said farewell to the seventies and ushered in the eighties under a blanket of snow.

Aberdeen's fixture list was hit hard. A 1–0 defeat in early January at the hands of their then bogey team Morton left them ten points behind Celtic, albeit with three games in hand. They lost again at home to Kilmarnock on 23 February and all looked lost. Celtic were geared up for a 32nd title but Ferguson and his side had ambitions of their own. It was to be the fire in their bellies that would eventually thaw a long cold winter. 'Beating the Old Firm was the spur that drove us on,' says Miller. 'It was all the talk in our dressing room and Fergie used it as a tool. He'd go on about the west coast bias in the country. "If you're looking for help from other people you're not going to bloody get it," he'd say. "If you want to achieve anything the only people who can help you are in this dressing room and that means going to Glasgow and beating the bloody Old Firm."'

Ferguson, as a manager, has long since used his 'us against the world' mentality and it has worked to calculating effect at Old Trafford. His squad of players at Aberdeen hardly needed reminding though. 'We were lucky at Aberdeen,' reflects Kennedy. 'Everyone in the country is brought up on the Old Firm *being* Scottish football but Ferguson inherited players who were desperate to upset that tradition and bloody-minded enough to do something about it. Willie Miller, myself, Steve Archibald and of course Gordon were all very dogmatic guys who wanted to win at any cost and if any of us ever dropped below a certain level of commitment we had a manager who was straight up on his soap box telling us the score.'

Morton had beaten Aberdeen three times already in that season's disrupted league programme. The fixture looked like it again could be cancelled due to snow in the north-east but come seven o'clock that morning an army of men armed with shovels and brushes worked incessantly to make sure the backlog didn't get any larger. Even chairman Dick Donald mucked in and helped clear over six inches of snow so the game was deemed playable. Aberdeen produced a gritty performance and thanks to a solitary goal from Drew Jarvie, their veteran striker turned midfield man, eked out a valuable win. The opposition wasn't a fashionable outfit and the win wasn't secured by a wonder strike from one of their fashionable new players but it was a victory that gave the side the scope to move forwards. Celtic's chairman hadn't been out clearing the snow from the Parkhead pitch and so the Celtic game had been called off. The deficit was down to six points and Ferguson would have to take his side to Celtic twice before May.

The first of those fixtures underlined Aberdeen's intent as they won 2–1, thanks to goals from Jarvie, doing his best to win a cherished league medal, and Mark McGhee, beginning to get a taste for the big occasion. On 19 April Aberdeen won another tricky fixture at Kilmarnock and Celtic capitulated 5–1 at Strachan's former club Dundee. It was an incredible result especially as Dundee would again be relegated that season. Were the mighty Celtic about to let their lead slip? It seemed that the hot breath emanating from the north-east was beginning to burn on their exposed necks. It meant the second game at Celtic would be crucial. An away win would still leave Aberdeen with a bit to do but a Celtic win would make it especially hard for them despite their monumental efforts. Rearranged due to the weather, the game was played on 23 April, a fine Wednesday night in front of 50,000 delirious and unyielding fans.

Strachan hoped that the pressure cooker of Celtic Park would get to the home team, who, having led for so long and been so far in front, had slowly watched their lead eaten away by a team with the bit between their teeth. Strachan and his team-mates, on the other hand, strolled into the ground full of the joys of spring. Laughter and banter was juxtaposed with a nervous silence from the home dressing room. Only the Aberdeen goalkeeper seemed at all perturbed by the job at hand. 'I hope you lads are laughing tomorrow,' Bobby Clark tentatively contemplated. Goalkeepers are different after all.

On a balmy late April evening in front of 50,000 fans Aberdeen laid out their intentions. Archibald – by now gaining some admiring eyes from south of the border – put them ahead from close range. Their joy though was short lived. Celtic were Champions and under Billy McNeill weren't going to give up so easily. A penalty after only ten minutes and they were level. The noise levels were deafening and would rise in the 30th minute when Strachan stepped up and missed his own spot-kick. It should have got to the player and the team. It didn't. After good work from Strachan and Kennedy down the right, McGhee scored and the Dons would go in at half-time 2–1 up. They returned now looking the part, their football smart and precise, the atmosphere unable to distract them from their task. It was Strachan himself who made amends for his earlier lapse by sealing the win after good work from Ian Scanlon down the left.

The home terracing at Celtic affectionately known as the Jungle had dished out their own form of commiseration when Strachan had missed the penalty but now the object of their 'affection' was purposefully running alongside them, fist clenched and each little step taking him closer to the crown that only weeks before they thought was all theirs. A tempestuous relationship was born. Strachan by now was a threat. His side would not lie down and be beaten and his tenacity, spirit and skill had brought him to the fore. In short he had got right under the Old Firm's skin.

Aberdeen still had lots to do. The following Saturday saw them take on St Mirren and there was no chance of Ferguson letting his players admire their efforts, especially against his former and contentious employers. The game was won 2–0 and after a draw at Dundee United it was set up that, if Aberdeen could go to Edinburgh and beat already relegated Hibernian and Celtic failed to beat St Mirren at Love Street, they would be – barring a mathematical disaster – Champions for the first time since 1955.

Strachan sensed his side were in no mood to let this opportunity pass them by and the anxiety was starting to get to him. He had been taken ill on the Friday before the St Mirren game with a stomach bug, brought on, not by a dodgy fish supper on Aberdeen's seafront, but by the onset of nerves. In and out of the toilet is not the perfect warm-up for any game but Strachan managed to soldier on.

Now he was back at Easter Road. A bus ride from where he had grown up loving and learning the game. On 3 May 1980, almost 20 years since his first visit to the ground as a five-year-old, here he was playing potentially for a Championship medal. He had managed to fit in a trip to his old school, Craigroysten, the day before the game but old memories were the furthest thing from his and his team's mind. It was time to make some new ones.

Easter Road had been far from a fortunate place for the Dons to visit. They were yet to win there since the formation of the Premier League in 1975 and had been knocked out by Hibs in the previous season's Scottish Cup semi-final. Aberdonians travelled down to the capital in their thousands. Their previous title had been won at Clyde's Shawfield stadium in front of only a handful of Aberdeen fans. If they were to repeat the feat of 25 years earlier they would do so in front of a sea of red and white.

In a blustery wind at Easter Road, Aberdeen took Hibernian apart. There would be no last-minute nerves, no willingness to allow Celtic an escape clause. They would finish the job and finish it in style. Two goals from Ian Scanlon, and efforts from McGhee, Archibald and Watson sealed a 5–0 victory.

The final whistle went but seemed to be drowned out by the high-pitched shriek of transistor radios. Celtic were still being held 1–1. The players on the pitch awaited a cheer or a groan while their manager looked frantically to the press box for clarification. Alistair Guthrie, a long-time writer for Aberdeen's *Evening Express*, caught Ferguson's eye and gave him the thumbs up: St Mirren had done the business and, unless Aberdeen lost their last game at Partick Thistle by ten goals, they were Champions. Football had again thrown up one its teasing ironies. Tears rolled down Ferguson's cheeks thanks largely to a club who less then two years before had seen fit to sack him. It was a special moment as he got hold of each player and embraced him as if he was his long-lost brother. They all deserved it: from the headline grabbers such as Strachan and Archibald to the veterans like Bobby Clarke and Drew Jarvie who had been waiting so long for this moment, and through to the unsung and often underrated pros such as Andy Watson whose work rate and vital goals in the run-in had secured many a tight win.

A bright early summer's afternoon turned into a red-skied evening in Edinburgh as the Aberdeen fans partied unhindered on the capital's cobbled streets. Far from begrudging their North-Eastern visitors a moment in the sun, the locals were just pleased to see the Championship finally housed somewhere other than Ibrox or Parkhead. For the first time since Kilmarnock took the title in 1965 the crown of champions would be worn outside the Old Firm's hallowed walls. Like a fairy-tale, the enchanted land was no longer under the evil witches' spell and all across the kingdom they rejoiced.

For the Aberdeen players their achievement was far from fantasy. This was the coming together of hard work that brought on a level of excellence that, while surprising the country, had seemed to them no more than they deserved. 'Winning the title just seemed like a natural progression,' says Alex McLeish. 'We went on that fifteen-game unbeaten run but it seemed normal. We just went out, played well and won points. Slowly it became obvious that we could win the bloody thing. Why shouldn't we win it? Rangers and Celtic didn't have a divine right. Having said that, when we heard the score from St Mirren, it was the first time I'd ever seen grown men cry.'

From chairman to fan, player to local scribe, the joy was unbounded. Jack Webster, a chronicler of the club's history and a former journalist for local papers the *Press and Journal* and the *Evening Express*, was by now a features writer on the *Daily Express* and in his column the following Monday his glee was unashamedly apparent.

> *Oh what a day to be an Aberdonian. I have lived through forty years of Pittodrie history but make no mistake; this was their finest hour. Today's youngsters will tell their grandchildren about it. When the final whistle blew and the truth dawned through a mounting excitement, the whole frenzy of celebration exploded in a riot of red.*
>
> *There was Alex Ferguson running about the field in a mad delirium, crying like a baby and hugging his players in disbelief. The coincidences began to dawn. It was fifteen years to the day that Bobby Clark, Aberdeen's most capped player, had signed for the Dons. It had seemed that the prize would elude him. But now, just recovering from the sudden death of his father, Bobby was able to shed a tear which told its own story.*
>
> *Willie Miller's mother Jean was recalling the amazing fact that her son had been born exactly twenty-five years ago – his birthday was the previous day – just as Aberdeen had been celebrating their only previous league championship in 1955. Then came the champagne that flowed through the night and, yesterday, the most beautiful headache in the world.*

'THE MONOPOLY BREAKERS', bellowed the back page of that Monday's *Scotsman*, but in some corners there were disgruntled noises made about the easy nature of their win at Hibs. It is a suggestion that Stuart Kennedy scoffs at: 'That's rubbish. There was some nonsense about them lying down and taking it easy on us. Utter nonsense. We were in unstoppable form, simple as that. We were snowballing down a hill and no one was going to stop us. Look at the facts. We had to play at Celtic twice in the run in, twice.' His voice becomes determined as if they had won the title only yesterday. 'How can you play two games at Parkhead against Celtic, our nearest rivals, and win both times? It's unheard of but we did it. Celtic hated playing us and we knew that. We had a manner about ourselves, not arrogance but a belief, and the Old Firm had never come across that before. I was so pleased for the manager. His career had been mostly about defeat up to that point but now he was a winner, he liked it and wanted more.'

The last game at Partick Thistle was an anti-climactic 1–1 draw. On the ground that Aberdeen had lost their first game of a roller-coaster season they were now crowned Champions. For Strachan the title was just reward for his new-found form. Having celebrated after the Hibs game on the Easter Road pitch, he remained in his home town and took in his achievements with Lesley, Gavin, his parents and a horde of well-wishers. The Strachans visited Edinburgh City Football Club's bingo evening and he was immersed by congratulatory goodwill, which may have subsided a little as Strachan himself walked away with that night's jackpot. How much good fortune is a man allowed in one day after all?

For his father Jim, his son's achievement was the culmination of years watching a talent develop. He had kicked every ball and felt every tackle. That night he glanced over to his son, a champion of Scotland. 'Son,' he said, a lump growing in his throat. 'You winning the league has been the highlight of my career.' His mother Catherine shook her head, but she must have shared her husband's joy. Her doubts had not been realised. All she wanted was the best for him and now that's exactly what he was, the best. The doubts over his future while at Dundee, his inability to settle under Billy McNeill during his formative years at Pittodrie, they all lifted and in that moment he truly felt that his future lay as a top-class footballer.

Strachan was given his debut for Scotland in that summer's Home Internationals and he pulled the famous blue jersey of his country on as Player of the Year, as voted for by the nation's press. A hugely popular winner, Strachan joined his and his countrymen's heroes. Billy McNeill, his hero and coach Pat Stanton, John Greig, Danny McGrain, all had worn the honour in the past, and, after Martin Buchan in 1971, Gordon Strachan had become only the second Aberdeen player to get the writers' vote. A proud young man, he had pulled out the stops to look the part that night and, on his more experienced team-mates' advice, hired a dinner jacket, bow tie, the works. Very dapper he looked too. The only problem was these functions only require a suit and tie and so their new Player of the Year went in front of Scotland's football writers looking more like 007 than Aberdeen's number seven. 'To this day,' says McGhee, laughing cruelly, 'I have not let him live that down.'

A few clubs were beginning to flutter their eyelashes in the direction of their talented young players. Gordon Strachan, Alex McLeish and Steve Archibald had all got pulses racing and the ever-available

English clubs hoped to continue their courting and wooing of Scottish talent. Archibald, a determined and persistent striker, had planned to leave months before. His single-mindedness on the pitch was mirrored off it and Ferguson was never going to curb his ambitious streak. The club had arrived back in Aberdeen as Champions to a heroic reception. No longer a commiserating pat on the back or disappointed scribble on the wall, this was a reception for winners and something they would have to get used to. Amid the howls of delight, cries went up of 'Don't go, Stevie' but it was – and to be fair the majority of fans knew it – to no avail. Tottenham Hotspur had put in a massive bid of £750,000, a record fee at Pittodrie and one Aberdeen had to accept.

Archibald had come to the end of his contract as had McLeish and Strachan. Despite their good form, no firm offers were received for the latter two and soon they were putting their red heads together. Strachan did not want to sign anything new and find out that someone of Alex's standing had left. Like two schoolboys bartering over a conker, they agreed that if one would sign a new contract the other would follow and so both were tied to the club until the spring of 1984. Archibald's migration south was followed by the sudden departure of Ferguson's assistant Pat Stanton. Stanton's family had found it hard to settle in the north-east and he had decided to move back to Edinburgh and eventually took over the reins at his beloved Hibs. Archie Knox, his replacement, would prove a worthy successor but it was still sad for Strachan to break the ties with a man he had not only worshipped as a boy but also whose good cop to Ferguson's bad cop had been the perfect foil for Aberdeen's players.

Knox had played against Strachan a few times during his time at Dundee United and had a successful stint as manager of Forfar. A no-nonsense sort of player, Knox became an extra growl, a deputy with a snarl as wicked as his sheriff's. Knox was not one to mince his words and whether it was with a player not pulling his weight or with Ferguson himself he would be heard and eardrums would suffer. His methods on the training pitch were not there to win friends but Strachan soon came to respect him, even if coming home after training to a barking dog and a screaming baby constituted a bit of peace and quiet.

The following season, however, offered far too much in the way of serenity. The 1980/81 season had started very well. The reinstated Drybrough Cup in which Strachan had made his top-flight debut seven years earlier was won with a 2–1 victory over St Mirren at Hampden. The old stadium that had famously packed in over 120,000 people for the 1960 European Cup final housed only 7,000 people that day and, although the tournament clearly held little in the way of romance and interest to the Scottish punters, Aberdeen hoped it would catapult them into a season where they could cement their position in the game.

The club won eleven of their opening fifteen games and were unbeaten in the Premier League until a 1–0 defeat at the hands of their old adversaries Morton on 6 December. Strachan had chipped in with five goals up to Christmas; his vision and energy was again vital to Aberdeen's defence of their crown and come Christmas they were a healthy four points clear of Celtic.

Aberdeen had entered the European Cup for the first time – more of which later – and were outplayed by a rampant Liverpool side who would go on to take that year's European title for the third time. It proved a lesson on how to play the game on the Continent and one the players took heed of in the coming seasons. For the manager, too, there was plenty of scope when facing Bob Paisley's Liverpool on how to act both on and off the pitch. The Liverpool boss knew that the game with Aberdeen could be a very tricky affair. New champions of Scotland, a young manager and a hungry team eager to upset their English cousins – steps would have to be taken to defuse a potentially awkward situation, and for the quietly cunning Paisley flattery would get him everywhere. The object of his affection? Gordon Strachan. 'If Aberdeen ever relent and decide to sell Gordon, he'll become Britain's first £2 million player,' he told members of the press in his dulcet Durham tone. 'He impresses me greatly, as do Aberdeen as a team. They don't give much away and with a few wins under their belt they'll face us with confidence.'

Mind games in the modern game are common and championed by the likes of Arsene Wenger and his Manchester United counterpart Sir Alex Ferguson. Here, Ferguson was learning from a subtle master. Paisley's team had arrived in Aberdeen and the local paper had published a 28-page pull-out supplement citing how they would prevail in the 'Battle of Britain', and he was quick to – as he called it – 'give them a bit of toffee'. Strachan had clearly been pinpointed by the Liverpool hierarchy as the man to watch, a player of skill whom they needed to stop in order to hinder the Scots' progress. It was a ploy that worked and must have opened Ferguson's eyes to the power of a carefully planted comment before a high-pressured occasion. Both legs were won by Liverpool and Strachan was noticeably quiet. 'That was brilliant,' said Alan Hansen, Liverpool's Scottish centre-half. 'We all knew why Bob had said the things he said about Gordon. It was to put him off, to give him the heebie-jeebies when he read it. It worked like a dream because Strachan never kicked the ball in the two legs against us.'

The Liverpool players may have been aware of their manager's tactics but would not have known that Strachan had been struggling with a bothersome groin injury that had quietly affected his game in the last few months of 1980. He had dismissed Paisley's comments: 'What would a £2 million player do?' he asked at the time. 'Score fifty goals a season, never get injured.' Now he had a problem himself that although not keeping him from the action was distracting his high-octane game and that would soon get worse. On 30 December Aberdeen played Dundee United at Pittodrie and late in the game Strachan jumped with United's Iain Phillip. On landing he felt a tear, an innocuous moment but one that would see Strachan without a ball at his busy feet for the rest of the season.

The stomach muscles had been torn and Strachan was bedridden. Always a busy man, lying and looking at his ceiling was far from ideal. Here the doubts that had hindered him in the past began to creep back into his head. He tried acupuncture from a Vietnamese refugee, but continued to struggle to walk, let alone play. His mother's old concerns about a future without qualifications were rekindled and, on top of trying to move to a new house in the Ferryhill district of Aberdeen, these were worrying times in the Strachan household.

Life inside Pittodrie was not much better. The fantastic start had been tempered by only one win in the opening six games of the New Year and their title would soon be relinquished to Celtic. They were missing something and that something was Gordon Strachan. Ferguson needed him back and turned to an old employee for advice. Jock Stein had invited the Aberdeen manager to come on a trip to Israel for a World Cup qualifier. Ferguson was honoured and keen to learn from a managerial legend but instead came away with a tip from his ex-goal-getter Steve Archibald. The Scottish striker had enquired about Strachan's injury and mentioned to Ferguson that his Tottenham team-mate Tony Galvin had had a similar problem but thanks to a

Harley Street specialist was now up, playing and would go on and help his team stride towards that year's FA Cup.

Ferguson immediately took a phone number and had Strachan booked in for an appointment with Sir Patrick England, a renowned surgeon who had had, amongst others, Prince Charles and Earl Mountbatten under his knife. What transpired was an operation that had been carried out only three times before. The doctor found and dealt with not only the ruptured stomach muscle but also a hidden hernia and a blocked intestinal tube. Strachan's innards must have looked like a London tube map. The complexity of the procedure had Strachan into that year's *British Medical Journal* before it had him back playing and his progress was hindered further by a form of salmonella caught from a local Chinese restaurant in Aberdeen rather than the splendid steaks and prawn cocktails he was feasting on in Harley Street.

The hindrance his illness had caused to his recovery from a complicated and frustrating injury summed up a galling eight months for Strachan. 'Gordon found that spell very hard,' says McGhee, by now becoming a firm friend of the Strachans. 'He was a very hyper character. He wasn't someone who enjoyed having leisure time. He wanted to train, wanted to play. He wasn't one to miss training easily and if he did you could be absolutely sure that he had a good reason. He was the sort of player a manager could trust.' His frustrations could not even be taken out on a golf ball as he was banned from his other passion by Ferguson, who had him back for pre-season training, desperate to rekindle the fitness levels that had been the mainstay of his game before the injury and illness. It was the tonic his side needed.

The club and Strachan were keen to prove that their Championship-winning form had not been a one-off. Strachan was desperate to rediscover the level of performance that had propelled him from a young player not short of potential to Scotland international and one of the most recognisable faces in the British game. That cheeky smile, the red hair, the little side steps and the infectious grin had been missed at Pittodrie and so a pre-season tournament saw Dons fans welcome back with open arms a key part of their Saturday afternoons. West Ham, future employers Manchester United and Southampton were to be Strachan's opponents on his successful return from a frustrating lay-off. Southampton under Lawrie McMenemy were transformed into a formidable First Division team.

Kevin Keegan had arrived from Hamburg the summer before while Mick Channon, Peter Shilton and Mark Wright were all past, present and future England internationals.

The Saints faced their hosts in a final won 5–1 by Aberdeen, with the biggest cheer of the afternoon reserved for a Strachan penalty. It was the prelude to a run of form covering three years that Strachan regards as the pinnacle of his playing career. For now though order was resumed on the right-hand side and the Dons faithful, along with the manager, could again look forward to another successful season. Ferguson had delved into the transfer market and brought in Peter Weir from his old club St Mirren. Weir was an exciting left-sided midfield player who, although taking time to settle into his new red strip and £330,000 price tag (a record fee between Scottish clubs), soon, with his lanky stride and ability to get to the by-line, would prove the perfect foil to Strachan on the opposing flank. The club, the squad, the team, it all had perfect balance. A fit-again Strachan was the catalyst to three seasons of success and for his team-mates his presence not just in the dressing room was heaven sent. 'On the pitch he brought us composure,' purrs Willie Miller. 'Ferguson's teams are always similar with a strong line up the middle, a rigid four–four–two with the skilful players in the wide areas. We had a very strong back four, of course, but often Gordon would get us out of bother. He was the one who would put his foot on the ball, get his head up and play us out of trouble. It was the same at United with Giggs and Beckham, but with Strachan Ferguson had an early side that could turn defence into attack very quickly. I'll tell you what though; you always knew the wee man was there. "Give me the ball, give me the ball." It would never end.'

Always so hungry to be involved, Strachan would not be constrained to the touch-line. He hated the term winger and in the super-fit Stuart Kennedy had the perfect full-back to oversee his tendency to roam. 'I was encouraged to get by him and give him an option,' says Kennedy. 'I was happy to do that and take defenders with me. "I'll run up and down for you all day, wee man. Give me the ball, cut in and do your stuff, it's up to you and if you lose the bloody thing guess who will get back and make the tackle?" He appreciated me though and I gave him the confidence to go and do his bit.'

That's exactly what he was doing and 'his bit' was soon enough to ensue more personal plaudits. The Mackinlay Personality of the

Month was won halfway through the season and Strachan fittingly chose Tom Aitken to present him with the award. Sixteen years after spotting a snotty-nosed boy shining on his primary-school playground and giving him a game at Edinburgh Thistle, the old school janitor was as proud as ever. 'Gordon was a born player,' he said in his speech. 'It was obvious, even at the age of nine, that he had the talent to make a big name for himself and I'm delighted that he has done so.'

However, as the days grew shorter and winter fell so did Aberdeen's fortunes. A run of six games without victory over Christmas was not Championship-winning form and they would again have to settle for second spot behind Billy McNeill's Celtic. Despite their yuletide generosity Ferguson's side only finished two points behind Celtic thanks to a run which took in an amazing fifteen wins from their last sixteen games. The one defeat in that run cost them dear and was at, you guessed it, Morton. Success instead would be gained, for the first time under Ferguson, in the Scottish Cup. It was a Cup run that would eventually end in glory, not only at Hampden but ultimately in Gothenburg with victory over Real Madrid in the European Cup Winners' Cup sixteen months later.

That was the furthest thing from anyone's minds as Aberdeen prepared to play at Motherwell in the third round of the Cup. As the game kicked off, the punters settling into their seats and the press uncapping their biros, John Hewitt latched onto a mistake and within nine seconds Aberdeen were in front. Hewitt, soon to be so famed for scoring late, dramatic winners and whose goal in Gothenburg would mean so much, had set them on their path to glory. Celtic were disposed of in the next round thanks again to a Hewitt winner and victories over Kilmarnock and St Mirren meant another major cup final against Rangers.

The build-up to the occasion brought a little more than the usual Cup preparation. Sure there were the suit fittings and the relaxing rounds of golf but Strachan would also have to rush Lesley to hospital as young Craig couldn't bear to miss the big game and so arrived the Wednesday before. In a career that allowed no time for family sentiment Strachan was back with the squad the following day and training at Cruden Bay, about ten miles north of Aberdeen, hoping to add another winners' trophy to the family album. Despite the setbacks in finals against the Ibrox side in the late seventies, Ferguson was confident that the new decade had swung the tide towards the shores of the

North Sea. The title may again have settled at Parkhead but Ferguson, so steadfast on the need to beat the Old Firm regularly, was happy with the aptitude his team were showing in these games. They had beaten Rangers three out of four times that season and knew his team were now relishing their encounters with the blue half of Glasgow.

Hampden, as ever when hosting a Rangers game, was a wall of blue noise. A sea of blue scarves ebbed and flowed across one half of the old stadium as they hoped that the minnows from the north would soon be engulfed by their vengeful tide. Aberdeen had beaten them 4--0 the week before in the Premier League and Rangers were desperate to make amends. Competing for every ball, crunching into every tackle, Rangers seemed to have grown tired of these rude visitors laying claim to their family silverware. The ever-brilliant Davie Cooper was teasing Rougvie, who couldn't fathom just where he'd pop up next. Challenges were fought for; the pace was set and it looked as if Rangers were destined to continue Aberdeen's wretched cup-final luck. A John McDonald goal after fifteen minutes seemed to confirm that theory but an unexpected source was to rectify matters and turn the game firmly on its head.

Alex McLeish had proved a menace in many an opponent's penalty box. A towering header or a scrappy strike were his usual forte but today he fancied something different. Twelve minutes before the break the Rangers defence failed to clear a Strachan corner but all looked safe as the ball fell at McLeish's feet. Like the shy boy at the school disco, he awkwardly shaped his body to shoot. As the ball boys were priming themselves to retrieve the situation, he swerved his body and with perfect technique curled the ball sublimely into the top corner. Game on.

'That was something I'd worked on in training,' boasts McLeish amidst my somewhat rude sniggers. He is quick to put this impertinent writer to task. 'No really, pal. We'd been playing five-a-side at our training camp in Cruden Bay and I bent one right into the top corner. I suppose my team-mates thought it was a one-off but I showed them. On a personal note it was a magic moment although after the game our late, great chairman, Dick Donald, asked me whom I'd been aiming for when I crossed the ball into the goal!'

It was the lift the team needed and, for all Rangers' early efforts, they were pinned back for the majority of the second half. Chances came and went but even going into extra-time Strachan was sure that their Hampden hoodoo was about to come to an end. As if willing for that to happen himself, he sent in the perfect cross for McGhee to head home a second and from that point Rangers were out of it. McGhee returned the compliment, crossing for Strachan, who with bloodied nose slipped the ball into an open goal. His somersaults, cherished by the Aberdeen hordes, summed up the feelings of joy in their stomachs at certain Cup glory. By the time Neal Cooper lashed the ball in to make it 4–1, the previously raucous terraces holding the Rangers faithful were sparse of bodies let alone noise. It was only Aberdeen's second Scottish Cup success since 1947 and, while no one could have envisaged such an emphatic scoreline, the club had once and for all proved that they were a team for the big occasion and certainly had the measure of an unfortunate, and wilting, Rangers outfit.

Aberdeen celebrated into the night at the Gleneagles hotel where Stuart Kennedy, rather than worrying about his club's fortunes, waited to have his picture taken with fellow guest and cinematic hero Burt Lancaster who was filming *Local Hero* in Scotland. That summer Strachan went on to make an international name for himself as he shone in Scotland's World Cup campaign where he faced the likes of Zico, Falcao and Socrates of Brazil, and Oleg Blokhin and Rinat Dassaev of Russia. Scotland had again failed to qualify for the latter stages but Strachan's eyes had been opened to a world of possibilities.

Not once had he looked out of place amongst such footballing dignitaries and his talents had been noted by a global audience. 'His persona was growing by the minute,' says Kennedy. 'He was growing in stature, playing against the best in the world and soaking it all in like a sponge. His time in Spain whetted his appetite I think and he returned to Aberdeen with a new spark.'

Strachan was now seriously thinking about a move to pastures new. Had he achieved all he could at Aberdeen? At 25, was the time right to leave a club that he had helped bring success but that had also made him the player he was today?

Before travelling to Spain with his country, Sunderland had made contact with Aberdeen about bringing Strachan down the east coast to Wearside. Their manager, Alan Durban, had seen enough of Strachan's game to warrant a move that would include the transfer of Ally McCoist to Aberdeen but was met with a firm 'no'. His performances in the intense heat of southern Spain had increased the interest and papers were full of talk that would have turned the head of the most settled player. Valencia, Barcelona, Tottenham, Arsenal, Southampton, Juventus and Nantes were all reported to be keen in obtaining his services. What was a man to think?

Strachan was confused and said as much in an interview with the *Evening Express*. It was a confession he would soon regret. Between his ill-advised chat and its publication Strachan had had second thoughts about what he saw as deserting a club that had been so good to him and he explained to a disgruntled Ferguson that his words were unfounded and his curiosity had waned, for now at least. It was a headache to a manager desperate to build on what had already been achieved. Willie Miller, his captain and the cement keeping Aberdeen's defensive wall so resolute, had been unsettled by an offer to join Rangers as skipper but Ferguson's power of persuasion and the fact that the Scottish game's balance of power had shifted heavily towards the north-east meant he stayed and continued the good work.

While the attention of bigger clubs from home and abroad must have seemed exotic to the players, they would soon be glad that they remained firmly on the green grass of home. The 1982/83 campaign turned into one that all Dons fans will treasure whether they were witness to it or not. Success in the European Cup Winners' Cup was, of course, the highlight of the campaign but Aberdeen would not be deterred from their task on the domestic front.

After a poor start and with only one win in the opening four games there were no signs of the celebrations and memories that would be forged so dramatically nine months later, and for Strachan there were concerns over a World Cup hangover. Paper talk and the feeling of anti-climax would in time recede but he was now a marked man, literally. Defenders were advised to wise up when it came to Strachan and the space which he so effectively scrutinised would be at a worrying premium. The concern was that he would be forced out of games and his influence would diminish. For lesser players it would have. Strachan had shared space with the masters of Brazil and seen first hand how the most sublime of players will create space and time, however closely they are marked. He went about improving his left foot and was resolute to score more goals. His efforts paid off.

Four goals at Dundee in the League Cup underlined his hunger in front of goal while his form and aptitude for training and the week-in-week-out business of the Scottish game dispelled any talk that his mind wasn't in it. Again it was Celtic and Aberdeen competing for the title but they were now joined by the serious challenge of Dundee United. Jim McLean's team along with Aberdeen had upset the Old Firm domination but two League Cup victories were so far all they had to show for it. They had a fantastic team, with Richard Gough, Paul Sturrock and David Narey the pick of a ripe orange bunch.

The Tannadice men had underlined their intentions with a 2–0 win over Aberdeen on the opening game of the season but as the season went on their 'New Firm' rivals settled into their stride and in November wreaked a savage revenge with a 5–1 victory, Strachan again amongst the scorers. The Dons were well in contention, winning at both Celtic and Rangers, but as they progressed deeper into Europe the concerns that they would be side-tracked suddenly seemed valid. A marvellous win over Bayern Munich saw them cruise emphatically into the semi-final of the Cup Winners' Cup, but there was no quick cure for an impending hangover and the following Saturday saw them lose a crucial game at Dundee United. More headaches were to come after the first-leg rout over Belgian opposition in Europe. A 5–1 victory practically ensured them a place in the European final and it seemed they had one eye on their passports as they again lost the next Premier League fixture, this time at Rangers. They were defeats that cost them the title.

For Ferguson what he saw as a lack of drive was a hindrance and, rather than bemoaning his own ability to raise his troops after their European battles, was furious at the way a potential treble was lost. 'He was very, very disappointed and felt we weren't as hungry for success as he was,' says McLeish, who now himself a top manager understands the need to hold a side's concentration. 'We had lost to Dundee United after the Munich night and that had cost us the title. Fergie's expectations were very high of course and maybe the club's and its players were that bit lower. If the club had demanded higher expectations over the years, we may have ignored all the pats on the back and the good press we received during our Cup run and focused better than we did. Dundee United after all had no interest in how well we were doing abroad and deservedly took the title.'

Eventually pipped to the runners-up spot by Celtic, Aberdeen would also meet the Glasgow club in what turned out to be a bloody and vicious Scottish Cup semi-final. Celtic were staring down a barrel going into the game having lost the title. Aberdeen were about to travel to Belgium for the second leg of their European semi-final but with

Ferguson adamant that his side kept their minds on the task closer to home.

Both teams were urged into action by fans and managers alike; the game was a battle from the first whistle to last. Tackles were unforgiving and challenges harsh. Strachan called it the roughest game between the two sides he had ever known and that was saying something. Struggling early on with a twisted knee and bruised ankle, Strachan was soon joined by Eric Black and Dougie Bell, also seeking the trainer's sponge. Neal Cooper, the catalyst for so much of the side's play, was as ever in the thick of things and before the game was up would be sitting in a local infirmary getting treatment for a broken nose. He had taken the blow and was lying on the Hampden turf when Strachan came over to check on his bemused team-mate. 'I can see two ball boys,' he moaned to his team-mate. 'That's OK,' teased Strachan. 'There *are* two ball boys.'

Inevitably for a game more akin to a gladiatorial movie than *Match of the Day*, it was a substitute who settled matters. Peter Weir came off the bench and headed his team into the final where, in defence of their trophy, they would again face Rangers. The rout of the previous season was never going to be matched and the game turned into a strange afterthought coming after Aberdeen's triumphant victory over Real Madrid in the Cup Winners' Cup final only ten days before. Despite an Eric Black goal securing a 1–0 victory for Aberdeen, Ferguson was not happy and let his players know about it. It had been unfair on a squad who had given their all and secured domestic as well as European kudos for the club. Strachan had played nearly sixty games for club and country that season and took exception to his manager's criticism.

Ferguson had seen the error of his ways and apologised, but Strachan was now sure that his time in Scotland was coming to an end. His contract was up at the end of the next season and, while he intended to see it out, the article that had been published after his return from Spain had woken the public and press to his thoughts of migrating to England or abroad. He soon had to defend himself against charges of being 'got at' by those in the Scotland squad playing in England and being attracted by the money available outside the Scottish game. However, sports cars and the sight of Charlie Nicholas – recently signed from Celtic by Arsenal – being paraded around London's nightclubs wasn't Strachan's idea of bettering himself. He was now a player of international repute and one capable of competing against the world's best but couldn't escape the notion that he was playing in what he saw as a mundane league.

'When I came back from Spain having played against some of the world's greatest players I was immediately into the old routine,' he said a week before the Cup Winners' Cup final. 'Same old dressing rooms, same old opponents, same games week-in week-out. I'd eaten all the pies, met all the tea ladies and I'd like a new challenge.'

But would a run in Europe, playing against and beating some of the best players in Europe, change his mind and convince him to stay in a league in which he had spent, hitherto, his whole career? 'You get tired sometimes and I thought then that a change of scene would do me good and I still think it would.'

Strachan reported back to training having spent the summer falling deeper and deeper in love with the idea of a new challenge. His itchy feet were not unbearable but an unwelcome distraction. It was as if his boots had been laced with pepper by a Pittodrie prankster and were preoccupying his mind from the job at hand – another season in the Scottish Premier League. Pre-season friendlies against Ipswich, Arsenal and Manchester United had fuelled his curiosity as had a trip to Nuremberg, more famous for rallies and trials but whose football team, once a power in the German game, were now showing a keen interest in a small footballer from the north-east of Scotland.

German football was no stranger to Strachan's ability. Their clubs had faced Aberdeen plenty of times in European competition and Strachan had stuck firmly in their psyche. A local scribe had penned an open letter in his paper to the president that he should sell his private jet plane and use the cash to buy Strachan. It seemed to have worked. The players were changed and making their way onto the pitch when Strachan, bringing up the rear, was suddenly approached by a small German man in a pin-striped suit.

'You like Nuremberg?'

'Yes,' replied Strachan, surprised to be asked such a question minutes before a game.

'You like the city? You like the park?'

'Yes, yes,' Strachan said warily.

'I am the president you see.'

Strachan was horrified and must have looked more eager than usual as he came sprinting out of the tunnel hoping his manager hadn't witnessed his pre-match chat.

It was to set a pattern that would dog Strachan's season. Interest from clubs, interest from agents, interest from the nation's press. Ferguson was far from impressed. As the season commenced, he, too, had been the subject of massive speculation after John Greig had been sacked from his post at Rangers only weeks into the new campaign. Ferguson, a Govan boy and ex-Rangers striker, would be perfect for the job. All the Old Firm had to do was click their fingers and men would come running but, having worked so hard to turn the tide, Ferguson resisted his home town's charms. Willie Miller and Strachan, during the height of the rumours, had walked past his office and were met by their manager's frosty glare. 'You better wipe that smile off your faces,' he growled. 'I'm here for another five years.' Deep down though, under his gruff exterior, he knew that the team he had reared would not.

Steps had to be taken. Billy Stark, an exceptional right-sided midfielder was brought in from St Mirren that summer, an obvious statement that Ferguson was resigned to losing Strachan. The club were unable to match the sort of earning potential Strachan could generate from a move to England or the Continent, but more importantly they could no longer offer a challenge. There was no quick fix. Neither time nor circumstance was going to eradicate Strachan's need for change. He'd better start looking at his options. Aged 26, his next move had to be the right one.

On the pitch there were no signs of the problems raging off it. Aberdeen had proven themselves a resilient bunch and wouldn't let the game's rumour-mongers and their back-page headlines dampen their spirit or their concentration and progressed through autumn and into winter challenging for three trophies at home and abroad. For Strachan, it wasn't so easy. Where he might have thought that, once he crossed that touchline he could get on with the job at hand, he increasingly found he could not. A small pocket of his own fans had begun to turn on him and nights before games were spent agonising at the latest call from an agent promising him wealth beyond his most extravagant dreams. He would sit getting changed before a crucial game, chatting to McGhee not about how he wanted him to peel off to the back post today because the opposition's left-back was useless in the air, but rather what he thought about the latest offer.

Both men had moves on their minds. For McGhee, not only was he leaving a club he had enjoyed helping become great, he also would be losing a deep and gushing source of creativity in Strachan. 'If you look back on all the important goals I scored for Aberdeen and briefly Scotland, Gordon provided most. The significant moments in my career, Gordon had a hand in them. Peter Weir was great too, but I think, percentage wise, if you counted up assists I doubt there is any player at any time who would have more assists than Gordon.'

Rumours persisted and for Strachan there was no getting away from them. Arsenal and Spurs from the English First Division continued to be linked with his name. In addition, Fiorentina and Verona from Serie A and Real Madrid from La Liga had been mentioned, while Bayern Munich, Borussia Dortmund, Hamburg and Cologne kept up the interest from the Bundesliga. It had turned into the Eurovision Strachan Contest! The town was resigned to losing one its most cherished adopted sons. One local businessman even offered to install a free kitchen for the Strachans, albeit on the condition that he stay and play at the club. 'Hello, Real Madrid you say,' Strachan said mocking an imaginary telephone call. 'No, no I'm sorry I can't sign. You see I've got this kitchen ...'

Strachan continued to contribute to the Aberdeen cause, scoring and creating goals, but his relationship with Ferguson had become strained by events off the pitch and he hated the constant limelight that his situation had placed him in. Ferguson went as far as 'resting' his star man but would not divulge to the press his reasons why. He feared that his preoccupation with a move away would hinder the team, but, despite the feuding, Ferguson knew that deep down the player who had been suffering in the reserves when he had arrived over five years previously was now vital, and trophies, Ferguson's lifeblood, were up for grabs. The title was won by seven points (an impressive margin made more so by the fact that they failed to win any of their final four games) and, for the first time a non-Old Firm club won the Cup as well. Aberdeen, double winners, took the Cup north for the third year in succession and this time it was Celtic, beaten 2–1 after extra-time, who had to make the short journey home with their heads bowed.

It was a remarkable way to finish his time at a club at which he had played such a big part in attaining success. A typically probing cross from the right by Strachan had laid on the winning goal for the also departing Mark McGhee and, amid the smiles and congratulatory hugs at Hampden, Strachan was positive he was doing the right thing.

It had been the seventh time they had faced Celtic that season and the novelty, even for turning over the Old Firm, had worn thin. Strachan loved his club, the city and his team-mates. He had become a microcosm for what Aberdeen had come to represent – a small man taking on and beating the establishment. Now it was time to move on. But where?

6. NOT BAD FOR A FISHING VILLAGE

> REPORTER: *This may sound like a daft question, but you'll be happy to get your first win under your belt, won't you?*
> GORDON: *You're right. It is a daft question. I'm not even going to bother answering that one. It's a daft question, you're spot on there.*

He holds his arms towards the Swedish night sky. The referee's final whistle still hangs joyously in the air like a baby's laugh as team-mates hurl their arms around each other in disbelief. The rain that had drenched Gothenburg's Ullevi Stadium all afternoon and evening begins to recede and, like a rainbow, ABERDEEN 2 REAL MADRID 1 shines onto the pitch from the stadium's electronic scoreboard. All that is left of the storm is on the players' kits that cling to their weary bodies; almost sleepwalking around his team-mates, he shakes their hands one by one not quite sure if what has just happened is real. Moments later, Willie Miller triumphantly lifts the Cup Winners' Cup aloft and the 12,000 fans who have made the trip over the North Sea respond in kind. He can only think of his dad somewhere amongst that red and white throng, an Edinburgh man through and through but right now as proud as any Aberdonian. It was real all right. Very real indeed.

Since the birth of competitive European club competition in 1955, Aberdeen Football Club, by geography and misfortune, seemed destined to remain on the periphery of the continental game. The closest they would seemingly get in Europe's tempestuous but ultimately glorious waters was via the town's countless fishing trawlers chugging their way through the early morning fog and out towards their murky North Sea workplace.

By rights, however, the club should have been Scottish pioneers into a new age where the game's frontiers were to be so emphatically broadened. In 1954 Switzerland had hosted a marvellous World Cup won by West Germany and commended for its typically fine Swiss engineering. It galvanised the countries of Europe to form the Union of European Football Associations; UEFA was born. The idea had been to create a tournament where the Continent's nations would compete but soon it was decreed that a club competition, pitting Europe's best against Europe's best, would be the more practicable and desirable option. The idea was passed around the Union's table for a while before Gabriel Hanot, the editor of the French sports paper *L'Equipe*, took matters into his own hands and in the April of 1955 invited delegates from the Continent's top clubs to a meeting in Paris.

Honved of Hungary, Real Madrid – who would go on and monopolise the competition for its first five years – AC Milan, Rapid Vienna and Chelsea – on their way to winning the English Championship – were all among the eighteen leading clubs represented who gave their blessing to a new and exciting European Champions' Club Cup. It was a brave new world of possibilities. For managers and players it was a chance to compare styles and tactics while the fans would get the opportunity to experience, first hand, the stars only ever seen on their local cinematic newsreels. For Aberdeen, the timing of the tournament couldn't have been better. In 1955, the club had marched to its first ever Scottish Championship and would proudly take their good name and that of Scottish football into Europe. Or so they thought.

The Scottish Football League had not followed the policy of their blinkered and reactionary English counterparts who deemed the tournament an eyesore on their precious fixture list and ordered Chelsea to withdraw. The Scots would be involved but, rather than Aberdeen, it was Hibernian who were asked as a token of goodwill to fly St Andrew's flag. Aberdeen were furious but, as the Hibernian chairman Harry Swan had attended the meeting in Paris and cemented the Scots' involvement, his club were given the honour of competing and admirably reached the semi-finals. Jack Webster in his chronicle of the club's fortunes summed up north-eastern ill feeling in his book *The First 100 Years of the Dons*. 'It may have been intended as a noble gesture but it was an outrageous decision, when the Dons had won the right of entry in the place where it was supposed to matter – on the field of play. So Hibernian became the first Scottish club in Europe's premier competition and Aberdeen, denied its proper place, had to wait another twenty-five years for the opportunity.'

The quarter of a century before they would again wear the crown of champions had not left them starved of European experience. A European debut in 1967's Cup Winners' Cup had seen them dismiss KR Reykjavik of Iceland 10–0, while further excursions through the seventies saw them take on European big-wigs such as Tottenham,

Juventus and Borussia Moenchengladbach. Billy McNeill's one season at the helm, in many ways a catalyst for their latter success, saw Aberdeen take on a tricky Belgian outfit RWD Molenbeek and the new-found belief that was beginning to run through the Pittodrie water flowed heartily after a composed performance earned them a 0–0 draw on Belgium's flat soil. One UEFA observer was most impressed: '[That] was one of the best performances, if not the best, by a British club playing in Europe that I have seen,' he remarked.

Celtic, Manchester United and Liverpool fans must have scoffed at such high praise and it seemed to distract McNeill's team, who couldn't build on their early momentum, losing 1–0 at Pittodrie. For Stuart Kennedy, Willie Miller and John McMaster, three players who would all be involved in the club's surge to glory in 1983, it was an early lesson on just how wily European opposition can be.

Strachan, trying hard to find his feet on the stodgy sands of his new Aberdeen career, missed out on that year's short stint on the Continent but with the advent of Ferguson's reign at Pittodrie his and Aberdeen's moves into Europe would slowly become more impressive, lasting longer than the Christmas booze run to Calais. A European final against Real Madrid was to be the definitive test but the four seasons prior to that were to prove the ultimate in revision sessions and for the first two campaigns under Ferguson the subject was harsh: double German.

Fortuna Dusseldorf and Eintracht Frankfurt saw off Aberdeen's challenge in those two seasons but Strachan had his taste of what the European game had to offer. Just months into Ferguson's management Aberdeen travelled to Bulgaria to face Marek Dimitrov in the Cup Winners' Cup. A three-hour bus journey out of Sofia, pigs roaming the streets, the primitive toilet arrangements and the lack of sleep – they were all eye openers to a young British footballer, as were the hospital facilities. Willie Garner, the centre-half and Strachan's room-mate, had broken his leg in a 3–2 defeat and had to wait for attention next to an unfortunate young lady having hers amputated. 'It could be worse,' quipped Strachan. 'You could live here.'

Strachan hadn't played in the first leg but got on as a second-half substitute and scored a goal in a 3–0 victory. The second round saw Aberdeen exit the competition after a 5–0 aggregate drubbing against Dusseldorf but their next German encounter, although again ending in defeat, was a much closer affair and Strachan, now a regular, was beginning to turn heads abroad. Eintracht Frankfurt were unfortunate first-round opponents in that year's UEFA Cup. A tie so early in the 1979/80 season against a team challenging for major honours in the Bundesliga was harsh and a 1–1 draw in the first leg at Pittodrie left them with an uphill journey to Frankfurt's Waldstadion. However, Ferguson's team was beginning to find its feet and put on a brave show, losing to a solitary second-half goal. Given a standing ovation by the 20,000 spectators, their industry and flair was not lost on Frankfurt's manager Friedal Rausch. 'My team is within one point of the top of the Bundesliga,' he boasted. 'We beat Hamburg – Kevin Keegan and all – last week but they did not give us as many problems as Aberdeen. I was really impressed, particularly in the first half when they could have scored twice. We had to work hard for this victory. Keeper Bobby Clark and Gordon Strachan were the top players. In defeat, Aberdeen were gentlemen and did not resort to tough play. We found friends in this team.'

The Germans were not the only ones impressed; even the Spanish referee saw something in the team worth championing. 'Both teams played as true professionals. There were no men posing injuries or play-acting. Aberdeen got on with the game and showed a high degree of skill. I am convinced they will become a big name in European football.' How right he would be. By winning the Scottish title that same season Aberdeen would at last get their chance in the European Cup. A 1–0 win over Memphis Austria at Pittodrie was defended successfully with a 0–0 draw in Vienna and next came Liverpool, twice winners of the tournament and gearing up for a third successful assault.

English opposition, even so early in the season, had already been taken on and beaten. Arsenal were invited to Scotland in pre-season and defeated 2–1 in a game commemorating the Championship flag being hoisted above the Pittodrie faithful. As it triumphantly swayed in a North Sea breeze, it was an excited and confident Ferguson then who took Pat Stanton down to Liverpool on a spying mission. Both were soon confronted by Bill Shankly, no longer the manager but still a massive presence at the club he had made great. 'Hello, gentlemen, good to see you – you are doing a terrific job up there,' he said to the Aberdeen pair, stuttering like a pair of awestruck Bay City Rollers' fans. 'So you're down to have a look at our great team?' continued Shankly. 'Aye, they all try that.'

It was another daunting challenge and one that again would prove too much for the side. Strachan, disabled by an injury and Paisley's 'kind' words, was ineffective and over the two legs of a tie branded 'The Battle of Britain' the only Scots laughing were Liverpool's contingent of Kenny Dalglish, Graeme Souness and Alan Hansen. Liverpool had taken the sting out of the game in Pittodrie and through a marvellous Terry McDermott goal – lifting the ball nonchalantly over Jim Leighton – took a 1–0 lead back to Anfield. Aberdeen, however, in the second leg started well; Ray Clemence had made a fine save from Mark McGhee, who went through one on one with the England 'keeper but, just as Souness was starting to growl at his slow-starting team-mates, Willie Miller put the ball in his own net. A Phil Neal effort before half-time put paid to the contest and Ferguson was not amused. They had given the ball away far too cheaply, especially their now seasoned internationals who, if anything, were paying Liverpool far too much respect.

It was a sombre dressing room until, as the players were getting ready to run out for the second half, Drew Jarvie, their old stalwart of the seventies with the Bobby Charlton comb-over, piped up with a rallying cry, 'Right, lads, three early goals and we're right back in it!' Strachan had to suppress a laugh but as he looked over to check Ferguson hadn't noticed his misdemeanour he saw the manager himself trying very hard not to laugh at Jarvie's admirable optimism. Those three goals didn't arise and the tie was lost 5–0 on aggregate.

'We were a young team,' explains Alex McLeish, making light of a situation that would hold them in good stead despite their manager's ever so obvious disappointment. 'We had nowhere near the experience of that Liverpool side but it was important to get those games under your belt. We were going to have to endure some pain in Europe before we won anything but that was normal.

'You have to go through it and we certainly did that night. We had started well but were chasing shadows by the end. The boss went mental at us despite our inexperience but then again he couldn't stand losing, especially so heavily. I remember we all sat on the bus after the game tucking into a goody bag from KP, the crisp and nut people, who had sponsored the game. Fergie walked onto the coach and said, "Anyone on this bus smiles, they're fined a tenner." That was that, heads down and no one said a word.' Scared to even crunch on their peanuts, the mood was hardly lifted as they arrived back at their hotel in Liverpool. 'Graeme Souness had chosen to dine out at our hotel,' says McLeish through gritted teeth. 'There he was with his wife, sipping on a nice glass of wine, with a smile spreading from ear to ear.'

Galling times for Strachan and his team but the revenge they craved over the English would not be long in coming. The following season Aberdeen were drawn against Ipswich Town, holders of the UEFA Cup and brimming with international quality. The 1981/82 season was to be their manager Bobby Robson's last at Portman Road before taking on the England job and in his twelve years at the club he had turned Ipswich from a small but friendly rural club not only into a force in the English game but also into one of the best teams in Europe. But for Liverpool's dominance they would have been crowned champions of England and the comparisons with what Ferguson was trying to do at Aberdeen made for a fascinating prospect.

Again it looked as though a tough early draw would hinder Aberdeen, yet to go past the second round of any European competition. 'We feared no one, I mean that,' says Alan Brazil, Ipswich's striker and team-mate of Strachan's within the Scotland set-up. 'We had beaten the best Germany, France, Holland and Poland had to offer the year before to win the competition so went into every game very confidently. We knew how good Aberdeen were and over the two games there were suggestions that we took them lightly, but I can tell you the Scots in the team, myself, George Burley and John Wark, were never going to let that happen. This was us against Scotland. Bobby Robson too wouldn't stand for complacency and he reminded us how good their players were. McLeish, Miller and of course Strachan were all internationals; McGhee was a dangerous and quick forward and they had the makings of a fantastic set-up.'

Just as Ipswich had gone about upsetting the European establishment, Aberdeen showed a similar disdain for supposed regiment and battled to a credible 1–1 draw at Portman Road thanks to a fine team display and an equalising goal from John Hewitt. The Scots had matched Ipswich in every department; a point celebrated in the Scottish press but played down by Robson. He argued that, while they had played brilliantly on the night, they couldn't be expected to reach those heights again and that his team's experience would see them through. For Strachan, back from injury and happy to be involved, Robson's words displayed arrogance not uncommon amongst his nationality. If anything the Dons would be even more up for it.

Strachan was buzzing around his home turf with intent. Popping up all over the pitch, refusing to be shackled by his supposed right-midfield berth.

Dropping deep to collect the ball, then darting on to whatever action he had so potently started, Strachan was like a horsefly around a millionaire's pool and, after scampering into the penalty area, robbed John Wark and went down under his fellow countryman's clumsy challenge. Penalty. Strachan himself stepped up and sent Paul Cooper – renowned for his penalty saves – the wrong way. Although Wark redeemed himself with his own spot-kick before half-time, it was Aberdeen who came out for the second half the more likely victors. Peter Weir now underlining his considerable talent was talismanic and, while brilliantly served all night by Strachan, it was he who mesmerised Mick Mills before scoring two brilliant goals. 'Weir ran poor Mick ragged,' recalls Brazil. 'I'm not blaming Mick, he was a fine defender, but Weir chose to really turn it on that night.' The 23-year-old from Johnstone tormented the England and Ipswich captain and had him spinning one way and then turning another as if drilling for Aberdonian oil. The 24,000 crowd erupted with delight at an Englishman's misfortune and walked away into the autumn evening relishing their beloved Dons' progress.

Those same fans would soon be blowing the dust off their atlases and asking the question Arges who? Arges Pitesti were a Romanian unknown quantity, but a 3–0 win in the first leg at Pittodrie – with Strachan opening the scoring early on from close range – settled any tension concerning their opponents. If anything they made the trip into Romania's agricultural heartland a little too lightly and found themselves 2–0 down at half-time. As we will find out later, Ferguson was beside himself. He had specifically sent them out with a game plan and now they were facing a humiliating turn of fortune. Strachan, who more than most had his manager's harsh words ringing in his ears, went out and scored from the penalty spot, and another effort from Hewitt, getting a taste for European goals, sent them home comfortably.

If that game had had Aberdonians wondering who and where they were playing, the next opponents, Hamburg, were bringing one of the most famous names in the history of the game. Franz Beckenbauer was playing out his career on the River Elbe, and, despite Kevin Keegan having returned home, Hamburg were on their way to winning the

Bundesliga title that season and the European Cup the next. At 38, Beckenbauer – having himself returned from across the Atlantic and the fading glitz of America's rocky flirtation with soccer in the late 70s – was no longer the marauding sweeper of his heyday but could still dominate a game with his exceptional footballing brain. As if finding a Picasso hung at an A-Level art show, the Pittodrie crowd – another full house – were hushed into stunned silence each time the 'Kaiser' received the ball on their home turf.

The players, however, would be less star-struck. Ferguson had instilled a belief that no one was worth being scared of, which had brought success domestically. Now, big European nights at Pittodrie were no longer to be seen as a novelty, whoever's reputation they were up against. With little regard for their guests then, Strachan and his team-mates confidently went about their business, dictating the tempo. They were playing with a youthful exuberance that seemed to rock the Germans, and appropriately it was one of the youngest of Aberdeen's new breed, Eric Black, who opened the scoring only 23 minutes into his European career with a fine header past Hamburg's keeper.

Still on top and hungry for more goals, Ferguson's side were brimming with confidence but a terrible mix-up between Jim Leighton in goal and Stuart Kennedy allowed the Germans to equalise and the tense-looking Glaswegian was suddenly grinding that bit harder on his chewing gum. From that setback, Aberdeen proved they had the character – if not yet quite the tactical European nous – to challenge abroad. So, undeterred, they began again to dissect their visitors' defence. As if rolling off the north-eastern shores, wave after wave of attack had the Germans drowning under a red tide. When Andy Watson put Aberdeen ahead in the second half, Hamburg were thinking only of damage limitation. Strachan missed a penalty to make it three but wouldn't hide and continued to pick holes in a defence – even under the guidance of Beckenbauer – that was beginning to huff and puff. With only nine minutes remaining, Hewitt latched on to a loose ball in the penalty box and made it 3–1 to round off a spell of football that Strachan regards as the pinnacle of his time at Pittodrie. There would be greater results and achievements in the red of Aberdeen, but for Strachan, clearly revelling in the class of opposition, the flowing football that night was hard to match.

It could have been, and should have been, five or six, but the same approach and pace to the game that had seen them upset Hamburg eventually cost them dear; brave adventure was replaced in the dying moments with juvenile naivety. With the clock ticking down on a memorable November night, Aberdeen were still searching for goals when big Doug Rougvie went down with an injury. The sensible thing to do would have been to play the ball out for the big left-back to receive treatment, therefore wasting some valuable time. Instead, committed to attack, they marched forwards, lost possession and were punished by an, as ever, unforgiving German team.

That meant that Aberdeen travelled to Hamburg in a far more precarious position than their performance merited, and Hamburg with blood in their nostrils were in no mood to let their unexpected standing in the tie slip. Aberdeen were ruthlessly dispatched. There was no shame: Hamburg were one of the strongest teams in Europe and would prove that over the next eighteen months, but they had thrown away a golden opportunity to progress. Again German lessons would have to be heeded. Strachan had had, by his now set standards, a very ordinary night in the second leg but vowed to improve. The domestic game was off due to adverse weather in Scotland but Strachan got his head down, trained even harder than usual and returned fitter, hungrier and, as the next few years proved, even better.

The Scottish Cup had been won in May and so it was the Cup Winners' Cup that would entertain Aberdeen's hopes of reaching a European quarter-final for the first time in their history. Usually the poor relation amongst UEFA's family of trophies, the competition in that year's tournament looked far from third rate: the holders Barcelona, their Spanish rivals Real Madrid, Tottenham, Bayern Munich and Inter Milan were an impressive array of European names. To be amongst such illustrious company was the spur Aberdeen needed as Strachan and his team-mates gave their club and its fans a season of glory, but a lifetime of memories that still, over twenty years later, lighten up any Aberdonian's face.

The road to Gothenburg. Not quite Crosby and Hope, and for most European purists the idea of a little club from Scotland's outback taking on and beating the Continent's finest was as amusing a gag as anything Bing and Bob could muster. That Aberdeen were regarded as innocuous by their European masters was obvious when they were among four clubs forced to play a preliminary round. Ferguson and his players were far from happy at the obvious contempt shown towards the team by the game's hierarchy but were powerless. They went into the draw, avoided their Welsh counterparts Swansea City and instead drew FC Sion of Switzerland. Ferguson strolled into the dressing room during pre-season training and told his squad the news only to be greeted by a bemused look from his players, which suggested they knew little about the Swiss challenge that lay ahead. 'Sion you say, they're going to be tough, boss,' piped up Stuart Kennedy, clearly a fountain of knowledge. 'They've got four or five internationals them. It's true, boss, *Shoot!* magazine says they're the team of the future.' Of course, Kennedy knew little of their team but his words seemed to have the desired effect. 'I managed to talk our bonus for that game right up. We hammered them 7–0. I even scored and we all got a lovely wee bonus.' Strangely enough Sion went on to knock the Dons out of the same competition in 1986, so *Shoot!* magazine were proved right after all.

Their ample lead meant Aberdeen's players could enjoy Sion's Tourbillon Stadium and its beautiful Alpine setting. Amidst the snow-capped mountains and their log cabins, Aberdeen played out a 4–1 victory and went peacefully into the first-round draw. From a winter wonderland Aberdeen would play the opening two rounds of the competition in the less picturesque surroundings of Eastern Europe. First up was a trip to Albania and a slender 1–0 win over Dinamo Tirana at Pittodrie was not the ideal score-line to take to the unknown capital. On the morning of the match it seemed that the team would have to avoid more than embarrassing defeat. Machine-gun fire rang across the searing streets as the son of the late King Zog attempted to overthrow the country's Communist regime. The players, mildly aware of the supposed coup, went about their business, despite perhaps inflated reports reaching home. 'FLIGHT INTO FEAR', rang the *Daily Record*, much to Willie Miller's amusement. 'It was all hyped up that we had fallen into some sort of revolution and were in danger of our lives. The truth was, we didn't know much about it. Our only real concern was getting a good night's sleep.'

The game finished goalless amid a friendly atmosphere hardly befitting a violent rebellion. Strachan had come in for some heavy treatment from the Albanian left-back Gega, who having harassed his Scottish counterpart for pictures before the game seemed more interested in a chunk of his ankle as a souvenir. Job done, the players were pleased to be making their way through the poverty-stricken streets of

Tirana and there seemed little sign of the obviously quashed troubles. When asked what he made of it all, Neil Simpson, a midfielder of growing stature and a local boy though and through, replied in his north-eastern drawl, 'A coo? The only coo I can see is ower in 'at park.'

It was another European win but UEFA's balls again awarded the Dons and their small band of travelling fans with a far from luxurious trip. This time Poland. While far from being a venue lauded on TV's *Wish You Were Here*, Polish football was enjoying a picture-postcard era. Semi-finalists in the previous summer's World Cup, Poland, inspired by their striker Zbigniew Boniek, had been one of the most attractive sides in Spain. Their champions Widzew Lodz would knock Liverpool out of that year's European Cup and Aberdeen's opponents Lech Poznan were on their way to winning that season's Polish Championship. Aberdeen carried out a thoroughly professional job at home winning 2–0 thanks to goals by Weir and McGhee. Strachan would score only once in his side's European adventure that year – an effort in the 7–0 drubbing of the Swiss back in August – but his overall play was far from unnoticed. The Polish crowd had taken to him immediately, recognising his fine performances in the World Cup only months before that had gripped the nation. The cheers he received may also have had something to do with the vast amount of chocolate he and his team-mates gave out to the Polish children before the game. Despite 30,000 Poles on a sugar rush, Aberdeen won 1–0 and returned triumphantly home.

Aberdeen Football Club were in the quarter-finals of a European tournament. To many observers that alone was an achievement, but an extremely underrated victory over the Poles proved that they had become a steely side capable of making a name for themselves. Strachan, although becoming concerned about his own future, was as excited as anyone about the prospects of a big European night. Like a cramming schoolboy, he studied the names of the teams still remaining. Out of the big names who started in the tournament, only Tottenham had been eliminated, so the likes of Real Madrid and Inter Milan still remained. Strachan was desperate to face the best. It was the nagging doubt in his head that suggested that his football may soon be played elsewhere, but he desperately felt that his beloved Aberdeen – and they were beloved – would raise their game against a big name. But this big? They didn't come much larger than Bayern Munich.

Managed by Uli Hoeness, the majestic blond right-winger of West Germany's 1974 World Cup-winning team, Bayern sported German legends. Amongst them Karl Heinz Rummenigge, twice European footballer of the year, and Paul Breitner, a veteran of two World Cups and one of only three men to have scored in two World Cup finals (Brazilians Vava and Pele being the other two). It was going to be tough. Bayern's ex-captain and recent conqueror of the Dons Franz Beckenbauer gave them little hope. 'Aberdeen are technically inferior to Bielfeld, who Bayern beat 5–0,' he said. 'I expect Bayern to outplay them. As soon as the Scots set outside their country, they are only half as good as they are at home.'

The great man's words were unfounded and simply judged on his experiences against them the previous year but who was to argue? The hugely ambitious Strachan, however, wanted it no other way than the hard way. Having played against West German sides so often over the years, Strachan had come to respect their football. To Strachan, the game in Germany and the Bundesliga was the best in Europe. Its teams were hard but fair and, when competing against the likes of Bayern Munich, the game would be determined by sheer skill rather than what he saw as the more cynical Latino game.

Ferguson too had the utmost respect for the West Germans but was adamant that his players should not fear anyone. Reaching the quarter-finals was great but his team were not to sit on that achievement, even when faced with the challenge of what he, deep down, regarded as the best team left in the competition. 'We'd been unlucky against Bundesliga clubs previously but they were the teams to beat,' says Miller, reflecting his manager's thoughts. 'Make no mistake, the German league was the best in the world at the time and they kept beating us, but through the boss we always thought, if we could beat Bayern, then we had a chance to go all the way.'

The team had successfully seen off the 'Old Firm' phobia that had hindered them and so many other Scottish clubs over the years, so why not go one better and put paid to the jinx holding them back against German opposition? 'Yeah, we'd become a bit too used to losing to German sides,' says Alex McLeish, laughing. 'But we now had so much confidence and went to Munich for the first leg brimming in self-belief, perhaps most notably Gordon, who by now feared no one. Aye, he was crucial to the squad going into those big games.'

Strachan had every right to have such feelings of grandeur. If the fact that his name was beginning to be branded across the Continent was unsettling his mind, at this point he wasn't showing it. Days before the Munich clash, the *Sunday Mail* ran a report suggesting that Munich themselves were keen to take Strachan off their opponent's hands for £1 million as a replacement for the soon-to-retire Breitner. A supposed agent had approached Bayern's manager Hoeness, saying Strachan was available but only when the German realised that Strachan was still under contract did he state that no move would be made despite his very authentic interest. Ferguson played it down as mind games, similar to Bob Paisley's toffee two years earlier. Yet again, however, it was his little playmaker who was used as the supposed tool of deceit but for now that issue could wait. Strachan could laugh it off and while accepting it as a compliment had to endure some friendly stick in the Pittodrie dressing room where for a number of weeks he was affectionately known as 'Herr Strachan'.

It had been four months since the win in Poland and in that time Strachan had managed to pick up a nasty hamstring injury that kept him, his manager and the Germans guessing over his availability. In that time Ferguson and Archie Knox had managed a number of scouting trips to Bavaria and had returned with six videoed matches. The players sat through them and, while not quite video nasties, there was enough quality to highlight just what they were up against. While Strachan sat admiring the likes of Breitner, at the end of his career but still so fast and so able to play the game at a pace that suited him, he was aware that his hamstring might not hold up and hopes of starting in Munich's famous Olympic stadium were now slim.

Ferguson was all too aware of his player's woes. He was back training but between the two of them they concluded that he was not ready for ninety minutes. It was a blow. Strachan was desperate to play in the world's best stadia and Ferguson recognised the necessity of having the strongest front on show as possible, but that was football and there was nothing either could do about it. The squad arrived in Munich and the Sheraton Hotel, a far cry from anything they had encountered in either Tirana or Poznan. A few of the wives had made the journey which was rare, and must have wondered if it was usual practice for Pan's People – the seventies dance act from *Top of the Pops* – to be rehearsing and milling around the team's headquarters. Aberdeen, though, were preparing to put on a show of their own and trained at the magnificent Olympic Stadium, truly a fantastic European venue steeped in history, on the morning of the match.

The Germans raised their eyebrows at such a request. Train at the ground on the morning of the match? 'But nobody has ever done this before,' argued an officious Bavarian official.

'Aye,' said Ferguson, dismissing their concerns, 'and nobody has ever won here before.'

Well rested and fully prepared, Aberdeen went out and put on a superb display, maybe their best. Strachan, tracksuited and itching to be part of it, admired his team's performance sadly from afar. Just as Ferguson had hoped, Bayern's array of reputations counted for nothing on the night as Willie Miller nullified Rummenigge; Neal Cooper shackled Breitner, and Dougie Bell – who most impressed Strachan – looked the best player on the pitch.

Aberdeen had been creating chances, but with fifteen minutes remaining, Ferguson felt he had to make a move that would keep the ever dangerous Germans on the back foot. Strachan was asked to strip off and get on. He now came with a reputation; his game would be recognised from his performances in the World Cup and the sight of him coming on in the final stages might just lower German morale and give the Dons that extra breathing space they needed for a famous result.

Strachan, still feeling his leg, didn't try anything fancy; this wasn't the time for his nippy game; clever football like an understanding friend could and would wait. Now was the time for discipline and with it coursing through the team's veins they held on to a memorable goalless draw. Held on actually is the wrong term. If anything it was Bayern whose ears were the more grateful as the final whistle went. Beckenbauer must have sat in the ground he would always call home, munching on his ill-advised words like sauerkraut, wondering at the new-found professionalism of his country's guests. Gone were the team who capitulated at Hamburg sixteen months earlier and, amid the furore amongst the Scottish media, a more accomplished set-up returned home.

The ever erudite Jack Walker, Aberdeen through and through, was among those scribes so taken by the side's Bavarian performance, and wrote in the *Sunday Standard*:

> *The lingering roar of celebration which rang around the great Olympic Stadium of Munich was more than a joyous expression of 1500 Aberdonians. It also marked the entry of Aberdeen FC into that upper echelon of continental football, with the announcement*

that this city which is already the oil capital of Europe is now set to take its place with the best of them.

All the years of promise and disappointment were finally put aside as the Dons took on the legendary Bayern Munich on their own ground and taught them a lesson in the arts of the game.

Of course it was a night with an historical omen. The pitch on which this memorable game was played out marks the exact spot where Neville Chamberlain's plane touched down for his crucial meeting with Hitler in 1938. There may have been no 'peace in our time' for the Aberdeen defence as the Germans came at them in raids of growing desperation but, to quote Mr Chamberlain's successor, this was indeed their finest hour.

After the match the focal point was the Sheraton hotel, where the players mixed with supporters in the lounge bar, enjoying a quiet glass of beer. Two American oilmen who had worked in Aberdeen and had flown in from Cairo and Tunisia for the night paid their own tribute. It was the least they could do for 'mighty fine people' they said. There might still be a long way to go in the second leg but, in Munich at least, Aberdeen had won 0–0.

The hyperbole was understandable but Ferguson was eager to ignore the plaudits and concentrate on the very hard job at hand. Strachan too had now been around long enough and had endured enough second-leg disappointments to realise the danger that still lay ahead. Bayern had not become second-class citizens after one goalless draw, and Strachan, like his manager, was more than aware that all they needed was a score draw in Scotland, and they were more than capable of doing that. That, though, was of no concern to the Aberdeen fans. All that talk levelled at the players to keep their minds on the job was for the dressing room only. While the team could concentrate amid the stench of boot dubbin and liniment oil, the fans were breathing in the clean air of expectancy and levels of hope were crashing above the town's seawalls.

In the two weeks between the night in Munich and the return leg, Strachan was still feeling his hamstring but there was no way he was going to miss out on such a massive occasion. Twenty-five thousand fans crammed into Pittodrie, creating an atmosphere not exactly synonymous with the old place. 'The atmosphere was incredible,' reflects Miller, goose bumps still not far away. 'The Aberdeen fans were not known for their exuberance and passion but that night changed all that.'

From the off, the fans were able to tone up their sometimes lazy vocal cords as Aberdeen set the tone, forcing two early corners and setting about the job with the gusto their fans deserved. The Germans, however, were not in the business of being dictated to and soon hushed the crowd in the most efficient manner with Klaus Augenthaler unleashing a long-range free-kick that screamed past Jim Leighton in the Aberdeen goal.

It was going to take something extra-special. The team showed they were up for the fight, equalising towards the end of the half through Neil Simpson, but when Bayern again took the lead through Hans Pflugler after 61 minutes the crowd's optimism was silenced. Strachan, though, was buzzing about the pitch. He had noticed some of the young players dropping their heads and, while his manager made the substitutions that he hoped would turn the tide, Strachan was busy rallying the troops. Even with fifteen minutes remaining Strachan felt that it could still be their night and looked to be right up for the challenge ahead. He wasn't alone. 'Sure they had scored the goals and silenced the crowd,' says Stuart Kennedy, who watched the final stages from the bench having been substituted. 'What they hadn't counted on was that our team wasn't going to stop playing, whilst there was a chance we would go for it.'

Hewitt had come on as an extra attacker and the play seemed to become centred around the Bayern penalty area, where Aberdeen soon had a free-kick. Strachan and John McMaster stood over it deliberating over who would take it. What happened next was a well-rehearsed bit of 'tomfoolery' as they intentionally ran into each other, and mocked each other as if a double-act playing the London Palladium. Not known for their sense of humour, the Germans were still wondering about the 'show' when Strachan quickly took the free-kick, and amid the defenders' uncertainty McLeish stole the extra yard he needed. It was 2–2, and suddenly the noise returned.

Bayern kicked off, still in the driver's seat, but as the Aberdeen players lined up bouncing with intent the fans followed. As Aberdeen immediately won back possession and swung a ball into the German box a roar went up into the Aberdonian sky that must have shook oilmen out to sea, let alone German goalkeepers. Eric Black, a nineteen-year-old forward with prolific tendencies, rose and put in a good clean header goalwards which Muller, the Bayern keeper, could only parry into an empty space gleefully filled by Hewitt who slammed the ball into the net. Amazing. 'They were the best team, in the best league in the world,' says Miller. 'We were 2–1 down; I'm marking the twice European Footballer of the year; the crowd is silent and yet we found the drive and determination to grind out the winning result. Gordon has to take a lot of credit; his energy that night was incredible and lifted the whole team.'

The stunned Germans had no reply and the likes of Rummenigge and Breitner could only watch speechless as Ferguson danced down the tunnel. His tactics had been better than his rhythm that night but now his legion of supporters would join him in a jig until dawn. Jack Walker again spoke succinctly for his home town when he wrote:

> *Grown men who had believed that Roy of the Rovers belonged to fiction might have disputed the fact, if only they could have raised the energy. It would be time enough in the morning, after a restless sleep of action replays, to accept that their team had really joined the European elite.*

How do you match that? Pittodrie's greatest ever night would mean precious little in years to come, though, if they didn't build upon such glorious foundations. The semi-final would be against Belgian side Waterschei. Not exactly a giant within the game but Strachan was making the usual noises to quell any feelings of contentment – no team could reach a semi-final of a European Cup without having something about them, etc. – as if putting Ferguson's mind at rest that complacency, that evil goblin that haunts all managers, would not rear its ugly head. 'Fergie built them up to be like AC Milan,' says Kennedy, laughing. 'He said he'd done his homework on each player, and that this winger was like Pele, could score goals; their forward was like Cruyff and lightning quick, and their keeper was as safe as bloody Lev Yashin. We went out for the first leg at Pittodrie all hyped up and wanting to smother this talented team right away. They were fucking mediocre! We scored in the first minute and won 5–1. Job done.'

So it proved. Waterschei were far from watertight and despite losing the second leg 1–0 the hard stuff had been done. Aberdeen, a little provincial club outside even their own country's football gentry, were in the Cup Winners' Cup Final in Gothenburg on Sweden's west coast. There, Real Madrid awaited them. Not that there was much in the way of celebration, such was the desire to win every game. 'We sat in that Belgian dressing room, our heads down in an eerie silence,' says John Hewitt, with a chuckle. 'You'd have thought we'd have been knocked out.'

Fair enough, it had been the team's first defeat in Europe, but the fact that they played with a severely dilapidated side (Strachan missed out due to injury as did four other regulars) meant nothing. It took Archie Knox – a man not known for ever being thrilled after defeat – to underline what had just happened. 'We're off to a European final boys!'

The Aberdeen fans, slowly becoming used to the big occasion, took less convincing. Immediately, maps were bought, routes decided and tickets purchased. 'Are ye gyan to Gothenburg?' became the question on everyone's lips as fifty planes were hastily booked up, cars filled with petrol for the long journey and the *St Clair*, the local ferry, primed ready to take 500 fans across the water. Lesley Strachan, despite a terrible fear of flying, would take to the skies for a game that she 'wouldn't miss for the world'. Like a military invasion, a red-and-white army descended by air, sea and road on Scandinavia; latter-day Vikings hoping to pillage European glory.

Strachan was like a boy on Christmas Eve, itching to get under the tree and unwrap Madrid's defence. He had played in Cup finals at Hampden, faced Brazil in the World Cup, but this, a European final against perhaps the biggest name in world football, was special. 'It will be the biggest game of my life,' he purred before heading off to Sweden with the team on just another in a queue of planes bound for Gothenburg.

The team were put up in Farshatt, a quaint little hamlet, fifteen minutes out of the city, where they relaxed, swotted up on the videos of their opponents meticulously put together by Archie Knox and tried to forget the pressures of what was just around the corner. The weather was fine for now but the storm clouds were soon to roll in and, as kick-off approached, a cloud of nervous expectancy began to hang over the camp. A message of goodwill from Margaret Thatcher couldn't even relax the squad fully and by the morning of 11 May 1983 the players were on edge. The usually placid Peter Weir was itching to get on with it and Mark McGhee contemplated taking out his tensions on an unfortunate fan who jokingly reminded him of a missed chance in a league game the previous week.

The rain had started to fall, at first slowly but then in torrents, as black clouds enveloped the formerly springlike skies. A sprinkling of rain was fine; the pitch had seemed to dry when the players trained at the stadium the day before, but as lightning and thunder clapped around the city it was hardly the ideal or expected weather for a May final. On the team bus, Strachan, usually engaged in a game of cards with Stuart Kennedy and Alex McLeish, sat pensively alone. His Walkman was on in his ears, a buffer between his own thoughts and the tense atmosphere on board. He contemplated the weather, the Aberdeen fans in their drenched masses lining the streets and just what sort of game he could muster on the most important night of his career.

Purpose-built for the 1958 World Cup finals, Gothenburg's Ullevi Stadium was no stranger to the big occasion. It had hosted England's demise in that year's competition when they lost 1–0 to Russia and was the venue the day an unknown seventeen-year-old Brazilian named Pele broke Welsh hearts by scoring the winning goal in the quarter-finals. With its strange wave-like structure and lack of cover, it wasn't ideal for the kind of night the Swedish skies had in store and the legion of men setting up behind the goals in yellow macks and matching galoshes looked more like North Sea fisherman than Europe's sporting photographers.

Aberdeen's fans, despite the rain, would not be perturbed. They vastly outnumbered the Spaniards in the 18,000 crowd and soon the familiar chants went up. The players changing into their familiar red shirts with white pin stripes began to savour the atmosphere. Strachan had come in from a warm-up, his wet fringe hanging over his eyes. It wouldn't do and the sight of him and Ferguson arguing over who would cut off the offensive hairs brought temporary relief. Soon though there was an eerie silence. Glances said more than words for now, but Strachan took time to whisper words of encouragement into the ears of the young players who up to now had shown class beyond their years. For Eric Black, Neal Cooper, Neil Simpson and the unfortunate substitute John Hewitt, all under 21 years of age, this was by far the biggest occasion of their young lives.

Hewitt had become accustomed to the role of substitute. He, like any professional, disliked the mantle of 'supersub' but he would again have to take his place on the bench and hope his time would come. Joining him in a tracksuit was Stuart Kennedy. He had been a mainstay of not only the European run but also the club's new-found success but injury to his knee in that gory Cup semi-final with Celtic weeks earlier meant he was unable to play. As a goodwill gesture, Ferguson took the gamble of naming him as a substitute so he could get a medal. Scant consolation for a man desperate to run his heart out for a cause but better than nothing.

In a matter of moments the bell would ring and they would be out of their misery. 'Forget the badge you're playing against,' Ferguson told them. 'Real Madrid may have a history, but, let me tell you, you've already knocked out far better teams.' It roused his troops who, amid a torrent of motivational cheers, began their walk onto the sodden Ullevi pitch. Ferguson had a point. Real Madrid's famous white shirts were no longer filled by giants of the world game. The Dutchman Johnny Metgod, who would go on to play for Nottingham Forest and Tottenham; the Spanish centre-forward and top scorer in that year's tournament, Santillana; and German defender Ulrich Stielike; all had played at the highest levels but they were far from the sublime side who, in the fifties and sixties, enchanted Europe. A teenage Ferguson had witnessed the Spaniards taking Eintracht Frankfurt apart 7–3 at Hampden Park in the 1960 European Cup final, and now here he was pitting his wits against Alfredo di Stefano, Real's magical man that day and now the manager Ferguson would have to out-think for his own slice of European glory.

Exalted company indeed, but Ferguson had taken his own source of inspiration: Jock Stein. To the manager, he was a wealth of knowledge, the one man who most symbolised Scottish success on the Continent, while to the players he was not only a giant in the game but also their national team manager and his very presence demanded their best behaviour and conduct. Stein, the wily ex-miner from south Lanarkshire, suggested Ferguson play up his feelings of awe towards di Stefano and his side. Ferguson, on the eve of the game, approached his opponent and offered him an expensive bottle of whisky, a token of the high esteem in which he held him. It was Ferguson's first real mind game (although I can't see Arsène Wenger today receiving a cup of tea, let alone good Scotch) and just may have worked. Were these polite Scots only here to make up the numbers?

That question was answered swiftly as it became clear Ferguson's players were far from as generous as their humble manager. The pitch was more like an Aberdonian beach and not surprisingly it was the Scots who settled quickly into the conditions. Strachan was immediately into his game, demanding the ball, his short steps bouncing over pools of water like a swan taking off for flight. Within minutes he had received the ball on his chest, halfway in Real's half, looked up and swept a quality cross to his forward on the edge of the area. It wasn't the most dangerous position to receive the ball, but Eric Black, showing all of his youthful elasticity, pulled off a scissor kick that cut the ball onto the crossbar. If Real Madrid had wondered about their opposition, they didn't any longer. Aberdeen's swathe of red shirts was like a matador's *la capa* taunting a Spanish bull and soon they would go for the kill. After seven minutes Strachan's out-swinging corner – another brilliantly rehearsed set-piece – was met by the on-rushing McLeish and, although his header was blocked by a defender, Black reacted first and lashed the ball into an empty goal.

A Scottish cheer rivalled the thunder that had roared over Gothenburg not long before as players, staff and fans realised this might just be more than a jolly trip abroad. However, as ever in a sport that flirts and offers a wink of glory, a cruel rejection can be just around the corner. Alex McLeish, a lynchpin within the side, had been vociferous in how his colleagues should cope with the drenched pitch. 'I had noticed in the warm-up that the ball wasn't rolling, and sticking to the surface,' says the amiable Glasweigan, still not content with his own actions in the Swedish rain. 'I said to all the players, "Make sure you all lift the ball when you pass it."' Approaching the quarter-of-an-hour mark, though, McLeish himself failed to heed those wise words. 'We had begun so well and utilised the conditions brilliantly. I, however, played a pass back to Jim [Leighton], which on any other night would have been fine. The three of us, myself, Jim and Willie [Miller], had a telepathic understanding but on this occasion I misjudged the turf. Their centre-forward reached the ball first and Jim had no alternative but to bring him down. With one lapse of concentration they had a penalty and were right back in it.'

Jaunito, who tragically died in a car crash only weeks later, scored and the game ebbed and flowed until half-time, both teams enjoying decent spells. 'You're right in this game,' Ferguson told his players, although he had some special words for McLeish.

'Aye, the gaffer had a go at me about the penalty. He was angry but I'd been brought up on that and so was well used to it.'

Strachan had been everywhere. With his usual right-back, Kennedy, sitting it out, he had Rougvie (his old adversary from his days at Edinburgh Thistle) behind him to protect and to serve. To the untrained eye Aberdeen's right flank must have looked like a tug-boat pulling an oil tanker to harbour, but between them they had worked tirelessly for the cause and were a constant threat to Real. So much so, Ferguson pulled Strachan to one side and suggested he take a breather early on in the second-half and conserve his much needed energy.

It wasn't advice that came easily to Strachan. He continued to run at the heart of the Spaniards, and twice he was unfortunate not to score but, as the half wore on and with 'The Flower of Scotland' ringing around the ground, extra-time looked the most likely outcome. With three minutes left, John Hewitt was told to get his tracksuit top off: he was going on. 'The boss called me over and said to go out and do my best,' recalls the soon-to-be heroic Hewitt. 'There were no rousing words, no Hollywood-like speech, just the simple everyday orders. Go out and work hard and see what you can pick up.'

Into extra-time and soon Ferguson was lamenting his decision to bring on the local boy. 'John proceeded to have a nightmare,' wrote Ferguson in *Managing My Life*. 'I was considering a substitute for a substitute in the second half of extra-time.'

Aberdeen were working hard to avoid the dreaded penalties but Strachan was wondering what he was going to do with his. Hewitt, meanwhile, was still on the pitch. 'In [Ferguson's] book he has a dig at me saying I was trying to run with the ball on a soggy pitch,' says Hewitt, laughing and trying hard to conceal a smug tone in his slow Aberdonian voice. 'He said he was going to take me off, but luckily for him, he didn't.'

Lucky for everybody. With eight minutes on the clock and counting, Peter Weir, as ever, wriggled clear of three challenges and fed McGhee with a fine long ball. The striker took on his marker, had the unselfish wherewithal to look up and sent an arching cross into the penalty area, where Hewitt was on the prowl. 'Even now, Ferguson says in his book that I should have bent my run to the near post but my instincts told me to stay centre; I didn't have to lose a defender and you just can't coach those feelings. Once I realised that the goalie had come but wasn't going to make it I knew I just had to dive and I couldn't miss. What a moment. I wiped the mud off my hands, did a little star jump – for which I *still* get stick – and ran off. Next thing I know, big Dougie has got me by the waist and wrestled me to the ground.'

Hewitt, who had started this merry dance sixteen months earlier with an inconspicuous goal at Motherwell in the Cup, had led his club to the brink of a night no one present will ever forget. Madrid, though, still had time for a free-kick on the edge of the Aberdeen area. Strachan was standing strong in the defensive wall, and a hush descended around the ground as the game went into injury time. Survive this and they were winners. Real Madrid's Salguero lined up hoping to break Aberdeen's hearts. 'Please, God,' Strachan was aware of a small voice from behind him. It was Peter Weir, shoulders slouched, knackered but offering the only last effort he had left. 'Please don't let them score. They don't deserve it.'

The ball tantalisingly fizzed past the post and to safety. It was all over. Aberdeen had conquered Europe. 'The whistle was the most beautiful sound I'd ever heard,' recalls McLeish. 'We'd won, but to be honest I couldn't get my mistake out of my mind. There is a selfishness in us all and a great moment was tinged with personal regret.'

He was wrong to have such doubts. McLeish had shown incredible character to put his mistake behind him and had a rock-solid second half and extra-time. He wasn't alone, though, in feeling blue amongst the red party. Stuart Kennedy, too, had to force a smile. He would never play football again after his knee problems and Strachan, possibly his closest friend at the club, could see, despite the smiles, his pal's heartache. An arm was flung around his right-back's shoulder, for a man who had helped Strachan's game blossom with his tireless work. 'Wee man, don't worry about me,' Kennedy said, as ever the team man. 'Go and enjoy yourself. It's no time to worry about me.'

Mayhem ensued. On the pitch, players and fans applauded each other with equal gusto. Off the pitch, the party continued until morning and a new dawn for Aberdeen Football Club. 'Personally it wasn't a massive night,' recalls Hewitt, dizzy only from the many celebratory pats on his head. 'People slowly went off to bed that night after a few drinks but a few stayed up. I woke up at about six in the morning, drew my curtains and there was Mark [McGhee] and Gordon, still fully clothed, sitting on the pool's diving board. Pretty plastered they were too.' Strachan deserved it. This was the ultimate so far. He was glad he had stayed.

From Real Madrid there could be no argument, no excuses and, as befitting a man of di Stefano's calibre, there was in defeat only admiration and generosity of spirit. 'Aberdeen,' he said, 'have what money can't buy – a soul; team spirit built in a family tradition.' Like a good family outing it was time to go home. The invasion had returned and, as the players touched down, the city centre and its main road Union Street – a ghost town the night before – was now a mass of people desperate to catch the eye of their heroes and welcome home the new and welcome guest: the European Cup Winners' Cup.

Of course, Jack Walker was on hand for the *Sunday Standard* to record a day never bettered in his home town:

> *When we touched down at Dyce, emotions which were already spent had to be quickly revived to meet a welcome which defied description. I remember as a boy running up Union Street, reaching out to touch Winston Churchill as he sat in an open car after the victory of World War II. But Winnie had nothing on this day, when Aberdeen laid down its tools and formed a crowd of at least 100,000 welcomes.*

It was more than appropriate for a team that would, the following December, win the European Super Cup, beating Hamburg 2–0 over two legs. They could, without a doubt, call themselves the best team in Europe. 'Our achievements don't get the credit they deserve,' argues Kennedy, the passion he showed playing still so apparent. 'Ferguson put together a team that beat Bayern Munich and Real Madrid. A young team from a town that, before they discovered oil, was nothing more than a fishing village.'

7. LITTLE AND LARGE

REPORTER: *So, Gordon, in what areas do you think Middlesbrough were better than you today?*
GORDON: *What areas? Mainly that big green one out there …*

For seven years they had meant everything to each other, but like so many great, old friends they had had a history, a turbulent start. They met, both bristling with potential and eager to get along, desperate for a lasting relationship. It wouldn't come. They seemed to have nothing in common. The harder one of them tried the less likely it seemed that they would ever hit it off. Any friendship looked doomed. But with time, patience and nurturing it had worked. Their initial differences evaporated amid a trail of success as one soon defined the other. Each a mirror image of their companion's own personal progress and glory. Now though was the right time to say goodbye.

After seven seasons, six trophies and a hatful of memories Gordon Strachan needed new friendships and waved goodbye to Aberdeen Football Club. He vowed to keep a house in the area that he and his family adored, but his football needed fresh pastures in which to grow. Not only had the routine of playing the same people and the same old faces started to erode into Strachan's imagination, he also started to sense that his own game – so reliant on expression and innovation – was becoming stagnant, which he confided to the captain. 'Gordon felt bogged down and disillusioned,' recalls Willie Miller. 'I completely understood. As a defender my challenge was to work out how forwards played, what tricks they had under their belts and combat that. That was the challenge. For Gordon, though, it was different. He had to, and on his own, come up with fresh ways to beat men who he had played against and often got the better of for years.'

That notion was no longer fresh and that pungency was affecting the high standards he had set himself. During his last season at Pittodrie, it was European games and internationals that awakened that childlike imagination in him. There he could bounce new ideas off different colleagues and face the challenge of new competitors with all the glee he had enjoyed since kicking a ball around his primary-school yard. Back home that passion was curtailed every day, curtailed by an atmosphere that wouldn't go unnoticed. 'It had become difficult,' admits Mark McGhee. 'He now only had a working relationship with Fergie and that made things difficult. Fergie knew he was off and that caused nothing but tension. Gordon though was too important to the team to leave out and Fergie too professional to compromise the team's fortunes because of his own ill feelings.'

The longer it went, though, the more press speculation there was. Ferguson's front was that of a manager keen to keep a valuable player who could help their ultimately successful bid for the Double. 'Gordon knows the situation,' he told reporters earlier in the season. 'He is keen to stay with Aberdeen for the remainder of his contract – but that has always been the case. If I said "yes" to some of the clubs who have made enquiries then Gordon would have listened to their offers and could have moved. But he wanted to remain here. And Gordon could help us into another European final – and possibly another win. We would be silly to allow such an asset to go. His departure at this stage could hinder our chances in Europe and in Scotland.'

Away from the cosy press conferences, Ferguson was not a happy manager. Strachan had tried to explain how he felt, how life in Scottish football had lost its impetus, and that deep down he had become bored. 'Go and get yourself unbored,' came the curt response. To Ferguson, Strachan represented a future that he knew was imminent. A future where the team he had built to bring honours to Aberdeen would break up.

'Leaving Pittodrie was, in his eyes, like leaving him,' admitted Strachan years later. 'It was as if he was asking what was wrong with his management. To me his management was the best in the world. I just wanted to go somewhere else.'

By the spring the atmosphere between the two men had become even more tense. Strachan would appear in the press to answer the latest speculation about a move and Ferguson resented what he saw as flagrant distractions to his squad. By April, Aberdeen were again playing in the semi-final of the Cup Winners' Cup and seemingly oblivious to any shenanigans off the pitch, but still nothing had been resolved regarding Strachan's future. He had felt down at Dundee sitting in their reserves, and insecure about his future as a professional footballer while struggling under Billy McNeil at Pitttodrie, but this was different – it seemed like the eyes of footballing Europe were on him and it was attention he could do without.

The semi-final in Europe was against Porto. They lost the first leg at Porto 1–0 and would crash out of the tournament having lost by the same score in Scotland. It was in their hotel in Portugal, though, that tensions again boiled to the surface between Strachan and his manager. Ferguson had remarked on the link between Strachan's poor performance and his impending departure. Although funny to the players, his comments by this point were finally getting to Strachan. To him it was happening all the time. A quip here and a dig there, they were taking their toll, and he had had enough. After the Porto game, representatives of German side Cologne approached Strachan and discussed with him signing a letter of intent that, as he understood it, would entitle him to join the club if – and only if – he decided to move to Germany. That, however, is not how the Germans viewed it. What ensued was, in Strachan's own words, 'The blunder that almost wrecked my career.'

Ferguson for all his resentment had to act quickly and ensure that the right deal was struck when the time eventually came for Strachan to go. The wily Scot knew that it would benefit Aberdeen financially if he were to sell to a British club. A move abroad meant that a 'multiplier system' could enforce a restricted fee to foreign clubs. It sounded like something out of *Star Trek* but it meant that a club selling a player to a club outside Britain could only charge a complicated sum that multiplied his annual wage by a figure governed by the player's age at the time. In layman terms, it meant that, if Strachan were to choose mainland Europe to play his football, Aberdeen could expect about a quarter of the £800,000 that Ferguson had valued him at.

Despite their falling-out, Ferguson recognised what a great player Strachan was. He was reaching his prime, had bundles of experience and was worth every penny. He hoped Arsenal, who had always flirted with the idea of Strachan coming to Highbury, would increase their interest from a flirt to a full-on proposition. They went as far as checking his medical records but cited a pelvis problem as reason enough to pull out. Ferguson, like a modern-day Captain Kirk, feared the 'multiplier system' and offered Manchester United manager Ron Atkinson his prized possession at the reduced and fantastic fee of £500,000, and at that price Atkinson didn't need asking twice.

'Aberdeen had come down to Old Trafford the previous summer to play in Martin Buchan's testimonial,' recalls Atkinson. 'Gordon, as ever, played very well and I had a chat with Fergie after the game.

"Was he available? Would he be available soon?" That sort of thing. Fergie was coy but marked my card and hinted that we could do business at the end of the season.' It seemed perfect but there was to be a problem. A German problem.

Strachan walked into Aberdeen's training ground ready for another session. Ferguson was playing snooker as his estranged midfielder walked past. 'Martin Edwards wants you to phone him. Give him a ring,' said Ferguson, unable to raise much in the way of enthusiasm in his voice.

'Martin Edwards of Manchester United?' came the reply from a surprised Strachan. A simple nod was all he got back and, while his manager missed an easy black, Strachan rushed to make the call.

And rushed it had to be. Twenty-four hours later when what he had seen as his optional move to Cologne should have taken effect, the lure of Manchester United had been something he could not forgo. Not again anyway. He had been booked on a flight to Cologne but, having spoken to Manchester United's chairman, there would be a change of plan. The proposal put in front of him by United was perfect. Strachan had his dream move and a new challenge; United had one of the brightest names in British football and even Ferguson was content having secured half a million pounds for his club's bank account.

Then, though, came the bombshell. Edwards would have to know about his pre-contract with Cologne as well as one he had penned with the gentlemen of Verona. Shakespearean in its comedic value maybe, but Ferguson – on discovering what Strachan had done – was anything but laughing. To Ferguson, Strachan had proved to be deviant and underhand. In his book published in 1999 he alludes to Strachan's 'cunning streak' and untrustworthy nature. It had been far from the quiet, simple move away that Strachan had hoped for. Cologne, like Ferguson, were furious.

The Verona document was easy to sort out. The Italians accepted that any agreement would only count if he had agreed to play and live in Italy. They would take no further action and even called Strachan for advice on who they *should* sign. To Cologne, however, the agreement signed by Strachan was binding. They threatened to sue him for breach of contract and have him banned from playing any football until the matter had been resolved. They cited the fact that they had signed star names, such as international 'keeper Harald Schumacher, on the back of securing his talents. It was a mess and Strachan was bang in the middle of it.

Strachan was terrified that the move to Manchester would be under threat, and for what? He hadn't meant anything by signing the agreement with Cologne. He had been desperate to sort out his affairs and settle where he would be working. He was guilty of naivety and in his own words 'couldn't believe how stupid I was'. His worries were eased as Martin Edwards and Manchester United ensured him that they could work around the deal and nothing would stand in the way of a done agreement. 'We were aware that what Strachan had done was maybe a little silly,' says Atkinson. 'We knew it wouldn't hinder us getting him to Old Trafford; it was never that much of an issue ... to us.' German and English lawyers representing United and Cologne met in neutral France and, while they got richer, a deal was struck

'That was a confusing time for Gordon,' says McGhee, who was also sorting out a future away from Pittodrie. 'He wasn't 100 per cent sure of what was going to happen, where he would be playing and if he could even be sued. Ferguson wasn't happy, but I reckon I had more reason to be put out by his change of mind. I had agreed to sign for Hamburg on the strength of the Strachans moving to Germany as well. The next thing I know he's signing for United and I'm left out to dry.' McGhee begins to laugh ironically. 'I was put out, I mean what are friends for?'

Strachan would be playing for one of England's biggest clubs. He was thrilled. He felt sorry for what he had done and for the German club, as well as for his pal now stranded in Hamburg. There were only three English clubs he would have considered joining and they were Arsenal, who had turned down the chance, Liverpool, who seemed happy with what they had, and, of course, Manchester United. Financially he would have been better off going to Germany but, having turned United down once as a boy, Strachan wasn't about to do it again.

The lure of the name alone had him transfixed as it would in time his now ex-manager. However big the club, though, it wasn't always easy to leave Ferguson. He had a way about him that, regardless of how eager a player was to change his fortunes, would talk them around. Alex McLeish for one, a loyal servant at Pittodrie for over a decade, found it hard to resist his boss's 'charms'. 'We threw a party to say goodbye to Gordon,' remembers McLeish, laughing, whose contract was up as well. 'Gordon came over to me and said, "By the way, don't you do anything just yet, big man. Big Ron fancies you at Old

Trafford as well. He needs a good centre-half." My head is buzzing after that. I sneak off and tell my missus and we're both ecstatic.

'I had a game for Scotland against France as a warm-up for their European Championships and I'm facing the likes of Michel Platini and Jean Tigana. My eyes have been opened and I'm thinking I want this quality all the time. I've chatted to a newspaper and simply said I'm open minded whilst also hearing that Spurs are keen on me. What a great choice. "I'm going to march into the boss's office," I say to the lads, "and tell him straight, I'm keen on a move." So there I am standing at his door. I hear that wee cough of his and my knees turn to jelly. "Come in, big man, here's the contract, three more years. Sign here." "Oh right, yeah. No problem, boss."'

Strachan, though, was made of stern stuff and for that reason he and his similar manager had clashed. But more of that later. For now Strachan would have to forge new relationships with team-mates, fans and manager. The Strachans arrived and moved into a new home in Wilmslow, Cheshire, a leafy and tranquil area known for its inhabitants from the often intertwining world of north-western football and television soap-opera stars, just ten miles south of Manchester. There would be none of the uncertainty that surrounded their housing arrangements in Aberdeen. Lesley had grown to love her home in the north-east of Scotland. It could have been an upheaval, what with the boys and school but, having joined her husband on a visit to his new club, she was sure they were doing the right thing, 'It will be an ideal place for our sons Gavin and Craig to grow up,' she said.

Strachan had been subject to the red-carpet treatment by his new employers and he couldn't wait to start earning his corn. Ron Atkinson had brought his own brand of flamboyant management and buoyancy to United in 1981 having done a great job at West Bromwich Albion. The club had courted the likes of Bobby Robson at Ipswich, Ron Saunders at Aston Villa and Southampton's Lawrie McMenemy without success but were more than happy to bring in Atkinson, a man whose image seemed to fit the very essence of Manchester United Football Club.

The expensive gold dripping from an expensive tan, the suits and the car, they were unmistakable. Parodied to a certain extent in today's *Footballers Wives* but back then very real. In some quarters it invited scorn – United had nothing but a 'Flash Harry' – but Strachan knew from an early stage that he was to be managed by a man, like

Ferguson, fixated with the game of football who, under the Italian shirts and French *eau de cologne*, lived for his involvement in the game and who could bring excitement back to Strachan's game. He grew to respect and enjoy working with Ron and to this day will seek any advice he may need as a coach from his old boss.

Atkinson had arrived fantasising of a dream team and had the money to achieve it. His mission? To break Liverpool's stranglehold on the title of League Champions. The burden of retaining the Championship last won in 1967 had proved too much for many of Sir Matt Busby's successors and wouldn't go away. 'It was always there for everyone at the club right up until they eventually did win it,' says Frank Stapleton, the club's Irish striker. 'You get used to success and so when it dries up you feel like you're chasing it. The beauty of football, though, is the optimism each season brings and under Ron we had plenty of that.'

With Atkinson's glitz came glamorous names linked with moves to Old Trafford. Glenn Hoddle and Michel Platini were quoted as possible targets, but instead it was Bryan Robson who represented his biggest move when he signed from West Bromwich Albion in October 1981 for a then British record £1.5 million. Remi Moses, another player from The Hawthornes, accompanied Robson for £500,000 and Atkinson's dream was starting to take shape. Some weren't so charitable about his signings. Tommy Docherty, a recent manager, said that for £500,000 he could have bought the original Moses and his tablets.

Atkinson would have to get used to such jibes. Runner-up in his first two seasons was promising but it was the FA Cup in 1983 that offered a first taste of success. A disappointing fourth place behind Liverpool's Treble winners of 1984 meant another foray into the transfer boutique and Strachan was joined by Alan Brazil from Tottenham and the Dane Jesper Olsen from Ajax. Strachan was excited to be linking up with such a wealth of talent. It was exactly what he needed, what he had craved. Everywhere he looked there was quality: Bryan Robson was now England captain, Arnold Muhren, a pass master from the Netherlands, and Frank Stapleton, a strong forward similar to Mark McGhee at Aberdeen; this was going to be fun.

Stapleton was just as excited at the prospect of playing alongside Strachan whom he had first met at a youth tournament in the Netherlands. Stapleton was at Arsenal and Strachan was with Dundee and both participated in the under-18s competition. 'I remember back then even, he had a way about him, a confidence.' It was that confidence that he would carry into his new job and, as a striker, Stapleton was sure that his charismatic manager had made the ideal choice.

'Steve Coppell had had to retire through a knee injury the year before and I for one had missed him,' says Stapleton. 'He could deliver a great ball from the right and was really the first wide player to do both jobs of getting forward and attacking as well as tracking back and helping his full back. He had a great attitude, was a favourite amongst the fans and his loss was a huge blow for United and England.' In Strachan, Atkinson as well as his forwards hoped that he found the ideal replacement.

Indeed, Coppell had left an enduring image. A learned footballer, and a Scouser popular on United's Stretford End, he was a rare breed. His Saturdays were spent embracing the touchline, teasing defenders and whipping in crosses, leaving only havoc in his wake. It was flattering to be seen as his successor but Strachan had doubts about his role in the team. He was no winger. He had spent six years convincing Ferguson of that and now, as he chatted to his new boss, he realised that that's exactly what he was being bought to do. Strachan enjoyed coming in and joining the play. He could get bored on the touchline; those itchy feet needed to be in the thick of it. This though wasn't the time to argue. He would get on with it.

'It's true, Gordon wasn't the same as Coppell,' says Stapleton with a laugh. 'But he had that quality; he was very busy looking for the ball, and would drop deep or in-field in order to find it. I think it might have upset Ron a bit who wanted to see him further up the pitch, and with Gordon drifting we could sometimes lack width. He had been bought as a right-winger but didn't like it. He was not one to beat three men for pace; instead he relied on his football brain; he was very clever and because of that always wanted to be involved.'

Atkinson, for all of Strachan's roaming, was less concerned. 'I bought him to do what he had always done. Attack from the right and get forward. Like David Beckham today, Strachs liked to drift in and of course he could do that. It was effective. He was tremendous, definitely in the top five players I ever worked with. I knew that from that early stage and so gave him licence to go and cause damage.'

Nevertheless, it had been a concern to Strachan but his role on the pitch and on the terraces was helped by a fantastic start. He had been helped by the number of Scottish names and accents in his new dressing room. Manchester United of course had long had an affiliation with his country. Sir Matt Busby was of course a beacon above the place and there was a long list of Scottish players from Jimmy Delaney, a Lanarkshire winger and Busby's first major signing at the club in 1946, through to Denis Law and Paddy Crerand, who won the European Cup at United, and Martin Buchan, an ex-Aberdeen man and accomplished captain at Old Trafford. As Strachan sat in the changing room for his debut at Old Trafford, a low murmur emanating from a slowly filling arena, his nerves were calmed by his three fellow Scots starting that day: Graeme Hogg in defence, Alan Brazil up front and at left-back Arthur Albiston, his old pal from Edinburgh Schoolboys' football. With Arthur Graham – briefly – still there and Gordon McQueen too a great help, the English First Division seemed a far less scary place to be.

Fear wasn't part of his make-up but his new challenge was laid bare as he ran out against Watford that August afternoon in front of 54,000 expectant fans. This wasn't Pittodrie where often the seagulls can be heard over the sometimes twitchy crowd. The roar from the Stretford End was a noise willing their side to make true their dreams and fulfil a painfully unrealised potential. Soon though much of that roar was for a new Scottish hero who looked to have about him more than mere promise. Strachan played himself into the hearts of many, scoring that day and adding three more in the next six games, including one against the old foe, Liverpool. The crowd and the place had taken to him, but had he taken to them?

It had seemed strange joining a new set of faces for pre-season training at United's training ground, The Cliff. There were no first-day nerves – Strachan had seen enough already to combat those – but to him that first day of training after a summer break was always hard. Under Ferguson and especially Archie Knox, any indiscretions a player may have got up to over the summer were soon ran out of him, so Strachan turned up bracing himself for a thorough work-out.

Atkinson arrived at the training ground sporting an even deeper tan thanks to a holiday to Israel and eager to top it up. 'Start a seven-a-side game,' he shouted to his men. They did and Atkinson found a good spot, not to get the best view of his squad's sharpness but to lie down and catch some more rays. It was a culture shock to Strachan but he would soon get used to his manager's less authoritarian methods. 'Right, on you go,' came the shout from the bronzing boss. 'Let's see what I've spent all my money on this summer.'

Atkinson of course wasn't the only contrast in his new Mancunian existence. Life at Old Trafford and in England as a footballer meant no more jumping off the team bus because it's your turn to pick up the squad's fish supper. He was now a commodity, part of a business and it was something he could get used to. 'The way they treat you here is unbelievable,' he said just months after his arrival. 'Everything is done for you. They even have a steward on the team bus to bring you whatever you want. In a word we're pampered. And I must confess I'm loving every minute of it even though at times it can be a bit embarrassing.'

Just three months into his English season of glamour Strachan was brought down to earth in the best possible way, by an old teacher. United were entertaining Tottenham and on arrival the players were greeted as ever by hungry autograph hunters and cameras. Among the maddening crowd though was a familiar face, Ken MacAskill, his old teacher at Craigroysten who took the team for football every Saturday. Short of becoming shy and calling him sir, Strachan sorted out his old mentor with some tickets and a pass for the players' lounge.

Despite the glitz of the place, MacAskill recalls how little Strachan had changed. Still the cheeky wee chappy from Muirhouse. 'I of course was completely overawed,' says MacAskill. 'There I was enjoying the free drink at the bar, just staring as Bryan Robson, Mark Hughes and then Bobby Charlton strolled past. Gordon walked in and skipped over, as bubbly as ever, chatted about old times over a couple of beers and invited me back to see the family at his new place in Cheshire. It was fantastic. I loved every minute of it. He seemed really happy in his new home and wouldn't stop, just like when he was a boy, asking me tricky football trivia questions.'

The question on the red half of Manchester's lips, however, was would this expensively assembled squad bring home the Holy Grail? Strachan had had experience of winning titles, as had Jepser Olsen at Ajax, but that hurdle of winning a title played hard on the minds of a squad unable to shake off the spirit of Busby's glory years. Yes, games were won, big games. Strachan was involved in victories at Highbury, White Hart Lane and most notably Anfield. These highlighted the quality in the Old Trafford ranks, but ten defeats to the likes of Stoke, Sunderland and Coventry pinpointed just where they were going wrong and why they only finished fourth that year. A lack of consistency dogged their efforts, a fact not lost on Stapleton. 'That's what it's all about. We had fabulous players, nearly all of them internationals like today but we didn't and couldn't get over that hurdle of winning that first title. If we had, I'm sure we would have gone on and won more. With the calibre of player we had we really ought to have.'

A team of Manchester United's stature and history wouldn't have enjoyed being labelled a good Cup team but that's exactly what they were. Brilliant, and a match for anyone on their day, they were liable to raise their games for the one-off games that count. Strachan's first season saw a run in the UEFA Cup that promised a lot after victory over his old rivals in Scotland, Dundee United, but fell away against the lesser-known Videoton of Hungary in the quarter-finals.

It was to be the FA Cup that would hold United's attention for the longest that year. Strachan, of course, had won the Scottish equivalent for three consecutive years and so entered the third-round stage perhaps a little more excited than his quite rightly nervous team-mates. The season before, United faced Bournemouth on the south coast as holders but amazingly lost 2–0 to Harry Redknapp's Third Division outfit. Again, it was to be Bournemouth, but this time they would come to Old Trafford. Such upsets were a rarity to Strachan and the Scottish game so he was surprised just how seriously his side were taking the forthcoming fixture. Their concentration paid dividends and they ran out comfortable 3–0 winners, with the cool Strachan settling the nerves with a goal in the opening twenty minutes.

Coventry were dispatched in the next round before another potentially tricky tie away at Second Division Blackburn Rovers. Strachan was beginning to realise just how nerves can creep into these awkward occasions. It was a Friday night, in front of an eager home support and national television audience. A bumpy pitch made for giant killing maybe but again they weathered the storm and again it was Strachan who calmed the nerves with a delightful chip to open the scoring in a 2–0 victory.

United went into the quarter-finals against East London's West Ham in buoyant mood and unbeaten in seven matches. Strachan, however, despite scoring freely, had gone on a run of missing four of his five previous penalties. Having glided into the Stretford End's penalty area, Strachan was felled by a West Ham defender and the referee pointed immediately to the spot. A hush went around the ground. Who would pick up the ball and take responsibility? Forty-seven thousand fans held their breath, a silence as loud as any roar, as if to say, not Gordon, please not Gordon. It wasn't. Norman Whiteside buried the penalty, and scored a hat-trick; United won 4–2 and Strachan could laugh at how nerve-wracking for everyone his penalty taking had become.

Atkinson had bought him to add goals from midfield, a necessity for any side with ambition. The penalty misses aside, Strachan went on to score twenty goals that season, a very healthy return, especially as Atkinson had set him a seemingly harsh target of fifteen in his first season in England. Only the new wonder boy at United, Mark Hughes, scored more and Strachan was a firm favourite among United's legion of fans by the time a semi-final came around against Liverpool in April.

The game was given added spice by the fact that both Liverpool and United were to miss out on the Championship as Howard Kendall's Everton were sweeping their way to honours at home and abroad. Liverpool were still involved in a European Cup campaign that would end in tragedy at the Heysel Stadium in Brussels but the chance to overturn the neighbours from down the East Lancs Road was always going to get north-west pulses racing.

United had a very good recent record against Liverpool and, under Atkinson especially, went into every game with their fiercest rivals confident of a result. Atkinson had over the years derived a plan to face a team and a club he had admired from afar for a long time. Alan Hansen, that silky centre-half and quiet catalyst for much of their play, must not be allowed time on the ball, and of course Kenny Dalglish had to be watched over as tightly and as resiliently as possible.

Liverpool were in their first season without the perpetual motion of Graeme Souness in their midfield. They had struggled in the League but would claim second spot behind Everton come May. Strachan and his team-mates, though, felt confident as ever going to Goodison Park. Now was as good a time as any for Strachan to extract some revenge for the humiliation of Aberdeen's European Cup exit in 1980 at the hands of the red half of Merseyside.

Things looked on course for just that. Mark Hughes and Frank Stapleton had twice given United the lead, and as the clock counted down it looked certain that another Cup final was to be the climax to Strachan's season. With seconds left, and faced with an advancing Kenny Dalglish, he tried a tackle that was never going to stave off the cunning fellow Scot. In a flash, Strachan had been 'nutmegged', Dalglish had looked up and stroked the ball into the United box, where Paul Walsh bundled the ball over the line: 2–2 and a replay beckoned. They had been so close. Strachan had momentarily forgotten about Atkinson's feelings towards Dalglish and at that point felt like leaping into the Mersey.

'We were distraught,' says Stapleton, who now with time can afford himself a laugh. 'There was literally no time left. We couldn't even kick off, that's how close we were. Gordon walked into the dressing room and immediately held his hands up. "Sorry, lads, my fault," he said, but we weren't thinking about dishing out blame.'

But what about the manager? 'It was a blow sure,' says Atkinson philosophically. 'Strachs though isn't the type who needs telling off. I wouldn't have to give him a rollicking as he was such a good pro that he knew exactly when he had done the wrong thing and was the first to hold his hands up.'

Strachan wasn't one to dwell on such errors. His game was all about showing for the ball, being in the thick of things, and such fears would only inhibit his natural exuberance. The replay would be in Manchester at City's Maine Road. Almost 50,000 fans crammed into the old stadium, and as ever for an evening fixture the atmosphere was even more electric than at Goodison. On a mild spring evening it was Liverpool who took the lead and being behind for the first time in the two games at half-time meant concern in the United camp. 'Your stomach goes,' explains Stapleton. 'You realise, hold on, we haven't been behind yet, how are we going to react to this?' Strachan, especially, could have been forgiven for going over and over his error on Merseyside, and hiding behind his disappointment.

Not Strachan: under Maine Road's floodlights and amid a cauldron of noise he went about making amends the only way he knew how. 'Gordon was brilliant in that second half,' says Stapleton. 'He excelled in that sort of atmosphere. He showed no fear. We equalised through Bryan Robson and then Gordon skipped past Alan Hansen and played a sublime through-ball for Hughes to chase and he duly scored.' Just like his days at school and as a young member of the Dundee ground staff, Strachan would not be intimidated by his surroundings. 'Even if he played badly, Gordon wouldn't go missing,' muses Stapleton. 'He would just carry on showing and that explains a lot about his character and his will.'

United were back at Wembley and Strachan was in a fourth consecutive Cup final. His team-mates must have been impressed by his run of fortune? 'Oh yeah, he kept mentioning that,' mocks Stapleton. 'We just told him the first three counted for nothing down here.'

Strachan could laugh off such remarks and to some extent agreed with them. The FA Cup final offered all the prestige a player could want. To him, only the World Cup final could better an occasion he had enjoyed witnessing from a young age: the history, the glamour, the build-up. To Strachan, it was another world from the Hampden occasion that to him had become the usual end-of-season fixture for Aberdeen.

United would face Everton in the final who, having claimed the Cup Winners' Cup on the previous Wednesday, were gunning for a fantastic Treble. They had already beaten United 5–0 at Goodison that season in the League so were a confident and effective unit coming to Wembley. United fans, however, strolled into North London with history on their side and fortune hopefully wearing a red, white and black scarf. Only eight years previously they had prevented Liverpool winning the 'Treble' with a 2–1 win in the Cup final at Wembley and now they hoped Merseyside would again be cursing their killjoy tactics.

For Strachan, the day was everything. His experiences against Real Madrid two years earlier had seen him vow to take in every moment of such occasions and savour the day. He had enough experience to take these matches in his stride as far as playing was concerned, and enough wherewithal to not let them pass him by in a blur of excitement. Strachan took his place in the side as it made its way, alongside its opponents, into the May sunshine. The look into the crowd, the wave at family and friends, the handshake with the day's dignitary and into the action.

'Action' is perhaps not the most appropriate word, as the game proved to be a dour and stale occasion. The hot weather and the fact that both teams had played long hard seasons were used as excuses but that should have meant a game full of mistakes and incident; this, until the 78th minute, had neither. With twelve minutes to go, Everton's Peter Reid picked up the ball on the halfway line and seemed to be fouled innocuously by United's centre-half Kevin Moran. As if trying to inject some sort of talking point into proceedings, the referee pulled out his red card and Moran, after 104 finals, had become the first player to be sent off.

Today Moran, an affable Irishman, still feels hard done by when talking about the incident that put him in the history books for all the wrong reasons. 'I went for the ball,' he says, as if still addressing a resolute referee. 'My foot remained on the floor and as Peter came through I felt I never touched him, his body came over mine and he went down. Whenever I fouled anyone I would always go over and pick them up. "Sorry, mate, are you OK?" On this occasion I didn't think I had fouled him so I just started to walk away and the ref has blown his whistle and called me over. He's going to book me – I don't believe it. "What ya booking me for, ref?" The next thing I see is a red card and I just freeze. I just kept saying, "What have I done, I don't know what I've done. Will you tell me please?" But he wouldn't. Peter was just looking at me, his hands by his sides and he shakes his head at me as if to say, sorry, mate, you don't deserve that.'

Strachan looked back on it and was as ever incensed by what he saw as a shambolic bit of officialdom. Moran's had been an untidy challenge at worse but, despite the player's pleas, referee Peter Willis would not budge. Moran had to walk. To Strachan, it was a classic case of a referee wanting to grab the limelight. It would be something that riles Strachan the manager and on that May day, Willis, in his last ever game in black, certainly made his mark. To the neutral, though, Willis's decision would merit some kind of man of the match award.

'The game was dying,' admits Stapleton. 'It was so even but Kevin going got the crowd excited.' Atkinson would have to tinker with his troops. Stapleton was moved back as an auxiliary centre-half with Strachan's energy in midfield trying to make up for Everton's extra man. 'It was all right for Gordon,' says Stapleton, laughing. 'He hadn't done anything for most of the game, not like me holding the fort at the back. No seriously, he was brilliant that day. It was very hot and yet he was full of running which aided our winner.'

Atkinson's rearranged team saw out the ninety minutes and went into extra-time containing a weary Everton side. With socks rolled around most ankles and ten minutes until the gruelling option of a replay, Mark Hughes dropped deep to receive the ball and played a pass wide into an open space as if begging Norman Whiteside to pump his tired legs and have a go at the Everton defence. Strachan had started to come into the game, exploiting tired legs and wide-open spaces. He, too, was up with the Ulsterman and made a forty-yard run beyond his team-mate that defied the sapping conditions and stretched a back-pedalling back four. Whiteside moved tentatively, biding his time, before clinically curling the ball beyond the outstretched Neville Southall. 'Gordon was great that day,' enthuses Atkinson, who couldn't hide his delight at such a wonderful winner. 'He never gets the credit he deserves for his tireless display. It was that great run that gave Norman the space and the time to get at Everton and win us the game.'

Bryan Robson lifted what would be the second of three FA Cups for the club and Strachan had another prize. The Championship apart, he couldn't have dreamed of a better start to his career in England. There he was walking up and down those famous steps at Wembley, an FA Cup winners' medal in one hand and a scarf thrown by his army of ecstatic supporters in the other. As the team lined up for a photo-call, Strachan bounced with his team, the words of 'Glory, Glory Man United' rolling easily off his tongue. A great performance on and off the pitch, he was a fixture at his new club and that meant everything to him. He had done the right thing, made the right move; with Lesley content in her new home and himself now a father of three following the birth of little Gemma earlier that year, Strachan was a happy wee man.

For Atkinson his team had brought further success. So, it wasn't the Championship, but his side had proved a match for anyone and to win a trophy that then still meant so much to players and fans with such a spectacular goal was just how he liked it: flamboyant, sparkling and with a taste for the dramatic. It was a feeling the squad took into the following season with aplomb. Atkinson had kept faith in the same set of players that had won the Cup. It seemed at last the club had found a blend capable of exorcising the spirits of the Best–Law–Charlton era that had haunted its corridors for so long. United won their first ten games and remained unbeaten for fifteen. It was a run that Strachan relished being a part of. He had always savoured the way he felt the game should be played and in Atkinson he had a manager and a team willing to do the same. The football in that autumn of 1985 was sublime; players gelled; chances were created and points won, all in front of an Old Trafford ready to forget about the club's swinging sixties.

'The team were now together and brimming with confidence,' purrs Atkinson. 'After two or three seasons it seemed to have come together. We'd had experience in Europe, which had helped. The young players such as Hughes and Whiteside – now in central mid-field – were used to the first team yet still only 21 and my signings such as Strachs were vital to the chemistry of the team. It just seemed to fit. The balance was right.' Or so it seemed.

Defeat eventually came at Sheffield Wednesday's Hillsborough on 9 November, at which stage bookmakers were refusing to take bets on where the title was heading. However, that defeat, rather than a blip on a merciless march to glory, was to be the first of ten. They again came fourth and gallingly had to watch Liverpool claim the League and FA Cup Double. It was a blow to all, but why had it happened, why such a fall from grace? 'I can tell you why,' says Atkinson with purpose. 'It went wrong because we lost Robson for months, Strachs for weeks, both with shoulder injuries, and a handful of others out as well. Squads weren't as big as they are these days and we couldn't handle losing such quality. That was our chance and it had gone.'

Frank Stapleton, however, puts it down to more than a crowded treatment room and cites the comfort zone of the early season climate. 'We were enjoying the autumn pitches and really got into our passing game,' he says. 'The immaculate conditions and pitches were perfect for us but slowly we faced harder opposition on far from perfect surfaces and what with the injuries it all went wrong. Liverpool, of course, were very good. People had said it was ours because of the start we made but it's not about a start, it's about the whole season and we simply couldn't maintain it. You have to accept that a season is going to be blighted by injuries and make adjustments.'

Strachan – who had come off worse after a collision with the woodwork at West Bromwich Albion and missed a couple of months of action – concurs with Stapleton that the side lacked the depth of ability to sustain their challenge and cites a new style of football that relied on power and getting the ball forward as direct and as quickly as possible. Despite playing what he regards as the among the best football he'd ever been involved in, the tactics of teams such as Sheffield Wednesday and later Wimbledon, who were soon to be promoted to the top flight, were overpowering a team reliant on raw skill to win matches.

Atkinson was now under pressure. Was that great start as far as he was going to take the club? Could he muster the nous within his squad to go one further and claim the ultimate prize? To many the answer was an emphatic no. There had been talk for years about ill-discipline within the club, of lax training and an infamous booze culture. The image of players and drink was highlighted during the club's UEFA

Cup run in Strachan's first season. United had drawn Dundee United and the game against strong Scottish opposition had been stirred by his ex-manager Alex Ferguson's comments. His conjunction was that Jim McLean's team would be far too fit for United and when the Scots battled to a 2–2 draw in the first leg at Old Trafford it seemed that he might be right.

Ferguson's comments however had riled his future employers who put in a sterling performance and ran out 3–2 winners on the night. Ferguson had obviously stood by his words after the first game and so Gordon McQueen on the journey home at Dundee airport made a point of proving how fit an old international could still be. There he was, for all to see, doing one-handed press-ups and shouting, 'How would Mr Ferguson like to see this? An athlete at work.' An athlete yes, but like many at United not adverse to letting his hair down – the free hand held a can of lager, supposedly the staple sport drink of 1980s football.

'Yes, players did drink and sometimes to excess,' admits Stapleton. 'Ron didn't condone it but he was far more interested in what went on at the training pitch and on a Saturday afternoon.'

Atkinson and his exuberant character was great fun to have around and he came perhaps dangerously close to his players. Bryan Robson for one recognised this fact and said at the time, 'Ron loves being with his players. He enjoys the camaraderie of the dressing room and I wonder at times whether he is in danger of getting too close to us.'

The talk was of player power and binge drinking far too close to fixtures. Atkinson would give anyone hell if they came into training reeking of the night before but deep down he was of the old school. A school that wanted players to be as close as possible and the best place to get that bonding was the bar after a hard day's training. A lot of the speculation was unfair but, nevertheless, it was publicity that the club could do without, especially as Liverpool, no slouches themselves when it came to barroom activity, were lording it up under their very noses. 'Players did have a drink but you have to recall that fitness levels were not what they are today,' says Albiston. 'After the game, players would go to the bar and relax, but it was just letting off steam. Liverpool were the most successful team in Europe and you heard all sorts about how much they were putting away. The difference was they were winning Leagues and European Cups, so less was made of it. We were falling short so people made more of us.'

It wasn't an issue that overly concerned Strachan. His humour and bubbly personality meant he was a popular figure in the United changing room but a couple of beers and a drive back to his family were his preference over a day's racing and drinking with some of the team. 'I used to drive home from Manchester United training along the M56,' he joked years later. 'There was a left turn for Wilmslow where I lived, and a right turn for Hale, where Norman Whiteside, Paul McGrath and Bryan Robson lived. I used to say that it was left for under three pints a night and right for more than ten.' That left turn suited Strachan, not keen on repeating his escapades with the incorrigible Jimmy Johnstone when at Dundee. 'I'm a pint-and-a-packet-of-crisps man,' he said. 'I can't see that changing. I'm happiest with my feet up, watching television or messing about the house with the kids.'

Going into the 1986/87 season, Atkinson had more on his mind than his players extra-curricular activities. In his book *Big Ron*, Atkinson describes how he had spent the summer of 1986 in Mexico working as a TV pundit on that year's World Cup finals. Working with him was Lawrie McMenemy, who let it slip to him that Bobby Charlton, now a United director, had 'tapped up' Alex Ferguson regarding the Old Trafford job. A cold meeting with the usually affable Ferguson in Glasgow confirmed his fears. Time could be running out.

The uncertainty, rumour and counter-rumour surrounding the club had left Atkinson unperturbed. He had gone to his board eager to make that extra step out of Busby's shadow. 'I am ready to give it another crack. This is it. Let's have another go.' For now it had worked, but a bad start to the season meant the cracks, rather than being papered over, were getting wider and wider. Questions were again being asked.

'Ron was under pressure, that's for sure,' says Stapleton, one of Atkinson's first signings. 'The previous season's failings hadn't helped and the club selling Mark Hughes was a glaring mistake. We had had a game at Oxford in the January and on that very day when vital League points were at stake it was on the back pages that we were letting Hughes go to Barcelona. We couldn't believe it. We were still in the title race and here we are selling our best player. United didn't need to sell but they did and the whole episode was to prove costly.'

Atkinson's moves into the transfer market to replace the Welsh youngster were equally as costly. Peter Davenport and Terry Gibson were not in the Hughes class and a disastrous start to the season saw the side in the relegation zone and, after a League Cup hammering at Southampton, Atkinson's days at the club were over. Atkinson, in the form of his jewellery, tan and silverware, had brought the glitz and sparkle that had gone missing through the seventies back to Old Trafford. Strachan had been injured when his boss was sacked and he along with other casualties, Bryan Robson and Norman Whiteside, enjoyed an impromptu farewell with their now ex-manager. The party caused a few stirrings from the new manager who thought it was undermining his new position but it was nothing more than a genuine thank you and goodbye to a manager and a friend. Far from encouraging a huge piss-up, Atkinson as ever went on and on about football. 'Shut up Ron,' said Strachan, laughing. 'What do you know, you're not even in the game.'

Atkinson had given him his shot at the big time. Strachan had embraced the opportunity and he recognised that his manager's methods and style had allowed him to truly express himself in his new home. It was, he acknowledged, however, time for a change: the players needed the prompting of a new man, with a new set of values and methods. Only for Strachan, they were to prove far from novel.

8. A UNITED FRONT

> REPORTER: *Bang, there goes your unbeaten run. Can you take it?*
> GORDON: *No, I'm just going to crumble like a wreck. I'll go home, become an alcoholic and maybe jump off a bridge. Umm, I think I can take it, yeah.*

Hmmph! Another cork flies from another champagne bottle at the Royal Lancaster Hotel in London, just hours after Bryan Robson has lifted the 1985 FA Cup for Manchester United. The sparkle off the old trophy matches the players' smiles and drinks. It's time to party. Alex Ferguson, for once not involved in the Scottish equivalent, had called his ex-player to wish him good luck on his big day at Wembley and now had arrived to congratulate an old colleague and new FA Cup winner.

Strachan stands thanking his ex-manager warmly, an apparent détente in the cold war that had manifested between the two only a year earlier. As they chat, United's South African goalkeeper Gary Bailey strolls over and greets his team-mate's companion. 'Hello, Mr Strachan,' he said as the conversation and the air turn cold. Ferguson, only fifteen years Strachan's senior, was liable to take offence at such an error. His dad? How could anyone think such a thing?

His father maybe not, but big brother, initially that had seemed entirely possible. The relationship between the two at Aberdeen had begun very well. Not only employee and boss, they also had often been companions. Ferguson's passion for the game had found a welcome and eager ear in Strachan, himself a veritable sponge for all things football. Ferguson in his first years at Pittodrie would constantly take in night games of all levels and Strachan was more than happy to join him on the road. Be it Parkhead, Ibrox or Arbroath's Gayfield Park, the two of them were just pleased to be there, involved in the nation's game. Ferguson would live for it; even the in-car entertainment was geared towards ascertaining more knowledge. 'Let's listen to Shankly,' he'd say, shoving a tape eagerly into the machine.

Even with the great Scot's talk of 'bastions of invincibility' ringing in their ears, the two men could not sustain such close ties. But why?

How could it have gone so wrong just as Strachan looked perfect in the role of Cary Grant to Ferguson's Hitchcock in their joint quest to thrill north-by-north-east Scotland? It wasn't only due to Strachan's eventual departure from Pittodrie under a smelly cloud of Cologne. There was a past, a present and a future that would decree that even today relations between the two men remain frosty.

Researching this book has been a pleasure as Strachan's peers, acquaintances and colleagues have matched my protagonist's enthusiasm on the field with the manner in which they have freely talked and reminisced about him off it. Ask about Ferguson though and one is usually met with a silence suggesting we move on. Having worked together at Aberdeen, Manchester United and with Scotland, the two men – perhaps more alike than they would care to admit – simply don't get along.

A warm relationship between the men initially continued as Strachan's career was given the shot in the arm it so craved from Ferguson, and in turn Ferguson recognised he had a player of genuine class under his control. Their six years together and the trophies that affiliation helped bring to Aberdeen of course brought mutual respect between the two, a fact never lost on the nation's back pages. 'Gordon is one of the most skilful players I have worked with,' Ferguson told Scotland's *Evening News* in 1989. 'He has always had an excellent first touch and there are few players with his ability to beat opponents in tight areas, either by dribbling or playing one–twos.'

Strachan in turn was full of praise for his manager. 'Alex Ferguson is probably the best all-round manager in Scotland,' he said in his column for the *Daily Express*. 'He's certainly the best tactician and coach that I've worked under. Sometimes his enthusiasm takes him over the top, but it's only because he hungers for success. Winning is what Alex Ferguson is all about.' Behind the mutual appreciation, however, that 'enthusiasm' of Ferguson's coupled with Strachan's unwillingness to be bullied had meant that relations between the two deteriorated amongst a series of dressing-room spats and post-match squabbles.

He had become used to Ferguson's half-time blow-ups. They are of course legendary, with players repeatedly on the end of a tirade of abuse while he suggests where they are going wrong. David Beckham, most famously, was on the end of a sweet right-foot shot in 2003, involving a football boot and several stitches, but over twenty years earlier it was sandwiches rather than boots that would take flight across the Aberdeen changing rooms and more often then not it was Strachan who had riled his manager enough to merit those 'special' team-talks.

In the autumn of 1981 Aberdeen were playing against Arges Pitesti of Romania in the UEFA Cup and took to the field 3–0 up from the first leg. Ferguson had sent his players out in a new formation that involved Mark McGhee as a lone striker while he flooded the midfield and asked Peter Weir and Strachan to hug the left and right flanks respectively. Strachan did not take to his new role. Never happy when constrained to the wing, his game was suffering and orders were not being met. Ferguson was out of the dug-out screaming at him to fall into line and all the while the Romanians were taking full advantage of the lapse and were 2–0 up. Ferguson's abuse continued and Strachan had had enough of the Govan ranting in his ear. 'Fuck off and shut your face,' he shouted somewhat ill-advisedly minutes before half-time.

Ferguson had remained silent but, as they trundled into the dressing room, Strachan knew it was a silence that would soon be broken. He wasn't disappointed. What followed were screams and abuse loud enough to wake the un-dead in nearby Transylvania. Strachan, according to his livid manager, had been showboating, 'Playing like something out of Barnum and Bailey!' That comment brought a couple of strange looks from an otherwise stunned audience. 'What has a lawyers' firm got to do with Gordon's performance?' whispered one bemused player.

'No,' said Stuart Kennedy. 'Barnum and Bailey the circus.'

Ferguson was losing patience and swung a fist at a tea urn, hurting his hand and in frustration had swept aside a row of full tea cups, spraying half-time refreshments over the dressing room and the players. No one flinched or said a word as he continued his 'motivational' speech with tea dripping down the walls. Strachan went back out and managed to score a penalty and help the team etch out a 2–2 draw. That was usual and he had no qualms about his boss's tactics. He recognised how efficient a motivational tool Ferguson's confrontational style could be.

He had witnessed how well men responded to his manager's barking. Even giants such as Doug Rougvie would be put upon as Ferguson went eyeball to eyeball – make that eyeball to chest in

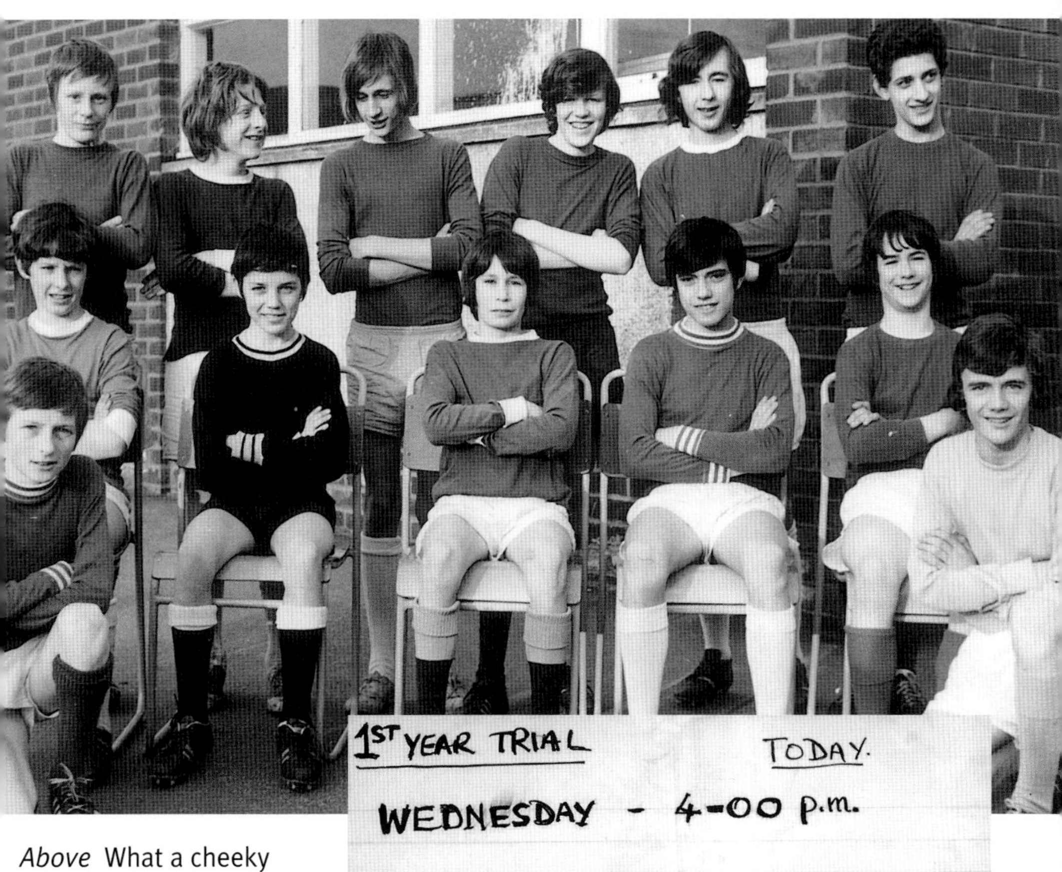

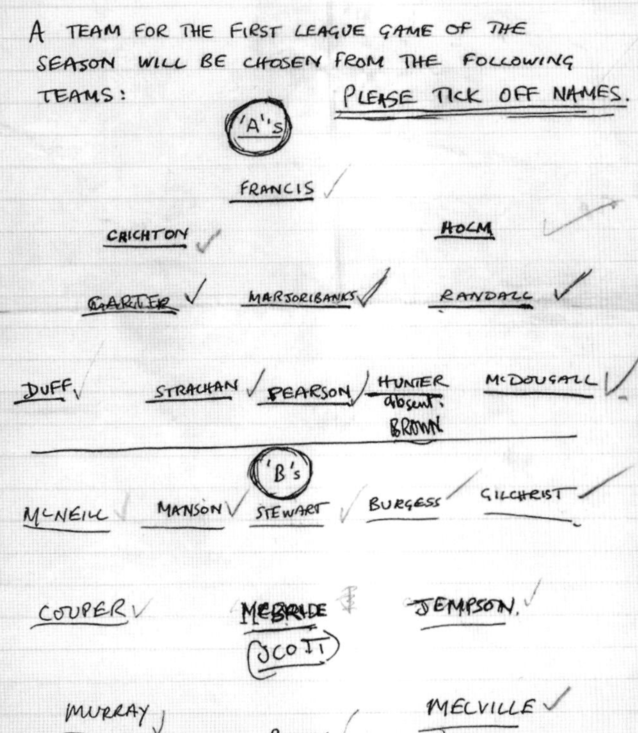

1ST YEAR TRIAL TODAY.

WEDNESDAY - 4-00 p.m.

A TEAM FOR THE FIRST LEAGUE GAME OF THE SEASON WILL BE CHOSEN FROM THE FOLLOWING TEAMS: PLEASE TICK OFF NAMES.

'A''s

FRANCIS ✓

CRICHTON ✓ HOLM ✓

CARTER ✓ MARJORIBANKS ✓ RANDALL ✓

DUFF ✓ STRACHAN ✓ PEARSON ✓ HUNTER absent. BROWN McDOUGALL ✓

'B's

McNEILL ✓ MANSON ✓ STEWART ✓ BURGESS ✓ GILCHRIST ✓

COUPER ✓ McBRIDE SCOTT JEMPSON. ✓

MURRAY ✓ POLLOCK ✓ MELVILLE ✓

Above What a cheeky grin. Strachan (*top row, second from the left*) lines up for Craigroysten High School 1st XI 1970–71.

Right The star of the A-Team at good old fashioned inside-right. (© Ken MacAskill)

Above A star in the making. Strachan lines up with his Dundee team-mates (*front row, second from the left*). (© Empics)

Left What a bubbly character in the dressing room. Strachan celebrates Aberdeen's Premier League Championship in 1980. (© Empics)

Right A Celtic fan attempts to do what his defenders couldn't and stop Strachan (*grounded*). Help is at hand, as ever, from big Doug Rougvie (No.3). (© Empics)

Below The Glory Of Gothenburg! The Dons have conquered Europe. (© Empics)

Left Me and my shadow. All Smiles at Aberdeen, but that wasn't always the case. (© Sporting Pictures)

Right Stormin' Norman! Strachan celebrates with his Manchester United team-mates after Whiteside's winning goal against Everton in the 1985 FA Cup Final. (© Empics)

Above A Brazilian wave. The magnificent Brazil team take the plaudits having outclassed Scotland during the 1982 World Cup in Spain. Strachan would soon have another close encounter with their captain Socrates (*centre, beard*). (© Empics)

Right I've still got it. Strachan turns on the style during his 50th and last game for his country. (© Empics)

Left 'What's he doin' here?' Strachan was as surprised as anyone when Vinnie Jones arrived at Leeds but they were to forge an unlikely friendship. (© Empics)

Below We Are Leeds! Strachan and his team-mates celebrate their championship in 1992. (© Empics)

Above Thanks ma'am. Gordon Strachan OBE shows off his gong watched by his sons. Not bad for a Muirhouse boy. (© Empics)

Right The Premiership's that way. Coventry have done the impossible and beaten Tottenham in 1997 and stay in the top flight. (© Empics)

Left Who'd be a manager? Strachan feels the pain as Southampton lose to Arsenal in the 2003 FA Cup Final. (© Empics)

Below I'm off. Strachan bids the press a fond farewell as he leaves Southampton for the last time.

Rougvie's case – with whoever he felt was in need of a talking to. 'You know,' Fergie would turn and say, having given another lecture to his giant left-back. 'The big man could have picked me up and used me for toilet paper. He's going to hit me one day.'

However, it was Strachan who so often had his manager wanting to hit him. In 1982, the team travelled to Switzerland to take on FC Sion in the first round of their ultimately glorious Cup Winners' Cup campaign. In the dressing room before the game, the kit was being laid out having been packed as ever by Pittodrie's jack of all trades Teddy Scott. On this occasion Scott had not made the trip abroad and, as Ferguson realised that the wrong socks were in the bag, he would have been glad he hadn't. It was a rare error from Scott who was the very fabric of the club and had been for decades, but Ferguson was not accustomed to taking such a lapse lightly. 'When we get back home,' he growled as the players sat around him, 'remind me to sack that wee bugger Scott.'

'Good point boss,' retorted Strachan to the disbelief of his teammates. What was Strachan thinking?

Ferguson looked at him suspiciously.

'No, boss, you're right, Teddy's got to go.'

'Thank you,' said Ferguson.

'One thing though. Where the fuck are you going to find the ten new men to do his job?' The dressing room erupted with laughter.

Laughter was abundant at Aberdeen and even Ferguson's rants could be followed by a knowing and comedic wink. With Strachan, however, his manager's criticisms were too often without humour and carried out in the public glare. Having seen off the Romanian opposition, Aberdeen had gone out in the next round to Hamburg. They had played very well at home but could not hold on to a slender lead and lost the second leg in Germany. Ferguson was a disappointed man, not least with his number seven. Strachan had had, by his own admission, a poor game, having dropped below the high standards he had begun to set himself but the gasps from the German press corps as he was substituted underlined how much respect he had begun to command all over the Continent. He was professional enough to know it and hold his own hands up to it. He didn't need telling and therefore took offence at Ferguson's comments to the press regarding his substandard display. His manager had compared Strachan's game to that of Hamburg's German international Felix Magath. 'I had no option but to take Gordon off, he just wasn't doing it for us,' he said. 'Magath was prepared to sprint fifty yards to get a ball, whereas Strachan was content to play in a five-yard area. Gordon must examine Magath's performance and learn from it by showing the commitment to create and make things happen.'

He didn't feel he deserved such a public dressing down. Why had his performance been highlighted? Others had played poorly but as ever, he felt, it was he who was to play the role of scapegoat. It affected him deeply, so much so that on returning to Scotland he went to his manager's office to talk seriously about his future. It wasn't a long conversation. 'Boss, I think it might be time for me to move on, play somewhere else,' he said purposefully.

'No chance. Cheerio.' And that was that.

Strachan had shown a rare courage in even confronting a manager capable of intimidating the burliest of footballers. Rather than looking sheepishly at the floor, Strachan would have an answer to most robust accusations. Ferguson had grown accustomed to what he called Strachan's 'nippy sweetie' moods but his tolerance towards his player had a very low threshold. It wasn't as if Strachan was the only one to question the manager's point of view. Miller as captain would have his say and Steve Archibald was far from being the type of man to shirk confrontation, even with Alex Ferguson.

In 1979, Archibald had scored a hat-trick against Celtic and helped himself to the match-ball, not common practice in those more thrifty days. Ferguson called him in and reprimanded his striker, sending him on his way with a request for the ball's return. The next day, while Ferguson was sitting enjoying a cup of tea with Pat Stanton, the office door was flung open and Archibald walked in, ball in hand, before booting it across the room. Once it had stopped ricocheting off each wall, he brazenly shouted, 'There's your fucking ball,' and stormed out.

Archibald's actions seemed to stifle Ferguson. Another occasion saw Ferguson query a bill that had come in from a local tailor for over £1,200, a lot of money. Ferguson was perplexed and discovered that Archibald had been buying new suits from this business and having the bill sent to the club. 'What the hell is this, Steve?' said Ferguson having immediately called for his suddenly smart forward's presence in his office.

'Listen, boss,' came the reply from a resolute Archibald. 'I am going abroad with the Scottish national team and when I do I am representing Aberdeen Football Club. Do you want me to look like a fucking tramp?'

Again, the cheek. But again, Ferguson felt he couldn't come down hard on him. If anything he was in admiration of the man's single-mindedness, his stubborn and determined nature. 'He reminded me of someone,' he said self-mockingly years later. Strachan though was different. His quick replies would leave his manager in a rage, fists clenched with intent, his west-coast blood at boiling point.

In 1983, ten days after bringing home the club's first European trophy and after a long season, the team battled to a 1–0 win over Rangers in the Scottish Cup final. It was another piece of silverware and Ferguson was approached by Scottish TV for an immediate post-match interview that would no doubt capture the ecstasy of a victorious and proud manager, right? Wrong.

'We're the luckiest team in the world,' he scolded, his face as ruthless and as hard as a day on a Clyde shipyard. 'It was a disgraceful performance. Willie Miller and Alex McLeish won the Cup for Aberdeen; they played Rangers by themselves. I don't care about winning other Cups. Our standards have been set and I am not going to accept that from any Aberdeen team. There is no way we can take any glory from that.'

Some called it a testament to what a winner Ferguson was. True, of course, but his players saw it as an insult to their professionalism and to the effort they had put into the club's most famous and glorious season. 'He lambasted us all,' says John Hewitt, with a chuckle. 'He did it on national TV and that hurt. He apologised but for many of us that wasn't enough. He'd forgotten that we'd played extra-time in a European Cup final, travelled, celebrated and yet still beat Rangers. That was the boss, though; he could fly off the handle.'

Ferguson, having let the nation know his feelings, had stormed into the dressing room just in time to stop Strachan opening a bottle of champagne. This, as it turned out, was time for a wobbly not bubbly. The fact that his club had just become the first team outside of the Old Firm to win successive Scottish Cups was lost on Ferguson and the atmosphere was nothing short of depressing. Strachan as ever tried to lift spirits during the following day's drive back to Aberdeen, stating that the procession through the city centre this year could be done on a tandem bike, as Miller and McLeish hardly needed a bus.

It was welcome comic relief to a situation that had come to a head the night before at the club's 'celebrations' in St Andrews. Whereas cheer and merriment should have filled the air, Ferguson's cutting words hung over proceedings and Strachan had had enough. 'Come on, Lesley, we're going,' he said before walking out of the reception. His absence was noted but Strachan simply had found it hard to take the lack of appreciation for him and his tired team-mates. He had no regrets but was concerned his actions may have embarrassed the club chairman Dick Donald and his vice-chairman Ian Anderson, two men he had nothing but respect for. Ferguson fined him £250 for his supposed impudence, again unable to tolerate Strachan's independence of spirit.

Ferguson's book published sixteen years later continues to recognise Strachan's abilities as a player but a sense of mistrust on his part manifests itself time and time again in the form of put-downs of Strachan, culminating in a remark that he would not leave his back exposed to Strachan in a hurry (alluding to what he saw as another knavish action – this time when departing Manchester United). On the book's publication, Strachan kept his silence, seeing it as the dignified thing to do. He would only, and with humour as ever as his weapon of choice, talk about an episode involving a favourite tape of Ferguson's that he would play incessantly on the team bus.

'Oh, God, that tape,' says Aberdeen's ex-right-back Stuart Kennedy, laughing nervously, as if my question has awakened a shrill of sound that he would rather not recall. 'The singer was a mate of Fergie's, but nothing more than a pub singer from Glasgow. Fergie loved him but, let me tell you, he was in a minority of one. He thought he was great and inflicted him on us all.

'"Wait till you hear this guy," he'd say enthusiastically. He was crap! One night we'd stopped at a service station and the tape went missing, thrown into a dark field. Fergie was furious. It was like Watergate all over again as he interrogated us all.

'"You must know who done it," he said to me. "You know everything that goes on round here."

'"Boss, I don't know what you're talking about, pal. We go back a long way, mate, but I can't help you." He wasn't a happy chappy.'

The silence was not broken for a decade and a half but Strachan used the story as his only comeback to his ex-manager's book. 'If he's still wondering who threw that tape from the bus,' he told Patrick Barclay in the *Sunday Telegraph*, 'it was me, so maybe he was right and I'm not to be trusted.'

Too quick to answer back and dishonest? Well, it was his footballing wit and his honesty of effort that meant, come the summer of

1986, Strachan and Ferguson continued to have a working relationship as the latter took the reigns of the national team's efforts during the World Cup in Mexico. Jock Stein had tragically died immediately after his team's victory over Wales, which put them in a play-off for Mexico, and Ferguson proudly agreed to follow up his mentor and good friend's work.

Strachan again enjoyed a good World Cup and Ferguson was pleased to have him in what was always going to be a very awkward test for his squad. There were no problems between the two and Strachan would even let his manager win the countless games of *Trivial Pursuit* they played that summer to pass the time.

The two men returned home, their own reputations thoroughly enhanced, and, after some choice meetings in Central America, it seemed their careers were to continue on their seemingly intertwined paths. Ferguson has since refuted claims that he was 'tapped up' in Mexico by an over-zealous Sir Bobby Charlton. The two men did have words before Scotland's final game but, according to the Scot, United's legend and director only suggested that if he ever thought of managing in England he should get in contact.

Not strictly 'tapped' then but for Ferguson there was enough in Charlton's words to make his thoughts and ambition swell. Coming home, Ferguson indicated to Strachan that there were only two jobs that would entice him away from the life and the club he had built in Aberdeen. Barcelona was one, and the other was Manchester United. Having turned down strong offers over the years from Rangers, Arsenal and Tottenham, and with Atkinson sacked in the November of that season, Ferguson's glorious spell at Pittodrie finally came to an end.

'To me, it all seemed to happen out of the blue,' says Archie Knox, Ferguson's right-hand man and enforcer. He's a very friendly man but players will testify that his methods could have the hardest of players quaking in their football boots. He would be an asset to Ferguson wherever he went. 'I was training one afternoon with the young lads and saw Ferguson's car pull up. I thought something's up here because he hardly ever came to see us. He called me over and got me into his car. "Listen, Archie, I'm meeting with the people at Manchester United tonight. Are you prepared to come with me?" Of course I was. We were no different to the players and like Gordon we saw it as a massive opportunity to move on to one of the biggest clubs in Europe.'

Like curious schoolboys asking about a new teacher, the United players went to Strachan for advice on what to expect from Alex Ferguson. 'He told us to brace ourselves for a lot of screaming and shouting,' says Frank Stapleton, with a laugh. 'They had won far too much together to be too negative but he did warn us about his temperament. I remember Gordon coming in the day it was announced that Fergie would be our manager; he sat down and put his head in his hands. "I thought I'd got away from him," he mockingly sobbed. "I never thought he'd follow me this far south!"'

They were reunited and there was little sign of the acrimony under which they had parted company from Scottish shores. Strachan had even given advice on where he thought Ferguson would look to improve things at the club and briefed him on how training could be changed for the better. Deep down, though, he knew that Ferguson's arrival could have implications for his time at Old Trafford. The fairy tale that had taken place at Aberdeen wasn't going to be told for a second time. They had been through too much, knew each other too well and their stormy past meant that lightning wouldn't be striking twice.

Ferguson arrived having been apparently briefed by Strachan and had concerns regarding the state of the team's discipline, fitness and physicality. Strachan's words about what to expect would soon be realised and it seemed that Ferguson travelled with a bogie-man-like reputation. Players had heard tales of his autocratic methods and should fear a man loath to suffer fools. Had he really once made four players sing nursery rhymes after they had misbehaved at St Mirren? 'If they act like children,' he said, 'I treat them like children.'

So just how scary was it? 'He didn't come in with a bang,' recalls Kevin Moran who would last two more seasons at United under the Scot. 'A lot was made about his strict disciplinarian methods but he actually came in slowly and made little changes initially. What he did do was give everyone a chance. Changes were made eventually but the whole squad got a chance to impress.'

Ferguson though had ideas about the clientele he wanted to call his own. Jim Leighton followed Strachan and Ferguson to Old Trafford, and Mark Hughes returned after two difficult years in Barcelona. A team that Ferguson could call his own began to take shape.

Strachan of course was a known talent to Ferguson but the manager immediately had concerns regarding his old acquaintance's form. The manager professed that his player's ability to answer back had not diminished but felt that he was secluded amongst the big personalities in the United squad. He felt that playing alongside big-name internationals with their own wealth of experiences and honours meant he was no longer the main man that he had been in Scotland. Ferguson decreed that this lack of attention had affected his game for the worse. They are harsh accusations. Strachan had arrived at Old Trafford and set the place alight in his first season with his clever game and eye for goal; he had been playing with and against bigger names while with the Scottish national team and had always done well so there was no reason to suggest he was affected by the awe in which he may have held certain players.

'Gordon had been awesome for United in his first eighteen months,' recalls Moran. 'He had got injured at West Bromwich Albion at the beginning of the 1985/86 season. I remember the day well because my son was born that Saturday, but Gordon was in hospital for different reasons with a dislocated shoulder. I think that that injury affected his consistency over the following few seasons, and, although he continued to be very good, he never quite reached the level of performance in United's red that he had found previously.'

Strachan's last two years at Old Trafford weren't as productive as anyone at the club would have hoped. The whole club was struggling to find itself a niche in a league they just couldn't get to grips with and Strachan, although very good in spells, couldn't rise above the general malaise of the place.

'The first thing we assessed was how we wanted *our* team to look,' says Knox. 'We wanted a team of youngsters, young men who had come through the ranks and could identify with the club and its supporters. We'd done the same at Aberdeen so we put a lot of work in at United to create that same atmosphere. We had to let every schoolboy go that year because we felt none were good enough but then went about recruiting what we saw as genuine talent. We already had Lee Sharpe, Lee Martin and Mark Robins who would go on and contribute for a short while, but the new batch of kids included Nicky Butt, the Neville brothers, Paul Scholes and David Beckham so it clearly worked.'

Ferguson began to create a team that he hoped would mirror his image and desires. United had finished a disappointing 11th in his first season and, despite coming runner-up to a very good Liverpool side in 1988, there was still a lot of hard work to do. Brian McClair had been signed from Celtic and Steve Bruce from Norwich, two men who would contribute greatly to Ferguson's incredible success at Old Trafford. While new players symbolised Ferguson's work in progress, the revolving doors at the club continued to spin heartily as players left in abundance. Peter Davenport, Terry Gibson and John Sivebaek all departed. But what of Strachan?

His form was still good – he had been picked to play for the Football League against a World XI that included Maradona, to mark the centenary of the League's existence – and the fans loved their player's intricate skill and dedication to the cause. His manager, however, was casting an admiring eye over players he felt might give him more on the right side of his midfield. Arsenal's David Rocastle had impressed him greatly and Trevor Steven, twice a Championship winner at Everton, was another he made efforts to get into a United jersey. Strachan realised that Ferguson wanted a more naturally wide player, a winger who would move up and down the touchline and whip in crosses without question.

Ferguson had plans. Strachan's position wasn't the only one that would have to be dealt with. Paul McGrath and Norman Whiteside, two strong Irish personalities, were content in many areas of the pitch. Unfortunately, they were just as comfortable in the players' lounge and their indiscipline would have to be dealt with. They would eventually both have to leave. Strachan, although not fitting into Ferguson's long-term plans, was playing well enough and scoring enough to warrant a new contract. United had drawn twice against an all-conquering Liverpool team, entertaining the country with the combined skills of John Barnes, Peter Beardsley and John Aldridge. Strachan had scored at Anfield in a 3–3 draw and Highbury where they won 2–1, but again defeats against lesser teams saw them finish nine points behind their big rivals. Strachan had known that his career would soon be changing. So often the catalyst to Ferguson's successes in the past, it was the young crop that clearly were the manager's and the club's future.

Under Ferguson he was again faced with the need for a new challenge. Their time together was becoming stagnant. Ferguson would roll into a half-time team talk and begin the rant. 'Hey, gaffer,' Strachan would say cheekily. 'Come on with something original, will you? You tried that one on me on a windy night at Morton ten years ago.'

In the summer of 1988, when an offer to move abroad came up, it excited him. Lens in the French First Division did not exactly represent the most glamorous of moves but it was a fresh start, an opportunity to sample the game in a brand new environment and culture. Ferguson again wasn't pleased. He felt that the contract offered to Strachan had been agreed and couldn't help but feel let down. Strachan had always wanted to play on the Continent and simply felt at 31 this was the time to live an ambition.

The move was not destined to be. Throughout the negotiations, the Lens coach had been under pressure, his job seemingly on the line. He was duly sacked; the move fell through and Strachan would have to think again about his future. 'Are you interested in a broken-down winger?' Strachan asked of Ferguson. The answer was still a yes and Strachan was given a one-year deal, much to the relief of his young sons who had been in tears at the thought of leaving Manchester.

His family may have not relished a new start but – and despite signing the contract – Strachan wasn't a content footballer going into the 1988/89 season. He felt he was just seeing out his time at a United team dubbed by the press 'Fergie's Fledglings' in a bid to arouse memories of a bygone era under Busby. He couldn't help but feel separated from his manager's ambitions and was waiting for Ferguson to find a ready replacement. His pride meant he was not overjoyed by such a prospect, while his patchy form in a poor United team underlined how much the uncertainty was affecting his game. The self-doubt that had nagged at him over the years had returned in earnest. He thought of the players who had left United in the past, only to see out their careers in a downwardly spiralling motion. The idea of becoming a has-been was too much to bear.

The fans weren't enamoured of the idea of Strachan being frozen out. Ralph Milne came in from Bristol City as a wide player, but was far from the dream player needed to wrestle the title back from Merseyside. 'I've seen milk turn quicker than Ralph Milne,' scoffed Tommy Docherty, and he wasn't alone. Strachan, to the fans, represented a rare commodity at Old Trafford towards the end of the 80s: quality. A move, however, was imminent.

Queens Park Rangers had shown a vague interest and, while a firm enquiry came from Middlesbrough's Bruce Rioch, Strachan didn't feel that the Teesiders were the club for him. He had played well in an FA Cup victory over West Ham, scoring a fine goal and underlining to any interested parties that his ability to open defences up with a clever pass had not diminished. As the club went into an FA Cup quarter-final against Nottingham Forest at Old Trafford, Ferguson even declared that his Scottish player's form could see United all the way to Wembley. They lost 1–0. After the game, Strachan was walking despondently along the corridors of Old Trafford when his manager, not happy with what he'd witnessed from a flat and despondent team, came running behind him with a question. 'Do you want to talk to Ron Atkinson at Sheffield Wednesday?'

It was to be Strachan's last game for Manchester United and his last with Ferguson as his boss. They had not been able to reclaim those glittery days in north-eastern Scotland. The only reminder of that previous encounter was the cool relations between the two that over the years has ceased to dwindle. 'It's a shame,' he told the *Sunday Telegraph* not long after Ferguson's damning book was published in 1999. 'For twelve years we've had arguments, niggles, bits and bobs, and I'd love it if the next time we meet we could just agree to forget it all and start again. He's on record as having admired me – at least as a player – and I certainly admire him as a manager. With his confrontational style I suppose this sort of thing was liable to happen. But it's a real pity. To be able to greet each other and talk about old times would be wonderful.'

Five years on and Strachan doesn't seem to have got his wish. One of his last games at Southampton as manager last season saw his team play well at Old Trafford before losing 3–2. The two men, who had shared so many trophies, memories and adulation of the fans, could now not even share a handshake. For Frank Stapleton, it is no surprise. 'Ferguson was Ferguson and Gordon isn't one to sit back and keep his mouth shut. If he felt he was getting unfairly picked on then he'd say and to me that is quite right. What happened over the years between them is between them, but Fergie then did his book that wasn't at all kind about Gordon, but he never retaliated publicly and to me kept a huge amount of dignity. He came out of it far better if you ask me.'

The truth was Strachan didn't bother to read the book. He had heard what had been said about his lack of honesty and dedication but saw it as just one man's opinion. 'Just one man, in all my time in football,' he remarked shortly after. 'He can be that way, though. He's a difficult man to like. I said I was bored and he's mentioned it a couple of times since. The thing is you can only do so much at a club and then, it's like David Bowie, you have to reinvent yourself.'

For now though it was a move apart that was the priority, and Sheffield Wednesday were given permission to talk to a restless Strachan. By working out a deal Strachan and Atkinson hoped to rekindle a working relationship that both men had enjoyed immensely. 'There's a grapevine and on that I heard that Strachs was about to become available,' says Atkinson. 'We were crying out for quality and I thought he was just the kind of player and character who could take the club on.'

So much so that he went to his former player with more than an offer of simply playing his way through the twilight of his career. The flamboyant manager hoped that Strachan would be tempted by the idea of becoming player-coach at Hillsborough with Atkinson stepping up into a general manager's role. Strachan, although touched by the obvious high esteem in which Atkinson held his football brain, did not feel ready to take on the coaching or managerial side of things.

He had seen his fellow countrymen Graeme Souness and Kenny Dalglish do brilliant jobs at Rangers and Liverpool respectively but he felt that by adopting such a role his abilities as a player would be compromised. Despite the doubts raised in his mind over his last several months in Manchester, he was still confident that he had much to offer. His 'engine', as he called it, was still purring nicely; he felt fit and the extra burden of looking after players could wait. Ron's offer though remained a good one and for now he could always just play the game he still loved with a passion. A move across the Pennines was going to happen, that was certain. To Atkinson's dismay and Strachan's surprise, however, it wouldn't be to Sheffield.

9. NO REGRETS

REPORTER: *Gordon, do you think James Beattie deserves to be in the England squad?*
GORDON: *I don't care, I'm Scottish.*

He strained but nothing. He had another gulp of water but nothing. It had been hours since the referee's whistle had put an end to an amazing display of football genius. Brazil had just beaten Scotland 4–1 on a sweltering evening in Seville. Their players, combining the most sublime ball skills and athleticism, had taken his team apart; their yellow jerseys buzzing over the pitch and opposition like wasps around honey.

The Scots had trundled into their dressing room and sat in awe, looking at each other in quiet disbelief; half bemused and half honoured to have been involved in such a display. There was no rush to get changed, instead they sat and talked sensibly about what had just happened. Why were they that good? Why were they so far ahead? Was it the way they warmed up? Their lifestyle, their climate, their professionalism? What?

Strachan had been asked to give a drug test and now, having chased shadows in the 80-degree heat, was struggling to find the required sample. He stood patiently waiting for nature to take its course when Socrates, the great Brazilian captain, strolled in wearing nothing but a pair of skimpy briefs and flip-flops. In his fingers, he held the necks of two cold bottles of beer, while in his mouth a half-smoked cigarette hung over his black beard. His tanned and sculptured torso shone next to Strachan's pale and sunburned limbs as he took the fag out of his mouth, turned to his opponent and said in pidgin English, 'You play good game. Good luck.' He took the bottles of beer, downed one after the other, had a large drag on his fag, pissed into the jug and walked out.

Strachan strolled into the dressing room. His club team-mate Alex McLeish was still sitting there. 'Hey, big-un,' he said calmly. 'You know we were wondering what we had to do to match these guys.'

'Aye,' said McLeish.

'Well, we'd better start smoking.'

It had seemed that, however hard the Scots tried, they were always just huffing and puffing away in world football. Their critics would say that they didn't have the guile or the nerve to get further in the big tournaments and many fans were driven to substances stronger then nicotine in the pursuit of national football glory. For others less cruel, Scotland – a nation of no more than five million – being there was where the glory lay. It was competing against the likes of Brazil and sometimes, just sometimes, getting a result that brought Scottish passion and pride to the fore.

For decades 'The Blues', as they were christened in 1928 by the *Scotsman*, have given their army of supporters something to shout about, something to moan about and often something to cry about. The 'Wembley Wizards' of 1928 who came to the Empire Stadium in Wembley, and with Alex James and Hughie Gallagher mesmerising their English cousins, won 5–1. Or the team that came south in 1967 to face the World Champions only to win 3–2 and send their fans into wild renditions of the 'Gay Gordons'.

Then there were the World Cup adventures of the 1970s. They had qualified for the 1974 tournament held in Germany, after a twenty-year absence. The entire squad had won that year's Scottish Football Writers' Player of the Year award in recognition of their achievements, but despite great names like Law, Dalglish and Bremner their tentative approach, especially against the novices of Zaire, saw them return home after the group stages, albeit unbeaten.

It was 1978 and, despite marching to the soulful tones of Ally's Army, they were again disappointed. MacLeod had predicted great things but, unprepared, they lost to an impressive and underrated Peru team and drew with Iran. A magnificent display and 3–2 win over the eventual runners-up Holland wasn't enough and again sent them home before the business end of proceedings. That summed up being a Scotland fan. The highs and the lows always travelled side by side, never separated by time or fortune, and Strachan was like no other, growing up loving and despairing at his country's game in equal measures.

By the time Ally's Army returned with a whimper from Argentina in 1978, Strachan was about to embark on life under Alex Ferguson and start to play like someone who could himself pull on the famous blue jersey. MacLeod wouldn't last long as national manager after his false hope in South America and so the country turned its lonely eyes to the one Scot whose name was synonymous with success both at home and abroad, Jock Stein. With Billy McNeill enticed away from Aberdeen that same summer, Stein had been offered a job on the board at Celtic but, for the ever involved Lanarkshire man, sitting with the suits wasn't a viable option and he was tempted to move to England and take over at Leeds United, a club holding on by their fingernails to years of success under Don Revie. 'I did not want to stay at Celtic as a director,' he groaned. 'I feel I have too much to offer football and I wanted closer involvement.'

Unfortunately for the Elland Road faithful, the position at their club wasn't close enough. He had only been in charge for 44 short days (the exact amount of time spent in the club's dug-out by Brian Clough four years earlier) when his wife Jean expressed her wish to return home. No contract had been signed and the national job had become available. The move home seemed right and not only for the Steins.

'Big Jock getting the job gave the whole nation a lift,' recalls Scotland's giant centre-forward of the seventies and eighties, Joe Jordan. 'For so long he had won honours in Scotland and Europe and everyone thought that one day he must get the job. It was similar to Giovanni Trappatoni in Italy. He had won everything for Juventus and so one day he had to get the Italy job. I think that's right, a national manager should be of an age when he has seen it all and can pass on his experiences to class international players. It was so exciting to have someone to look up to, admire and learn from. I was a Celtic fan too so that made it a little more sweet.'

Stein's first task was to qualify for the European Championships in Italy in 1980. They had been ousted by Belgium, but Stein took solace in the fact that the lowlanders had gone on to lose to West Germany in the final and were becoming a fine, albeit small, footballing nation. That's where he wanted his country to be and, with the players at his disposal, why not?

It was a new decade and, while Thatcher set about emasculating the trade unions, Jock Stein, a man raised from good mining stock, looked to his players as a group. He wanted a collective, where the great individuals in his country would co-operate together and become a *team*. He had every right to feel confident. Under his command he had fine players reaching the peak of their already distinguished careers. Kenny

Dalglish, Graeme Souness and Alan Hansen had won European Cups and would win more in the coming years at Liverpool; Archie Gemmill, John Roberston and Frankie Gray had also enjoyed winning Europe's premier club trophy at Nottingham Forest; and Celtic's Danny McGrain had a wealth of experience and determination on his side.

What Stein was excited about was that he could blend that talent with a host of fine young players earning a living in both the Scottish Premier League and the English First Division. Ipswich's John Wark and George Burley, Roy Aitken of Celtic and David Cooper of Rangers had broken through in the latter part of the seventies, while St Mirren's Peter Weir and Aberdeen's Steve Archibald would soon get their first caps. 'There's no doubt Jock wanted to look at what was available,' says Jordan, who, approaching thirty, would be kept on his toes by the exciting crop of youngsters. 'In my position alone I was competing against the likes of Archibald, Andy Gray and Alan Brazil. That was the competition and it could be hard.'

Like Archibald, Strachan and another Pittodrie stalwart Alex McLeish were also making a good case for international caps. The closest they had got was a visit to Wembley in the May of 1979. 'That was when Gordon and I began to cement a good friendship,' says McLeish, smiling. 'Myself, Gordon, John McMaster and Gordon's brother-in-law Kenny drove down to London and stood in the terraces with the Tartan Army. We had a great weekend. I remember standing behind the goal, but it was Gordon who was getting noticed by other fans. The game kicked off and Wark put us one up. There was a surge behind us and the wee man was on the crash barrier. It looked bad and he may not have had the illustrious career he did had McMaster and myself not helped him out. We shielded him and gave him some air. Do you know, looking back on that occasion and others, he may dwell on things and say to himself, "I owe Big Alec my career!"'

The following summer the two companions would go from spectators to fully fledged internationals. It was no less than Strachan's form deserved. 'There was a clamour to get young Gordon involved,' recalls Ron Scott, who had enjoyed observing Strachan's football from the country's press boxes for a number of years. 'There was a feeling amongst the more provincial clubs and the papers that followed them that their players were too often overlooked, that the Old Firm players along with those playing in England were given preferential treatment.'

What with Willie Miller and Archibald also involved, any suspicions of favouritism were dispelled. Instead there was just recognition for Aberdeen's illustrious, Championship-winning season. Strachan – who had managed only one cap at under-21 level in November 1979 – of course was overjoyed with the call-up and his first full cap was won in a Home International in Belfast on 16 May 1980. He had had experience of travelling with the squad before winning that honour but, and again along with McLeish, thought his international career might be over before it even started. After a game in Belgium towards the end of 1979, the team had boarded the bus and were ready to make their way to the airport. Jock Stein then climbed aboard with the hotel manager, not looking a happy man. 'Could I have your attention,' he said with a coarseness that suggested slight annoyance. 'Can the gentlemen who have chosen to steal the hotel towels please get off and return them?' Amid the sniggers, Strachan and McLeish, heads bowed, made their way off the coach and returned their souvenirs. 'That's it, big man,' said Strachan to his Pittodrie pal. 'We're never going to play again.'

As ever, he needn't have worried. It was the first time the Scots had visited Ulster for ten years due to the Troubles and they were beaten 1–0 by a Billy Hamilton goal but bounced back after with the same score-line beating Wales in Glasgow a week later. How had he taken to the very different world of international footballers and how had they responded to the quick-witted boy from their nation's capital?

'Gordon wasn't the confident character that we all perceived back then,' says Willie Miller knowingly. 'He put up a show but deep down there was self-doubt. He could be very nervous at times and the front that he put up was just to dispel that side of him. His ability was fine but when he came into the national team he was suddenly surrounded by some brilliant players and men. Dalglish, Souness, Big Jock; these were intimidating men to the strongest personality and Gordon still looked up to them. He was nervous and that little bit more reserved. Like all good players, though, once on the pitch those nerves left.'

He, along with his young club team-mates, would arrive at the hotel and sit quietly, observing, taking in their new and inspiring environment. Strachan though would not have to stay quiet long. Scotland kicked off their World Cup-qualifying campaign in Sweden (a country that seemed to appeal to Strachan's sense of glory) in the autumn of 1980. A draw away to strong Scandinavian opposition would have suited Stein and his team but in the latter stages of the game Strachan played a one–two with Gemmill and pierced the ball with his weaker left foot past the keeper Ronnie Hellstrom. It was enough to seal a brilliant start to their World Cup hopes and Strachan noticed that all of a sudden senior team-mates, press and fans had plenty more time for their Player of the Year.

He had made his mark and not just in a friendly, but in a game that had counted. Any lingering self-doubt should have blown away in a breeze of publicity but his stomach injury that December kept him out of the game for the rest of the season and he wouldn't play for Scotland again for almost a year. Laid up at home, bed bound and frustrated, Strachan would only have been comforted by Jock Stein's words of support:

> *Gordon Strachan played a major part in winning the championship for Aberdeen and when he came into the Scottish side he did all I expected from him. He settled in very quickly and was not the slightest way overawed. He is a good player in the old Scottish tradition. By that I mean he gets the ball and isn't frightened to take people on ... He has had a marvellous year and scored that vital goal in Sweden to give us those equally vital World Cup points.*

Strachan returned stronger than ever, helped the team in their last two qualifying games that took them to Spain and was playing what he thought was the best football of his life. However, and despite his esteemed manager's confident words regarding the apparent ease in which he had taken to the international set-up, Strachan was still too aware of those playing around him. Approaching a World Cup, it was something that would have to change. 'I'd always been a bit in awe of Graeme Souness in particular,' he said not long after that summer's World Cup. 'I'd ended up playing the Sammy Lee role of just giving him the ball. I had decided to play my own game and stand or fall on the consequences.'

He had been left out of all three of the Home Internationals leading up to the World Cup, including the 100th fixture against England, at Hampden. That day, the same Glaswegians that had booed his every touch only a week before while Aberdeen beat Rangers in the Cup final chanted his name, urging Stein to have him unzip the tracksuit and join a game the Scots eventually would lose by a single goal.

Strachan, though, need not be perturbed. Stein had told him he was saving him for the festivities in Spain. He could travel south an excited and expectant man.

Scotland had travelled to the two previous World Cups in buoyant mood, and this time their camp had tried to play down their hopes, especially as they faced daunting games against Brazil and the Soviet Union. 'In 1974, expectations were left on the shelf,' recalls Jordan. 'The whole country was just elated to be going after such a long time out; 1978 was different. The whole thing was built up too much before we left. We'd do this and win that; it was over the top and subsequently failed to materialise. In 1982, Big Jock was too cute to fall into that trap. He played it down and knew we would have a tough time.'

Having settled and trained in Portugal, the Scots crossed the border and headed for a tennis complex in Sotogrande, just a stone's throw from the Rock of Gibraltar. Strachan was starting to feel the part. The training, the dealing with the press, it all felt right. Despite the well-documented problems Scotland managers had had in the past involving discipline on trips abroad, Stein felt he had a group of men who could be trusted. Strachan enjoyed the extra responsibility afforded to him and the squad and was benefiting from being treated that bit more like a man than you would be with your club.

The opening game was in Malaga, a two-hour drive along the coastal stretch nicknamed 'the road to hell', due to the large amount of accidents. Scotland's base, such a long way from the majority of their matches in Malaga, was a strange choice, especially as their opponents on that ground had both camped nearby. Scotland had been to the last two tournaments but it seemed their FA had learned little from the experiences in Germany and Argentina. So it was New Zealand, in their first and only World Cup to date, that arrived the fresher but surely, unlike Zaire and Iran in the past, there wouldn't be any slip-ups this time?

Strachan had 11 caps to his name and took to the bowling-green surface confident of what he could contribute on this, the best of settings. As he took to the field he was struck by how hot the Malaga night air was but the occasion soon had him itching to get going. He settled quickly into his game, wary of conserving energy in the heat but still able to collect the ball and put it to good use every time. He picked up the ball and began to run at an awkward-looking Kiwi defence, seemingly in awe of his control and technique. A simple pass to Dalglish and it was 1–0.

Strachan went on to have a hand in two more goals before half-time and he and his team were flying. In orange country there would be no banana skins. Or so they thought. After half-time New Zealand were allowed to score two sloppy goals and, despite the Scots regaining some composure and scoring two more to win 5–2, their failure to keep a clean sheet in such a tight group would come back to haunt them. Strachan had been brilliant. His work-rate and deftness with the ball had not gone unnoticed among the locals; when replaced by David Narey late on he was met by rapturous applause and named Man of the Match. He had loved every minute of the game. It wasn't the glamorous opposition that people associated with the World Cup – he wouldn't have to wait long for that – but the occasion, the crowd, the conditions, it was all he'd ever hoped it would be and he couldn't wait to face Brazil in the next game.

It was only a three-day break between matches but they were to be three long days. Strachan loved the football side of a tournament but the waiting around and being confined to hotels, that he could do without. Players had different ways of dealing with the long hours not training or playing. Stein had allowed him and a few others to enjoy southern Spain's golf scene but what else was a man to do? While some played cards and Willie Miller slept by the pool, Strachan grew more and more bored. His skin isn't exactly designed for soaking up the rays and, mindful of his pale player, Stein kept a close eye on him realising he was going to be a huge asset to any progress made in the competition. If he thought Strachan had been out in the sun too long, he would call him in like an overprotective parent, and Strachan could twiddle his thumbs in the shade.

The monotony was broken soon after the first game when he was bothered by a man sitting near him smoking a cigarette. On the brink of asking him to put the thing out, Strachan realised the culprit was a Scotland fan. Not any Scotland fan, mind, it was Sean Connery. The actor had his own home up the road in Marbella and had popped into the hotel to offer support. Strachan's boredom was broken as the two men chatted, although it is doubtful whether they compared Edinburgh milk rounds. Connery wasn't the only Scottish star to pop in. Rod Stewart also had a local place nearby and Strachan jumped at the chance with a few of the others to visit the singer, even posing for photos with Rod in an unfeasibly skimpy pair of leopard-skin swimming trunks (Stewart that is, not Strachan).

If he felt at all star-struck in the presence of film and rock stars, it was Scotland's next game against Brazil that had him and his team-mates almost joining the 50,000 crowd in their cheers for an encore. Brazil were awesome. With each player on first-name terms with the ball, their ability to control the pace of the game in the even more intense heat of Seville and their almost rhythmic movement had the Scots flabbergasted, at times only able to sit back and enjoy a carnival of football.

Scotland for all that had started the stronger and had taken the lead through a Brazilian-like shot from distance early on from Dundee United's David Narey. After the dust had settled on the defeat, Narey's team-mates would mock him for scoring. 'Why d'ya go and do that, big man,' they teased. 'You went and made them angry.'

Zico, Falcao, Eder, Oscar, Junior, Socrates; the names roll off the tongue like their own brand of flowing football. They opened up Scotland with four sublime goals. Strachan again had run himself into the ground and gave a very good account of himself but he couldn't help but marvel at the joy the Brazilians got from playing. The shackles that so often grated at the ankles of the British game were off and Strachan, having been substituted, couldn't help but sit and enjoy the show. 'That team were just brilliant,' recalls Jordan. 'I had been playing for AC Milan in Italy and come across the likes of Falcao and Socrates. What personalities, and what players they were. They messed up though. They should have won the whole thing but messed up big time.'

The heavy defeat meant Scotland had to beat the Russians to go through to the second round for the first time in their history. 'If we had kept a clean sheet against the Kiwis,' bemoans Jordan, re-called for the last game, 'we would have put ourselves under far less pressure going into the Russia game.' Jordan's early goal had given them a fighting chance but conceding two goals due to first an Alan Rough error and then a bizarre collision between Miller and Hansen meant that even a stinging equaliser from Souness was not enough to see them through. They were out on goal difference. 'The Miller and Hansen mix-up wasn't dwelled on really,' admits Jordan. 'To me the two goals we let in during the first game were the disasters. You can go on about other moments but that was the slip-up. It was crazy but I suppose typical Scotland.'

His boredom aside, Strachan returned home with treasured memories and glowing reports. The Spanish press voted him the best player in the group which was an incredible feat considering those Brazilian names he had faced, and to top it off he was voted into the World XI. The locals had taken his game to their hearts, likening him to the tournament's mascot, branding him *Neranjito*, 'Little Orange'. The best praise though came from his fellow pros and not just anybody. 'Strachan's play in the World Cup excited me,' declared Portuguese legend Eusebio. 'He is one of the finest players I have seen in years. I had heard the name of Gordon Strachan before but did not know he was that good. He was better than some of the Brazilians.'

With Belgian manager Guy Thys chipping in by saying he rated Strachan more highly than Diego Maradona, it was not surprising that he returned home to the Premier League with his head and horizons somewhat broadened. Flattered definitely, but he was aware that a lot of the quotes were a little over the top. 'I'm not world class,' he declared back in the reality of his own country. 'I lack genuine pace to be considered truly world class. When you see the guys who really have it you see the difference.'

The whole experience was hard to leave behind, and the normality of his everyday working existence in Scotland was, frankly, hard to get excited about. Even dealing with Brazil's press brought its own form of exciting sport. Cameras flashing in his face, microphones shoved to his mouth, it wasn't exactly a cup of lukewarm tea and a soggy biscuit in the Pittodrie press room. 'There were hordes of them trying to talk to you,' reminisced Strachan. 'You didn't understand half of it but I just enjoyed the colour of the whole thing. They were probably swearing at me, but never mind, I loved it.'

No doubt, Strachan was now one of his country's most recognisable footballing faces among fans, press and admiring opposition managers but his personal good form was not reflected in Scotland's fortunes as they were again pipped by Belgium for a place in the European Championships to be held and won by France. Strachan did get to pit his wits against the midfield that would win that summer's tournament for the host nation as the Scots visited Marseille for a friendly in June. Michel Platini, Jean Tigana, Alain Giresse and Luis Fernandez were a formidable line-up, and he hoped, having tasted playing the best, that his country could improve and go on to qualify for a fourth successive World Cup, an incredible achievement in itself.

Scotland had got off to a great start with victories over Iceland and a 3–1 win over the runners-up in the European Championships, Spain. This being Scotland, though, things would not be smooth in what was a difficult group. Spain three months later had their revenge, winning 1–0 in Seville before Wales came to Hampden and won thanks to an Ian Rush effort. Under Mike England, Wales had built a strong squad of players. Rush was scoring enough goals to soon warrant a big-money move to Italy; Neville Southall was one of Europe's finest keepers and, in Strachan's new young club team-mate, Mark Hughes, Rush had a partner of power and often acrobatic skill.

Strachan had helped his country to a 1–0 win over England at Hampden and so went into the final crucial qualifying games in buoyant mood, and having beaten Iceland it came down to the last game in Wales. It was simple: Scotland only needed a draw to put themselves in a play-off. A packed Ninian Park in Cardiff bellowed out 'Land of my Fathers', in the hope that their side would win and stand a chance of reaching their first major tournament since 1958. It was to be a tragic night, but for reasons far more poignant than any football match.

Alex Ferguson by now was assisting Stein with the national team and as Souness was suspended (a typically robust challenge in Reykjavik had seen to that) he suggested that Strachan fill the available central midfield berth. With a Welsh roar behind them, the home team had taken an early lead through Hughes and were looking the more likely victors as the teams came in for half-time. It was to prove a strange fifteen minutes. 'It was a high-pressure night but half-time in the dressing room was quite surreal,' recalls Roy Aitken, playing alongside Strachan that night. 'Jim [Leighton] came in saying he'd lost his contact lenses and didn't have any spares. We didn't even know he was short sighted but it explained why at the end of the half he had come to take a catch, missed it and cleared it with his knee.'

A tired-looking Stein approached Strachan. 'Wee man, during the second half I'm going to replace you with Davie Cooper.' Strachan, so keen to be involved in such a vital game, was not happy and was about to argue his corner with the man who had given him his international calling.

Ferguson, no stranger himself of course to dressing-room 'chats' with Strachan, spotted the potential flashpoint and pulled his ex-employee to one side. 'Leave it alone,' he said calmly. 'He's not well. Just leave it.'

Strachan did as he was told and ran out for a vital second half thinking not much more if it. He had noticed on the afternoon of the match that the usually robust Scotland manager was a little quiet; the usual remarks about his height, or lack of it, were conspicuous by their absence as he sat that afternoon in the hotel foyer. This though was a massive game and with so much at stake it was no surprise that he wasn't acting himself. 'The expectation that day was immense, the tension immeasurable,' recalls Aitken. 'Jock though was the kind of manager who would protect his players from that tension and take it all on himself.'

The second half on the pitch continued in the same vein, with Strachan struggling to exert his presence on a midfield being swamped by Wales' Mickey Thomas and Peter Nicholas. On the hour mark, Stein made good his threat and brought on Cooper for an unhappy Strachan. It was a massive match and, despite being aware of his under-par showing, he was the kind of player who could change a game with a clever pass or run out of nowhere. He had been muttering his displeasure when Scotland equalised, through a Cooper penalty. Stein though remained unanimated. Ferguson had noticed that he was quite grey and now sweating profusely. He asked the team doctor to keep an eye open when a whistle went. Stein thought it was all over and moved towards the Welsh bench but collapsed before getting there. While their manager and a hero of the Scottish game was helped by medics into the stadium, the Tartan Army saluted the final whistle and another potential adventure into the unknown. Mexico? Tartan and tequila, what a splendid combination.

They were of course oblivious to what was happening in the dressing-room area. In fact, for a while, so were the players. They had heard Stein had had a heart attack but differing reports filtered through about his condition. It was Ferguson who came back into the room, the colour drained from his cheeks, to say he had died. How could it have happened? Their giant – and not only in stature – of a manager seemed infallible. There wasn't one player he hadn't touched, either as a schoolboy watching or supporting his Celtic teams, or as a player who had benefited from simply being in his company. No one even talked about the World Cup. 'We would rather have lost the game and still had the big man,' said one distraught fan outside. Strachan drove home to Manchester, an empty feeling inside. It was a void that would never be filled in Scottish football. The game in his country had lost its father.

Despite Stein's death, there was a job to do, one which he would have insisted on doing right. Australia were the opposition in the play-off and were dispatched 2–0 at Hampden. Strachan wouldn't make the journey Down Under where a goalless draw meant Scotland could start planning their trip to Mexico. Ferguson had been given the honour of continuing his mentor's work as a part-time manager that summer and took the team over to the United States without the worry of expectation that had befallen previous campaigns. Stein himself had used all his artistry to deflect the kind of wild optimism of previous years, but Ferguson would need no such psychological tools. This year no one expected anything less than a momentous task ahead.

'The pressure was off,' recalls Craig Brown, a future Scotland manager and part of Ferguson's coaching team that summer. 'We'd lost Dalglish which was a huge blow. He had pulled out causing concern over his reasons. Alex had chosen to go with McLeish and Miller as his centre-half pairing and omitted Kenny's skipper Alan Hansen from the squad. Some felt that Kenny had pulled out because of that and so that anti-climax hung over the country's expectations. Inside the camp though we left with quiet optimism.'

That optimism would have to be very quiet because the draw had not been kind to Scotland. They would face West Germany, Uruguay and Denmark. Not easy. Denmark were actually the unseeded team, incredible given the players they had at their disposal. Strachan was just delighted to be going to another World Cup. His form wasn't as good as it had been four years previously but he was still one of his country's main players, someone who could feel comfortable on the same pitch as the great players that lay in wait.

While the football was a mouth-watering prospect, Strachan was again perturbed by the arrangements regarding the team's living arrangements. A small hotel in the smog-filled streets on the outskirts of Mexico City was not ideal. The Aztec pyramids may have been nearby, but this was a football team, not `Time Team'. Having trained for the high altitude in Albuquerque and the comfort of the United States, Strachan and co. were aggrieved by where they would prepare for the hard task ahead.

Denmark came first. A game that with a little more luck would have been against another unseeded team. Canada, Iraq or South Korea might have given the Scots a chance to feel their way into the tournament, but the Danes were exceptional and only unseeded due to it being their first ever time at the World Cup. They had been unfortunate to go out on penalties in the semi-finals of the European Championships two years earlier and, with Michael Laudrop and Preben Elkjaer leading their attack, their chances were again looking good.

In fact, Scotland played well and Denmark were lucky to win through an equally fortunate Elkjaer goal whereas Roy Aitken had a perfectly fine goal chalked off for offside. As in Spain in 1982, the second game was against a world super-power of football. Strachan had picked up a slight knock against Denmark and reports emanated around opposing camps that he could well miss the next game against West Germany. It was a rumour that the officious Germans and their manager Franz Beckenbauer would need confirming.

The assistant to the 'Kaiser' in 1986 was Bertie Vogts, himself a fine defender for the Germans and a World Cup winner in 1974. The game was played in Queretaro, 100 miles north of Mexico City. The Scots enjoyed their last training session before the game in the stadium where they hoped to enjoy complete privacy from prying eyes. Vogts though was sent on a mission: find out if Strachan is playing. The strict door policy was a hindrance but, like an archetypal German general in a propaganda-fuelled war film, he had 'ze cunning plan'. One of the main sponsors that summer was Coca-Cola and so Vogts approached a vendor bringing supplies of the soft drink in for the following day's match. A quick chat later and the young man had himself an official German jersey while Vogts was dressed in Coca-Cola branding and enjoying free access into the ground. He could report back to base. Strachan was fully fit and they should plan accordingly.

West Germany would make it all the way to another final with the finishing and finesse of Rudi Voeller, the steely drive of Lothar Matthaus and the cunning experience of Pierre Littbarski; but it seemed even with their inside knowledge they couldn't keep the shackles on Strachan's ability and, as ever, the Scots, when facing superior opposition, started without the fear that so often hinders their progress against weaker sides.

The ball was played into the inside-right position where Strachan was loitering. His intent, the German goal. In one movement he had brought the ball down, skipped into the German box and fluently found the corner of the net. There was a tartan explosion as Strachan ran off to take the applause. It had long been *en vogue* for players to run and leap like thoroughbreds over the advertising hoardings to salute the fans. As Strachan advanced with purpose he looked more like a Shetland pony approaching Beechers Brook and was forced to pull up. Self-mockingly he hoisted a leg up as if to climb over before giving up, that infectious grin all over his face. It was a lovely moment, one that summed up the man. 'It would have been just my luck,' he later said, 'to find one of those eight-foot moats on the other side. I wasn't going to take a chance.' The wit, the cheek, it was all there in that split second and even today is mentioned and recalled with a smile.

As ever though, Scottish smiles were short lived. Disappointment was again to prove an overzealous companion on these trips and four minutes later Voeller equalised, while a second-half winner meant another loss. They had again been beaten by the better team but, unlike the defeat against the transcendent Brazilians, this felt hollow. This felt like more could have been done. However, there still was more to do. Despite two losses, due to the structure of the competition, victory over Uruguay would see them through to that dreamlike and uncharted land of second-round World Cup football.

Uruguay had won little fans so far in a tournament that they had cynically made their way through. They had been destroyed 6–1 by the Danes in one of the best performances of the summer but a draw with Germany meant another draw would strangely see them continue to the last sixteen. Ferguson went about picking a team to win the game but made two decisions that he would later be questioned over. Steve Archibald had impressed against Germany but was dropped seemingly for fitness reasons; Ferguson has admitted since that his concern with perceived bias regarding the number of players with connections to Aberdeen had influenced his decision. Leighton, Strachan and Miller would all start, with the latter made captain following the decision to leave out Graeme Souness.

'We had a chat amongst ourselves,' says Brown. 'Ferguson was very close to Walter Smith and they decided that Graeme had been struggling in the altitude. He was gone. A decision had to be made and a hard one. Sir Bobby Robson sums it up when he says that that summer he had been forced to leave out Bryan Robson and Ray Wilkins due to injury and suspension. England had been struggling but without them they won the last group game and went through. Bobby admitted that he would never have left them out even though they perhaps needed to be. He learned from that that a manager has to be proactive rather than reactive and that is exactly what Ferguson was. It might not have paid off but it was a decision based solely on football and for that Alex should be commended.'

It was, however, to be a physical game and one wonders just how Souness would have approached the cynicism of the South Americans, but there was no doubt his country missed his forceful guile. Scotland had an idea of what to expect and after only a minute their hypothesis was proved correct as Strachan was scythed down by Jose Batista. It was an atrocious challenge on a player the Uruguayans obviously had earmarked as a threat. Strong action was needed and the French referee Joel Quiniou made his intentions clear with an immediate red card. It seemed the Scots had a referee who would come down hard on any misdemeanour.

However, ten Uruguayans were even more abject than the full complement and they kicked, spat, hacked and punched their way to a goalless draw. Scotland missed some gilt-edged chances but were subject to horrendous provocation, all of which slowly went unchallenged by the referee whose supposed might wilted in the blazing Mexican sun; from cactus to weeping willow in ninety long minutes. 'I don't know what all the fuss is about,' said a resolute and unflinching Uruguay coach Omar Barros. 'We played a fair game.'

Ferguson hadn't thought so and refused any notion of a handshake, and wouldn't disagree with an SFA spokesman's notion that Barros and his team were the 'scum of the earth'. Archie Knox, as ever Ferguson's assistant, sat and watched as disgusted as anyone at what was happening to his country's chances. 'That wasn't a game at all. They had ten men and shut up shop but the other things that went on that afternoon had nothing to do with the game of football.'

As for Strachan, he too left the stadium with a nasty taste in his mouth. The football pitch was a place where he had always felt at home, a place he could live out his passions, but on that afternoon those passions were soured like never before or since. As the Scotland coach pulled away from the Estadio Neza, Strachan took a good look at the surrounding slums – the dead dogs strewing the roads, the cardboard housing and the malnourished children. He tried to rationalise what had just happened. Most of the Uruguay team would have come from similar backgrounds, poverty that made his Muirhouse look like Beverly Hills. They had football as one route out of that poverty and would clearly go as far as possible to make sure they were a success. He had tried nobly to understand but it was hard. Right now he just wanted to get back to Cheshire, Lesley and the kids.

Despite the setbacks, his experiences at World Cups had been the pinnacle of Strachan's playing days. He had returned to England, continued to play well at a Manchester United now under Ferguson, without truly reaching the heights, and in turn his Scotland career went flat after the twin peaks of Spain and Mexico. He had found it that bit harder playing for his country and earning a living in England. While at Aberdeen, he had sensed the difference between the two sets of players. The English-based players, while not aloof, would be chatting or eating together and cliques were formed. Once Strachan had moved south he realised a lot of it was in the minds of the Scots: it wasn't that the English felt enhanced or superior, it was that they had travelled together and just fell into natural groups. With the doubts though came rumours of preferential treatment of the Anglo-Scots, and with the rumours came a certain amount of resentment, distrust and, at worst, jealousy. Strachan himself admitted how emotions could be stirred during a get-together. 'I would drive up to Troon or wherever we were meeting in my old Vauxhall Viva, praying that it wouldn't rain because then the car would break down. I'd park this battered old rust bucket beside some of the flash cars that the English-based players had driven up in and I felt lousy.'

Now he was the Anglophile, the man with the flash car, but he soon realised that with that came added pressure. Arriving to play for your country from England brings a stigma, a stigma attached by the Scottish press cautious of the travelling 'superstars'. Strachan could feel it. He had to be that bit more impressive, put in that extra bit more effort, stand out that bit more in order to avoid the accusation and slurs of his nation's back-pages. It became a chore to prove himself and, when Alex Ferguson – due to a Manchester United friendly with AC Milan – pulled him out of the Scotland squad for a game at Wembley, his international career looked over.

The truth though was that having taken over the job as manager after the Mexico World Cup, Andy Roxburgh had not wanted to drastically change things but was concerned with supplementing Strachan's undoubted talent. He and his staff were aware that Strachan was eager to play on the right of a central midfield pairing. His old phobia of filling a straightforward wide role had again reared its head and so decisions would have to be made. In Paul McStay, Scotland had a right-footed central midfielder who was felt to be superior to Strachan in age and now ability. Strachan would have to fill the wide role or drop out completely.

To Strachan 'wing' was a revolting four-letter word and, on the occasions he did play out there, the Scottish bench were left frustrated at his lack of apparent discipline. He would pick the ball up, drift inside with the ball and start to dictate the play from a more central post. It could be minutes before he returned to his designated spot and the murmurings from the bench became more audible with time. 'Gordon's fucked off again,' they'd moan and it soon affected just how much he was picked.

Scotland were vying for their fifth consecutive World Cup to be held in Italy in 1990. By the autumn of 1989, Strachan had made one appearance for his country in over two years and that as a substitute in a fabulous 2–0 victory over the French that set them well on their way to Italy. Just days after that run-out Strachan had moved to Leeds United and in doing so dropped a division. Could a 32-year-old playing in the rough and tumble of the English Second Division still have what it takes at this level? To many it was clear that the new national manager Andy Roxburgh had a difficult choice to make and that just might mean saying, once and for all, good-bye to a national treasure. 'A wee gem,' as he called him.

Strachan had started the 1989/90 season brilliantly at his new club. He was captain with an extra spring in that already bouncy step. A player enjoying his football again. Roxburgh and his assistant Craig Brown had had Strachan up to Largs to do his Scottish coaching badges that summer and his fervour and fitness hadn't gone unnoticed. 'He had such a super attitude,' recalls Brown. 'It was clear his enthusiasm had increased if anything since his move from Manchester United.'

His form and his hunger persuaded the Scottish management that Strachan still had something to offer. That theory would be put to the test in the Parc des Princes in Paris where Strachan hoped his international game would still have a certain *joie de vivre*. His inclusion had been scrutinised by the press wondering whether the 'born again' international could relive past glories. The game was a disaster. France breezed to a 3–0 win and of course it was the gamble on an old man that brought the most inquests. Strachan's game had matured but in France that night it seemed more Dairylea than fine brie.

Strachan, unlike his team-mates playing in the top flight in Scotland or England, didn't have the luxury of a weekend off to prepare. While the squad got settled and tuned, Strachan was playing at West Ham's Upton Park in a vital Second Division dog-fight. It was no excuse of course but Strachan was aware that he would be judged on his performance in Paris and on that alone. The fact that he was playing some of his best football at Leeds meant nothing to the Scottish fans or media. Despite his 42 previous caps, he was almost the new boy with it all to prove and he returned home hurt by the criticism and deflated by the thought that all he had put in to his country's football would be undone, the memories eroded by an off-night in Paris. Even as a veteran, the self-doubt that had accompanied his playing days couldn't be silenced.

Strachan was disappointed but talk of a fall-out with Roxburgh was off the mark. He continued to attend the SFA's coaching courses over the summer, now as a First Division footballer at newly promoted Leeds and had continued good relations with a manager he felt was doing all the right things. He hadn't been taken to Italy, of course, which had hurt, but Strachan, not one to feel sorry for himself and feeling absolutely exhausted after his promotion push at Leeds, had concentrated on his club form and was reaping the rewards.

Scotland's qualification for the European Championships – a competition that had never borne the same fruit as their World Cup challenges – had started well with two wins and a draw but, and after another 18 months off the scene, Roxburgh's eye was again drawn to Elland Road. 'The thing about Gordon was his amazing Peter Pan-like presence,' says Roxburgh, admiration filling his voice. 'He seemed timeless and you felt he was going to go on forever. It had been hard to leave him out of our World Cup plans but, seeing him in the First Division, I had no doubt his fitness was second to none and he could still do it for us.

'When I took over I immediately lost Dalglish and Souness and that was a blow. To lose that quality at once was a problem. If anyone names their top ten Scottish players those guys would be in each time. That was hard, so I was glad to get Gordon involved and he did very well. I admit that I didn't have enough of him; I got some but not enough of him in his prime.'

Strachan had his doubts. Did he need those feelings of failure again? He was loving his football at Leeds and maybe he should leave it at that. It was a feeling that wouldn't last. His doubts were in conflict with a sense of injustice. The Scottish fans would remember him by his last game and this was his chance to show his country not only what sort of player he still was, but also remind them of the player he had always been.

He proudly accepted national service once again, and this time could count on being judged by more than one game. Things had changed, though, even in the eighteen months he'd been away. 'Strachan came back and we had our first kit-fitting,' says Roxburgh, laughing. 'Umbro had designed these new long, baggy shorts that came to the players' knees. They had only sent large sizes though and so Gordon puts these shorts on that came over his knees and up to his arm-pits. What a sight!'

Maybe the kit did not fit but this time Strachan's seasoned game certainly did and by the end of the 1990/91 season Strachan was captain of his country. His form was excellent and Roxburgh understood his character was perfect for the job at hand. 'Gordon was fiercely competitive,' he muses. 'But also he was very protective over his players and I'm sure he's taken that into management. I can recall one match that we'd lost and not played well. I laid into the team and individuals, really let rip and Gordon got needled and stood up for those I was screaming at. I was at first put out but realised that was exactly the sort of skipper I wanted to run my team on the pitch. I strolled over to him and said, "You know what your problem is, wee man?" A hush fell over the dressing room as Strachan shook his head. "You're just as crabbit as me." Crabbit is a Scottish term meaning awkward and argumentative which he was but I loved his passion. It could make him difficult but I liked that about him. I would rather have someone like Gordon questioning and making himself heard than someone who frankly didn't care.'

In Strachan, the Scotland manager certainly had someone who cared, and with that captain's armband proudly adorning his jersey he led the team out like a modern-day, miniature-sized William Wallace. Roxburgh would send his team onto the pitch, taking great pleasure as Strachan called out in the tunnel, 'No regrets!' 'That summed Gordon up,' says Roxburgh. 'He always gave his country his all, quality and heart.' They were the essential merits that again saw Scotland qualify for a major championship. The build-up to the European Championships in Sweden saw him honoured by his country with a 50th cap. Fewer than 10,000 fans turned up to see him lead out the team. It was against Finland which would explain the low attendance but how many more would have come, if, with the power of hindsight, they had known it was to be his last game for his country?

Having brilliantly helped Leeds to the Championship in the May of 1992, Strachan told Roxburgh that, due to long-term back problems, he would have to rest over the summer and call time on his international career. It was a blow to both men: Roxburgh was losing a captain, an inspiration; Strachan was saying farewell to his country, his mortality in the game suddenly a reality. His injury made the front pages in Aberdeen, the town that had launched his career. 'STRACHAN BLOW FOR SCOTLAND MANAGER,' cried the *Press and Journal*. Perhaps though it was the right way to go. He had reached fifty caps and his name and his portrait looked just fine alongside the others to have reached that milestone and made Scottish football's Hall of Fame: Dalglish, Law, Miller, Souness and McGrain among others. Always the neat and tidy player, it seemed the right number to bow out on. Regrets? You must be joking.

10. A CHEEKY WEE BASTARD

AN INTERVIEW WITH GORDON STRACHAN FROM A SCOTTISH NEWSPAPER IN 1978:

Favourite players: Tony Fitzpatrick and Ian Scanlon
Favourite 'other team': The Welsh rugby side
My international honours: Capped for schoolboys, professional youth and under-21s
Influence in my career: Hugh Robertson, Dundee coach
Biggest drag in football: Size of the park
If not a footballer, what would you like to be? A photographer with Mayfair
Would like to meet: John Cleese
Main likes: Cinema, golf
Main dislikes: Ian Fleming's elbows, my dog barking at night
Favourite meal: Steak and chips
Best country visited: Sweden
Favourite TV programmes: Fawlty Towers *and the* News
Favourite singers: Frank Sinatra, Dean Martin and Elvis Presley
Favourite actor and actress: Clint Eastwood, Miss Piggy
Favourite holiday resort: Carstairs!
Best friends: My wife, Alec Caldwell

There's no one around. The ball's at his feet, defenders are caught cold by a pinpoint through ball and he's in. His short steps see him ever closer to a goal dwarfed by its packed Kop. He draws nearer now, 25 yards out, 18 yards out, inside the box. He looks up. He can see the wild expressions of the Liverpool fans behind the goal. It's as if he has not only Bruce Grobbelaar to beat but 18,000 others intent on one thing: his failure. He breathes in, pulls back his right foot and slips the ball under the 'keeper into an ungrateful net. Silence. Then the faint, distant cry of a few thousand Manchester United fans. They've equalised. The old enemy have been clawed back. He stops, stands still and mockingly begins to smoke an imaginary cigar in front of a now incensed Kop. It is the ultimate in cheek. A gesture that can make you a lot of enemies, but also a lot of friends.

United fans even today cherish that impish moment of brazenness. It hasn't stopped. On announcing his temporary retirement this year, and while the Southampton fans mourned the parting of a man doing so much to raise their club's profile, the wider football community bemoaned the loss of an individual who had livened up the post-match interview. Able to offer more than the statutory and bland musings of so many of his kinsmen, he'd be missed. It's nothing new though. Just a side of his character nurtured from a young age and developed in more hazardous environments than the country's press rooms. As a manager the cheek hadn't changed, it had just become that bit easier. Upsetting a room full of journalists armed with nothing more than a dictaphone is one thing; but Strachan had made a habit over his career of doing just that to tens of thousands – Scousers, Glaswegians, he didn't discriminate.

With his game blossoming as a player under Alex Ferguson at Aberdeen, so too was a confidence in himself; a confidence that would manifest itself in many ways and in the future land him in hot water. Not that he was alone at Pittodrie where characters born from fiery Scottish stock were the norm. The team had a way about them that would bring them closer in time; a sense of mischief along with bloody-mindedness were useful tools in their armoury. The whole squad had to be reprimanded at one stage as for some reason, every time they scored at Pittodrie, they would run and celebrate near the same advertising hoarding. A strange ritual? An odd football superstition? No, the owner of the boutique being advertised had promised the players some designer gear for their troubles.

It was of course, though, in the games against the Old Firm that the team's togetherness and Strachan's ability to wind up opponents was most vibrant. Ferguson's policy had been to convince his players that when playing against Rangers or Celtic everyone was against you. The teams, their fans, the referee, his linesmen, the press, everyone. They were, if they wanted success, to fight fire with fire and for the majority of times there was no one more fiery than Gordon Strachan.

It was during the 1980 Championship season that Strachan announced himself to the game of Scottish football and its passionate fans. Sure, people had seen him during his time at Dundee and in his quiet formative years at Aberdeen, but then it was more likely to be his own fans who would be upset with what they saw as an inept talent. In 1980, however, Strachan's game was freed on a wave of ingenuity, his busy skills soon matched by even busier gestures. Celtic were beaten 3–1 at Parkhead; Strachan stole the show; his team stole the points and ultimately the Championship and, to the fans in Celtic's notorious Jungle, a new anti-hero was born.

At the final whistle and while his team-mates celebrated a fantastic victory together, Strachan ran straight to the Jungle, his arms aloft, his fists clenched in taunting delight. His face told a tale and it was one that the residents of Celtic's terraces would rather not have to listen to. They were no longer *the* dominant force. They no longer had *the* best players and there *were* footballers and a club willing to meet their game head on. Would they live happily ever after? No chance.

Football fans, specifically upset football fans, have good memories and it wasn't long before their tormentor was back in Glasgow heaping on more misery. This time, though, Strachan was letting his football do the talking but showing the sort of form that was just as mocking as any clenched fist or wry smile. He glided along the touchline in front of the Jungle, each side-step past another bewildered Celtic player another reminder to each fan of their loosening grip on the Scottish game. It was too much to take. He beat one, dropped his shoulder to beat another, knocked the ball gingerly in front of a defender and got his shot away. It narrowly missed but, no matter, something had to be done.

Strachan was running back to the centre-circle, turning to keep tabs on play and Celtic's Tommy Burns. Out of the corner of his eye, he saw a foreign figure. His mind registered a danger not dressed in green and white hoops but before he knew it he was being hauled to the ground, a strapping pair of Glaswegian hands gripping at his throat and hot boozy breath filling his nostrils. It all happened so quickly before help was at hand. 'Oh, aye, the Jungle had it in for Gordon all right,' says Willie Miller, laughing. 'Contact with the fans is frowned upon today, but Gordon had a special relationship with those guys. He'd get a lot of verbal but would offer a little wink back. To most, though, it was a place you wanted to avoid of course, unless you were Gordon or big Dougie [Rougvie]. We'd go to Celtic and the team would go out about twenty minutes before kick-off to warm up and stretch. We'd all keep our distance but Dougie would make a point of going right in front of the Jungle, stretching and sprinting, seemingly oblivious to the mayhem and stick emanating from behind. So when Gordon was attacked he was on the ground and curled up like a porcupine, wondering what the hell was going on, while his minders, Rougvie and McLeish sorted the imposter out.'

Strachan was unhurt but, like his childhood rock idol Elvis, all shook up, cutting a bemused figure for the rest of the game. 'That was out of order,' admits Roy Aitken, playing against Strachan that day. 'Gordon's nature was to win and that was reflected in his game.' Now coaching, Aitken is quick to instil similar attitudes in talented but shy youngsters. 'You have to show your personality on the pitch even if you're the quietest bloke in the world. We coach kids and tell them they have to find their personality on the field. That is the place to come out of your shell. That is where to show your true colours. Gordon had that. His persona, that cheeky nature, they all came to the fore when he crossed the touchline.'

For Lesley, though, on what was her first visit to Celtic, it was a worry. Was this what happened here all the time? Players attacked and in fear of their safety? People would reassure her that this was a one-off, but such was Aberdeen's and Strachan's rising form that it wasn't long at all before those same fans were looking for retribution once more.

It was Celtic again. If Strachan had been affected by his close encounter a year earlier in Glasgow, he seemed to have shaken it off as he tore into the heart of their defence, this time though in front of a more appreciative Pittodrie crowd. With more pressure, Aberdeen won a penalty in front of the travelling support. Strachan wasn't going to shirk his responsibilities and stepped up, placed the ball down with Celtic's fans crowing at their sworn enemy like enraged seagulls. He was focused; his run-up true and the ball was in the net. Turn around and get back for kick-off? You must be joking. Strachan was away and in front of a sea of hate, somersaulting his way further and further into their bad books.

Celtic's faithful weren't used to being made fools of and a fan was again going to take the law into his own hands. He climbed onto the pitch; ironically doing to a policeman what Strachan had been doing to his team's full-backs for two years and skinned him before getting to his target. Strachan though could again rely on back up in red and no harm was done. 'We'd scored and suddenly there's this furious-looking fan on the pitch,' recalls Stuart Kennedy with a mischievous chuckle. 'He's run past me; he's run past Neil Simpson and gone straight for Gordon. Why? It's not because Gordon's the smallest, it's because he's had enough of the wee man's ability. It's grating the Celtic fans and summed up how far we were getting up their nose.'

Mark McGhee agreed and, despite the threat, felt he had little to worry about as far as how much it was getting to his mate. 'If it affected Gordon, it was only in the sense that he couldn't wait to get back out there again and rub it in further. He relished it because he knew better than anyone that if that was happening then he was doing well. There was nothing wrong with what Gordon was doing. Celtic had been doing it themselves for years and didn't like seeing it happening to them, under their noses. I was a massive Celtic fan as a boy and loved watching wee Jimmy Johnstone in the 60s teasing opponents with the ball; they couldn't get it off him; he'd nutmeg them – he'd play one–twos around them and that is exactly what Gordon did. It antagonised them like hell.'

There would be more incidents. Rangers too had had enough of Strachan's incessant goading. He and his team would arrive at Ibrox undeterred and unfazed. The Old Firm's tea party had been gatecrashed by the maddest of hatters, and for now they sensed their fun was over. Aberdeen's continued success meant that soon ill feeling wasn't monopolised by Glasgow's giants. Boos and hisses followed Strachan around at many a Scottish away ground where he had become a pantomime-like figure of hate. 'Gordon did what opposing fans hate most and played bloody well all the time,' says a busy bodyguard Alex McLeish. 'There were those, especially in the Old Firm, who took exception to Gordon's brilliance, and with Gordon in our team, and big Dougie of course, we could go to Parkhead or Ibrox and say, "Look, we've come down to Glasgow and we're not afraid of you."'

It wasn't just Strachan's game that infuriated fans. 'He wasn't the type to gesture rudely to the crowd,' says McLeish, laughing. 'He would go and get the ball, take the stick and come back with a clever answer. He was prone to a little wink or wave and that wound them up rotten.' His ex-manager and the boss of a rattled Celtic in those early days, Billy McNeil, goes one step further. 'He was a cheeky wee bastard,' he rasps. 'People see it today on television. That's Gordon, that's his character and if you took that away you wouldn't have the real Strachan.'

The real Strachan? Most fans took their thoughts on who that was from one of his naughty retorts or puckish winks on a Saturday afternoon. That was fine by him, who – although not enjoying having to wear the odd drink thrown at him when out in public for no other reason than for who he was – knew that the more they booed, the louder the abuse, the better he was playing. It was a side of his character that could not be harnessed, even by his own weary manager, and it wasn't only supporters whose skin he comfortably got under.

Referees also had to deal with his chat and, while never having a discipline problem, Strachan wasn't shy when it came to discussing with officials how he felt the game was being managed. His game invited mistreatment from opponents eager to stop him by any means necessary. His opinions about referees and linesman have not subsided into management; it's a feeling born from frustrating days at Pittodrie. One Saturday, an aggravated Strachan was not having things his own merry way. His passing wasn't up to scratch, his dribbling a faint trickle. The referee wasn't offering the required sympathy and so words would have to be had. 'Hey, sir,' he said. 'Did you know you're having a nightmare?'

'Aye,' came the reply from an unfazed official. 'You're not doing so fucking well yourself.'

In Ferguson's early days at Pittodrie and with his side becoming the new kids on the tartan block, it was the blue half of Glasgow that would take the most offence. Rangers were dominant, winning a treble under Jock Wallace and it was against the Ibrox side that Strachan and his team would have the severest test of their game and physical resolve. Rangers were far from shrinking blue violets and weren't about to give up their high and historic standing in the game without a fight, often literally.

Colin Jackson, Tom Forsyth and Alex MacDonald were from the old school. Giants of body and heart, they were not about to give up titles, not to a set of up-starts from a seaside town 150 miles away. Strachan thrived on these encounters. They helped him come out of the shell that had enclosed his initial 12 months at Aberdeen, and gave him the savvy needed to reach the top level. Bloodthirsty crowds and even thirstier defenders propelled Strachan's game. Like a Scottish Robin Hood he thrived on upsetting the Ibrox gentry as he set about pilfering their silver and giving it to the hitherto underprivileged of Aberdeen.

Rangers were seen off but Strachan's presence on the pitch continued to be the focus of some overzealous opponents, unappreciative of his sweet moods, cute dribbles and tantalising backchat. After a coarse fixture at Pittodrie against Kilmarnock, tensions ran high. Strachan had scored two penalties, decisions that the Kilmarnock players had taken distinct exception to. He spent the remainder of the game being told what was going to happen to him after the game. Showered and changed, he made his way to the tearoom where Lesley was waiting for him, close to tears. The opposing player had been ranting about what he was going to do to that 'wee bastard Strachan' and continued – along with his wife – his assessment as the figure of his resentment walked in.

'Hey, you, Strachan, if no one else has done it, see the next time we play, I'm going to break your fucking leg!' Strachan quietly questioned the player's pace and wondered how he could break something he couldn't catch, before Doug Rougvie towered in and asked the visiting player to shut his face. These were common occurrences and are not rare wherever men choose to compete against each other in the name of sport. Threats are usually empty of course but as time went by Strachan became aware that games were becoming more ugly, incidents more common and if someone said, 'You wait, I'll get you next time pal,' next time was usually just around the corner.

'It was the same for all of us,' says McGhee, not adverse to a game of verbal tennis himself. 'I had centre-halves telling me the next time I had the ball I'd have my ankle done and in turn I was telling them that the next time the ref turned away I was going to break their fucking jaws. And so it went on.' But what of Strachan, wasn't that aspect of his Saturday something he could do without? 'No way,' says McGhee, laughing. 'It didn't intimidate Gordon, quite the opposite in fact. It got his back up and he went back for more. Mind you, one of the great things about our team at Aberdeen was how much we cared for each other.

'If Gordon got kicked, which was often, the next thing that would happen is that someone would step in and cement the culprit right away.' Even today as a manager McGhee instils in his players the importance of looking out for each other. 'Listen, Gordon is lightweight by nature, so when he was kicked you could count on myself, Big Alec, Big Dougie, Neil Simpson, anyone would be in to help.'

Strachan though was war weary; the feuds of the Premier League were getting him down and it was a major factor in his desire to get away. It was the fixtures against Celtic that saw the flowing of most bad blood. On the terraces Strachan was a figure of hate among the Celtic supporters (perhaps only King William of Orange himself would cause more of a stir in the Jungle) and that often translated to the field of play. It was intense, the stakes high and Strachan wasn't enjoying it.

He had already decided to leave when Aberdeen faced Celtic in the 1984 Scottish Cup final. It was to be his last game in Aberdeen's red and an afternoon that validated his need for a less stagnant environment. It had built up over the years, Celtic's resentment brimming over while Aberdeen's dogmatic stars refused to be overawed by the giants of their game. The SFA had seen trouble on the horizon and took steps to combat any ill behaviour in their showpiece event.

The previous six games between the teams that year had all been bruising encounters and Alex Ferguson and his counterpart at Celtic, David Hay, were summoned to a meeting at the SFA headquarters where they were warned that a lack of conduct would not be tolerated. It only helped to create an atmosphere, one not akin to the usual celebratory tone of Cup final week. Aberdeen were going for a Double, had been named Europe's best team by Adidas and the magazine *France Football*. Celtic had won nothing, and neither had Rangers, and so Aberdeen arrived in Glasgow like a busload of spring lambs to an abattoir.

The SFA had appointed their most experienced referee, Bob Valentine, in preparation for what they saw as a potentially explosive game. They weren't disappointed. Eric Black had put Aberdeen one up in the first half when the fun began. Minutes before half-time Mark McGhee picked up the ball, and Celtic's brawny midfield henchman Roy Aitken had him firmly in his sights. Weeks earlier the two had clashed at Parkhead, and now those Premier League feuds that clung like cobwebs to the game's furniture were about to gather more dust.

McGhee picked up the ball in midfield, looked up and was hit. Hit hard. Valentine had gone into each dressing room prior to the game and said he would come down hard on anything untoward. He would have to stand by his words; steps would have to be taken. Aitken feared the worst. 'It was a hard tackle,' he recalls sheepishly. 'The thing was after I made the challenge I looked up and the Aberdeen players, including Gordon, were surrounding the referee, putting pressure on him to act and he showed me the red card. I don't think I would have gone if it hadn't been against Aberdeen and the background to the game had been less fraught. In those days you didn't have red cards for professional fouls but Valentine chose to knuckle down.'

Aitken was aggrieved and the focus of much of his and his club's annoyance was Gordon Strachan. Over the following days, claims from Parkhead that Strachan's demonstrative pleas had influenced a put-upon Valentine were rife. Strachan hadn't been the first on the scene; he agreed that it was a passionate crowd around the referee, but then it was a passionate afternoon. Doug Rougvie had got to the referee first, but, as Strachan pointed out, it's easier to blame a man like him before a bad word is said about the larger frame of Rougvie.

Aitken though was unconvinced and even pulled out of Scotland's game in France two weeks later partly due to his disappointment at what had gone on at Hampden. The dust has settled, of course, but Aitken jokingly reminisces to this day about the supposed injustices of 20 years ago. 'We're all pals now,' says Aitken reassuringly. 'To this day, I still give McGhee stick about that. I made the challenge and Mark went down like he'd been shot. I got the red card and he gets up, plays like a demon, scores the winner and gets the Man of the Match award. What a fucking recovery.'

Jokes aside, Strachan had been hurt by accusations that he would try and get a fellow pro sent off. That was a harsh assessment of the verbal aspect that accompanied his game. 'If the misinformed could see the bruises on my body,' he protested, 'which usually begin on my chest and work their way down, I think they would alter their opinions of me.'

Strive to get someone sent off, no, but the truth was he did have an active tongue. His words on the pitch had become a tool he could rely on, and at times, very handy they were too. 'Gordon loved all that,' says Aitken, with a laugh. 'He had the mop of red hair; he was always moaning. I called it "mumping and grumping", always having a go at something or other. The ref, his team-mates, us opponents, the fans, we'd all get it, but that was Gordon, that was his game.'

It was an aspect of his game that, while never drowned out, was dampened during his early days at Manchester United. 'Here he was among bigger personalities,' recalls Arthur Albiston. 'He had the England captain with him, Norman Whiteside, Paul McGrath. These guys were larger than life so Strachan probably didn't stand out as much as he had in Scotland and therefore was that bit quieter.'

It was on the field of play though where his retorts and moans would serve more than simply winding up those pitted against him. 'Oh aye, he was verbal all right,' says Mark Lawrenson, laughing, so often his opponent in United's clashes with Liverpool. 'He'd be at you all game, but do you know what, there was always a smile at the end of it. By the time I finished playing him I realised it was more about getting himself going. He'd do it not to necessarily wind others up, although that was a bonus, but to get his heart pumping and up for the game.'

His time at Manchester United did bring more accusations questioning his professionalism. Strachan had scored a number of penalties during his first season at the club, many of which had been won by his own brand of trickery. What some in football however saw as skill, others condemned as cheating to win free-kicks and penalties. His manager, Ron Atkinson defends his player's tactics. 'He was seen as a bit of a ragdoll merchant. All I can say is he made the most of his attacking opportunities. He was brave enough and good enough to carry the ball into the box and hold on to it so of course penalties were won off the back of that. Maybe sometimes he invited them, but that was justice to all the times he had lumps kicked out of him and nothing was given.'

Having been that bit more subdued at United, his move to Leeds awoke the leader in him. Leeds were no Manchester United. There was no call for etiquette. No need to be conservative. His move to Yorkshire rekindled the fire in his belly and, emphatically, in his gob. Howard Wilkinson had built a team of characters. Hard men were needed if his dreams of bringing success back to Leeds was to be realised. Strachan was the key to that and when he spoke even Vinnie Jones shut up and listened. 'Gordon was great in that dressing room,' says Howard Wilkinson like a proud father boasting about a son. 'With his tongue he had a punch like Sonny Liston.'

Like Liston, Strachan's tongue brought a reputation into the ring. One that could strike fear into the most heavy of heavyweight opponents, but could also alienate and form enemies of those around him. An example of the latter came in his early days as manager at Coventry City. The Sky Blues were entertaining Arsenal and Tony Adams who had recently gone public regarding his problems with alcohol. The fans around the country of course were dishing out their own form of stick.

Chants from afar can become far less hurtful; Adams had been brought up on terrace taunts likening him to a donkey, and now a man striving to fight the demons in his head was going to deal with the expected rantings from sections of the crowd. No, what upset Adams that day was Strachan. During the game, Strachan, who was playing himself that day made gestures towards Adams, simulating the downing of a pint. It was a harsh thing to do, one not worthy of a good man trying to make his name in the management echelons of the game. Adams and his partner Steve Bould were furious, and wanted to carry out their own form of retribution before Strachan wisely substituted himself late on.

The Arsenal captain wasn't going to let it lie though and marched into the Coventry dressing room and demanded to talk to the Coventry manager immediately. 'Come in to my office,' said Strachan softly, knowing exactly where the big centre-half's grievances lay. He closed the door and before Adams could blow his top defused a tricky situation. 'I've always had the utmost respect for you, big man. I'm very sorry, I don't know what came over me, please accept my apologies.'

Strachan insists on using humour and that audacious wit as a managerial tool. To him it was and is as important to coaching young players as tactics and skills. To bring humour to the training ground creates more than tomorrow's players, but also tomorrow's characters. Commodities to Strachan that are too few and far between. He grew up idolising Denis Law's smile as well as his touch, and was coached by Tam Gemmell and Ron Atkinson, men who would bring a hearty laugh as well as a grimace to the job at hand. Strachan would use that in management. On the sideline he can scream, gesticulate like an epileptic octopus, have wild fire pouring from his eyes towards a referee or slack centre-forward; but come the press conference he is a different man, ready and willing to offer humour to defuse and exorcise the demons within.

Football can be like a child. Fun, amusing, excitable, but also very cruel; all qualities highlighted by Strachan and it is the latter that journalists today so often have to deal with. His offbeat remarks make great copy, but usually a young scribe is left wondering whether he should have chosen the more peaceful option and taken the job of covering Iraq rather than the Premiership. In Scotland a journalist approached Strachan looking for a line or two. The hack in question had ginger hair, freckles and generally shared his potential interviewee's colour tone. 'Excuse me, Mr Strachan,' he said tentatively.

Strachan turned around. 'Oh my god, it's my bastard son.'

It of course got laughs, and was Strachan's way of breaking the ice; the barrier was down but for some it means he can be an elusive character, someone hard to get close to and that for Strachan is mission accomplished. Strachan's nervous energy has transferred itself into the world of management and, whereas it would be put to good use on the field as a player, his new arena is pressrooms up and down the country. Roddy Forsythe covers Scottish football for BBC Radio Five Live and the *Daily Telegraph*, and while not pretending to have been able to get close to Strachan likens him to a very good car salesman. 'He wouldn't be selling you any old beaten-up second-hand car,' he says with a giggle. 'They'd be top of the range, and there would be nothing you could say to question that car that he wouldn't be able to combat with a quick answer.

'He's always had that repartee. Always had a quick response. In my experience he's a very intense wee man, but those retorts are not always just smart, he can often say something that really makes you think.' Think? Sometimes. Laugh? All the time. If journalists find themselves putting on their psychologist hats to decipher what Strachan's latest quote says about him, fans and viewers simply can't get enough of his quips, so much so that lists of classic Strachanisms are floating around the internet, a welcome aside to an average day in the office.

Punters want him back; the game needs a 'cheeky wee bastard'. His break may calm him down a little but let's hope not too much. 'I'm getting better,' he recently said of his touchline antics. '[Managers] are all different though. Trappatoni, Capello – maniacs. Lippi sits there with his fag, Sven just sits. Arsène is kind of cool but even he got an eight-week ban for a bust-up. That went from eight weeks to none on appeal. That's some going that. How do you do that? Must have had OJ Simpson's lawyer on the case.'

11. THE KEYS TO A RUSTY ROLLS-ROYCE

REPORTER: *Gordon, can we have a quick word please?*
GORDON: *Velocity. [walks off]*

Perhaps not surprisingly, Howard Wilkinson has a lot to say about Strachan. Strachan's link-up with Wilkinson at Leeds United changed the destiny of all three. He himself went from being a good player at a massive yet struggling club to Player of the Year and captain of a Championship-winning team, while Wilkinson went from being a respected and hard-working coach to a winning manager with a reputation to which even the Football Association could turn. And Leeds United? They went on a roller-coaster ride that even today won't stop to let anyone off.

In the spring of 1989 such notions seemed laughable. Strachan's move alone looked destined to be a pipe dream at best for the Second Division club. Ron Atkinson and Sheffield Wednesday had continued their interest and were confident of getting their man. Atkinson had sold players to help finance the package, a generous £200,000 had been accepted by Manchester United and Strachan would be offered more wages than any player in Wednesday's history. He looked like becoming a wise old Owl.

Strachan himself was 99 per cent sure that Hillsborough was to be the next chapter in a story that had run with a favourable plot, had some exciting twists and included both honourable and devious characters. Not quite a blockbuster but the ending would be well received if he were to pull on the blue and white stripes of Wednesday. He arranged a last meeting with Atkinson and other Wednesday officials to clarify matters but informed them that he first had to have an obligatory chat with Leeds United's manager Howard Wilkinson, who for a long time had coveted his services.

Wilkinson was aware that he had his work cut out but upped the ante by offering United £300,000. Ferguson was happy to accept an amount that he saw as great business for a 32-year-old player approaching the end of his contract. No matter, Atkinson could match that and was confident that by the end of the day Strachan would be under his managership once again. His ambitious nature was counting on it.

Strangely, it had been Sheffield Wednesday's lack of ambition that had tempted Howard Wilkinson away from Hillsborough only five months earlier. Wilkinson had bemoaned the lack of metal in the Steel City and instead trotted north to Leeds who, having sacked Billy Bremner, were languishing near the bottom of the old Second Division with nothing but a glorious past keeping the home fires burning. 'To all intents and purposes it was a rusty old Rolls-Royce,' says Wilkinson. 'It was a tatty old car in need of a new engine. It needed a heck of a lot of bodywork I can tell you.

'They were second from bottom; they hadn't won a game for God knows how long; they didn't own the ground and they had debts up to their eyeballs.' So why make the move? 'What they did have was a very good chairman in Leslie Silver, and directors who were allies and together they all formed a good and resolute board. I suppose I'd become a bit stale at Wednesday and what attracted me to Elland Road was potential. They had a fantastic history under Don Revie and I just felt, it had happened once, it can happen again. It wasn't a fluke. Leeds is a big city, with only the one team. They therefore had a huge fan base, and I arrived convinced I could bring those great times back once again.'

Those great times. They had been missing for fifteen years and the managers who proceeded Wilkinson had had links with the glory which they had so desperately tried to resurrect. Allan Clarke, Eddie Gray, Bremner, they were all students of Revie, yet couldn't repeat his master class once he had accepted the England job. Now here was someone new, someone unattached to that past and unwilling to hide behind it.

His own staff came in and that meant Norman Hunter, a darling of that bygone era and now on the coaching staff, was sacked. It was nothing personal but things were going to be different. The blanket of Revie's years had protected the club for too long. 'I was aware that that was all the club had, memories,' Wilkinson says in that slow measured Yorkshire tone of his. 'I felt that too often those ghosts were comforters for everyone at the club and I thought that they should be temporarily locked up, put away until we had a new club and a team worthy of those reminiscences.

'So, one of the first things I did was take all the old pictures down and all the old memorabilia from Elland Road's walls. I knew it was a big gamble, and in some quarters it didn't go down at all well, but that's what I wanted. I wanted to create a reaction about the place, break the apathy that had formed around Leeds United Football Club. It was my way of getting things started again.'

His other way was to deal with a tired and uninspired-looking squad that needed swift and immediate attention. On taking the job Wilkinson had told the board he needed the freedom to bring players in and quickly. Not to break the bank, but players that 'would fit into and live up to my way of doing things, and my standards'. Relegation was quickly averted thanks to some low-key signings such as Carl Shutt from Bristol City but soon the proper rebuilding could begin in earnest.

'I'd turned things around rapidly in my previous jobs,' says Wilkinson. 'I'd won promotion at Notts County and Sheffield Wednesday and so the board had faith in my methods. We were safe but I wanted to build a team capable of winning promotion right away. That meant getting players who were used to being at big clubs. The supporters and the team, despite being in the position that we were, needed players who had experience of the big time, had had experience of playing with the Arsenals, the Manchester Uniteds. I didn't want just good players, I wanted men with self-belief and a lot of nerve.'

Gordon Strachan came comfortably under that umbrella of course. A man used to the big clubs and the big occasion but not the lower leagues. As the two men met in the living room of one of Leeds' directors, Strachan prepared himself to say a polite 'Sorry'. After all, Atkinson was a man who believed in him and enjoyed working with him. He even had the option of coaching at Hillsborough.

'No, no, no,' cried Wilkinson to that suggestion. 'You're too young, too fit, too good to even start thinking about coaching, Gordon.' Strachan listened intently for hours as Wilkinson set about telling him what sort of future he could look forward to at Elland Road. The financial offer put in front of Strachan was also immense, bettering even that from Atkinson, but sitting there with Wilkinson it was his ego, as well as his bank balance, that seemed to be inflated by the Leeds manager's dream.

'Gordon, you aren't in the twilight of your career, your career hasn't even started. What I am offering you is a crusade, as a player and a skipper. Come to Leeds and help me get this club back to where it belongs.' Strachan couldn't help but be drawn to Wilkinson and, as the time passed in that house, he began to realise that the move made the most sense. 'That afternoon he bought into my vision,' recalls Wilkinson proudly. 'He bought into my idea of the Leeds United future and the key role he had to play in it.'

He was convinced, but he was also very late for an appointment with his friend Ron Atkinson. The Sheffield Wednesday contingent had grown impatient but Atkinson had told them not to worry, Strachan was known for his bad time-keeping. Finally he arrived but stopped Atkinson before he could say any more. 'Boss,' he said out of habit. 'Don't even start talking terms because it's a waste of words.' He was off to Leeds. Atkinson tried to talk him out of it. He even offered him his last biscuit and, as Strachan pointed out shortly after, that was a sure sign that the food-loving manager wanted his man. It wasn't enough; there simply wasn't a digestive big enough. It was hard to let down a mate, but the offer from Leeds was just too good. His family would be well looked after and he could go about trying to do for Leeds what he had done at Aberdeen. It was time to take on the big boys again.

Strachan immediately set about moving the family to Yorkshire. 'I want to live near the people I play for,' he said. Despite their love of the north-west, he didn't feel it was right to commute across the Pennines. He wanted to be part of his new club and its surroundings. Driving in his big car from Manchester would only fuel speculation that he had joined little old Leeds for purely selfish and financial gain. A mercenary seeing out his final days of active service while the money rolled in. For the fans his arrival was a gentle pointer towards the club's future. Maybe, just maybe, Wilkinson *was* the man to wake the town's sleeping giant and, in their new captain with his red head and boundless energy, *maybe* he had found the perfect Duracell to power the alarm clock.

In turn, Strachan hoped that dropping a division wouldn't prove too difficult, not because of his ego; it was just a very tough and physical league to get out of. It was strange. Twelve years earlier, his first club Dundee had sold him because they felt he was too lightweight for the lower and more corporeal regions of the game. Now he was being signed by Leeds specifically to help them get out of that same mire. It made a strange sense. In Wilkinson, he felt he had met a man and a manager he could trust. In many ways they were both taking a gamble but the odds seemed too good to resist.

Throughout Strachan's career he has courted comparisons with others. As a youngster at Dundee he was compared in one afternoon to both Billy Bremner and Alan Ball. His size and distinct style meant that that trend continued at Leeds where – and despite Wilkinson's wishes to create a future rather than enjoy a past – the fans and press couldn't help notice how similar he was to Bobby Collins. Collins had been the rock on which Revie's dream had been built. A man of small stature (even smaller than Strachan), he would compete like a giant and orchestrate the side into the big time during the early sixties.

It was heady company to be in as was the connection between him and another Revie legend, Johnny Giles. Again similar in stature and style, Giles' passing and shooting brought opposition teams to their knees and the Elland Road fans to their feet. Both players had been at Manchester United before dropping a division to help make great Leeds sides. Both had difficulty with overpowering managers at Old Trafford and would seek solace in swapping red roses for white. 'I wasn't at all happy at Manchester United,' says Giles, today a newspaper columnist. 'In the May of 1963 we'd won the FA Cup but personally things weren't any good. Matt [Busby] wasn't pleased with me and to be honest I couldn't do right for wrong. It wasn't pleasant, and after that final I knew my future wasn't at Old Trafford.'

Revie, like Wilkinson 26 years later, convinced a great player to join him and become part of his revolution. 'They were a team on the up,' recalls Giles. 'There was a great set of young players, Norman Hunter, Paul Reaney, Terry Cooper, only Bobby Collins had much experience. It was a much better spirit than what I had become accustomed to at United, where the big name players didn't always pull together.' With Giles and co., Revie and Leeds went on to achieve greatness within the English game, winning the Championship twice, the FA Cup and finishing runner-up in the ill-fated European Cup final of 1975. So how did he feel about the new era and Wilkinson's decision to pull a veil over those achievements?

'That was nonsense,' he says in a gruff Irish tone. 'Of course it was. All clubs have their history, you see, and they should be proud of that, especially such a glorious one. It should inspire players. I suppose I could see where Howard was coming from; he thought our success might intimidate his new team. I wasn't bothered though. If my picture is up at Elland Road or not, it doesn't bother me. It won't keep me up at night.' Whatever the pros and cons of Wilkinson's action he was the first to join the club, the city and the country that May in mourning Don Revie, as the father of Leeds success lost his battle with motor-neurone disease.

It was a sad goodbye but Wilkinson remained adamant that he could and would build a future of which Revie himself would be proud. Strachan though was less sure that Wilkinson could turn the club around as quickly as he had predicted. He had signed a two-year deal, and hoped that he would help take the club up, but saw it happening possibly in the second season. Straight away? That was going to be tough.

Wilkinson was undeterred and set about taking on playing staff that he felt could bring promotion to the club as quickly as possible. Chris Fairclough from Spurs, Mel Sterland from Glasgow Rangers, John Hendrie from Newcastle, these were all seasoned pros with experience of playing in front of an expectant crowd. Those fans, beginning to like the class of player they were seeing arrive through the gates of Elland Road, were as surprised as anyone when the name Vinnie Jones was linked to the club. Was this the sort of man Wilkinson wanted associated with his new Leeds? Wasn't he just the antithesis of all that was wrong at a club hitherto suffering a major crisis of image?

Wilkinson though saw Jones as the perfect foil to Strachan's impish ability. In Jones, he saw a footballer waiting to happen, a misunderstood individual who might just complement what he was striving to achieve. Jones had hoped to be made captain but that honour was always going to fall to Strachan, a man Wilkinson thought was best equipped to deal with the hurdles that were bound to come his team's way over the coming months. 'Gordon was key,' says Wilkinson. 'He helped me gel together the new group of players and in him I had someone amongst the staff who shared my values. We had the same thoughts on how the game should be played, on how people should live and what discipline should be enforced to make sure that was realised. It may have come as a surprise to some people, but spiritually, we were like close brothers.'

For Strachan, though, there were times in those early days when he wondered, not about the manager he had joined – he shared Wilkinson's enthusiasm for their working relationship – but for the club he had joined. On 25 March 1989 he made his debut in a

1–0 win over Portsmouth at Elland Road. He was brilliant and stood out like a flare above the humdrum of Division Two. Quite rightly he was named the Man of the Match, but, to his concern, he was given a 24-can crate of lager as reward. What sort of club was this? The image of beer-fuelled louts, on and off the pitch, seemed to ring true. Things would have to change, and then Vinnie Jones signed.

Strachan's first reaction was to simply laugh. Vinnie Jones? He was hardly going to rid the club of that bovver-boy preconception held by the rest of the football fraternity. The haircut, the tattoos, the man, they were what the club should be striving to get rid of from the *terraces*, let alone give a pivotal role to in midfield. It was going to be a meeting of two very different entities. Jones' reputation preceded him and a pre-season trip to Belgium did nothing to convince Strachan otherwise. Leeds took on Anderlecht in a friendly, but, as it turned out, 'friendly' wasn't something the new signing found easy to comprehend. The game, like all of these summer matches, ambled along at a leisurely pace, a calm before the seasonal storm. Strachan was jogging forwards when he heard a crack that suggested fist on face, the sort of noise mimicked on the old Batman and Robin TV shows and it wasn't going to take the Riddler to explain who was at the heart of it. Jones calmly trotted past his captain and winked. 'Well, that's the first of the season,' he said smirking, while a poor Belgian lay flat out, blood pouring from his nose.

Jones has since remarked that, when he first came to Leeds, Strachan thought he was 'crap'. 'Actually,' Strachan said later. 'I didn't think he was as good as that.' But then something odd happened. Strachan began to like the ex-hod carrier from Watford, and to even appreciate his part in what was trying to be achieved at Leeds. 'They very quickly developed a healthy respect for each other,' says Wilkinson, without a molecule of surprise. 'Gordon respected what Vinnie was trying to do and how much he was trying to change his game. With time he kept telling Vinnie that he was a much better player than he had previously thought. Vinnie, likewise and aside from Gordon's ability, respected the fact that Gordon could achieve so much using determination and mental bravery.'

Strachan took it upon himself to impress on his unexpected disciple that he would be no good to the team sitting in the stands serving out suspensions every other week. He should work on his football and channel the rough stuff to the team's advantage. It was early on though that Jones's impetuous nature helped iron out a few creases within the dressing room at Elland Road. Here, he and that temper could be a useful tool. Wilkinson's arrival and that of so many new faces had irked some of the players left by Billy Bremner. Bobby Davison, Ian Baird, John Sheridan and Mark Aizlewood were an old guard in the firing line due to Wilkinson's revolution.

A situation was developing at training, one that could damage the very fabric of the togetherness the manager and his captain had hoped to maintain. Remarks were made, especially regarding the signing of Jones. Why buy him when you had someone with Sheridan's talent? 'Vinnie,' said Strachan, pulling Jones aside. 'Listen, pal, it's a case of us and them.'

Jones was getting aggravated by the formed clique and took Strachan's words to mean he should do something about it. As if in rehearsal for his later roles in Guy Ritchie's movies, Jones stood up, walked over to the 'old' players and barked, 'This all stops, right here and now. If any of you want to say or do anything, here I am.'

Bobby Davison stood up. 'No, no,' he said. 'You've got the wrong end of the stick.' Jones didn't think so and Davison quickly had a split lip for his troubles.

Strachan calmed Jones down, but the trouble stopped. The players knew where they stood and slowly many of the aforementioned individuals were sold to help settle the books that had been turning crimson red during Wilkinson's summer spending spree. 'To me there was no problem with old players,' says Wilkinson, playing down the small mutiny. 'There couldn't have been anyone with an iota of common sense that couldn't see we were going in the right direction and that eventually we would succeed.'

With the season about to kick off, the team and the fans' expectations were in place. A hard trip to Newcastle should underline how well Wilkinson's new team was going to fare. They lost 5–2. The result had Strachan, as ever, dreading the worst. Was this gamble going to pay off? Wilkinson was unmoved by the result. 'Oh no,' he brags. 'That result didn't change my view in the slightest. We had a few missing and I knew with the full complement that we would get on track.' It seemed the press, particularly the London-based scribes, hoped that the manager's confidence was misplaced. That nasty reputation had been simmering like a newt's eye in a witch's cauldron for years. The riot by Leeds fans at the 1975 European Cup final in Paris had only spilled that ill feeling over the edge and all these years later the heat was still firmly turned up.

In that early part of the season, Fleet Street reported the dangers of a successful Leeds team, how awful it would be to see the club and its lunatic contingent back in the top flight. 'There was plenty of that,' admits Wilkinson with a sigh. 'It brought the lads closer together. It annoyed them and as far as I'm concerned an annoyed player can be a better player, so it was nothing more than a positive tool.'

After the setback at St James' Park, that togetherness, and the fact that they had the full complement fit, took them on a run that suggested the hacks in the capital were going to have to get used to Leeds' second coming. A run of fifteen games unbeaten meant they had stamped their authority on Division Two's steel-capped toes. Stamping was, in Wilkinson's mind, the best way of getting the team *out* of this league. It wasn't how he planned to keep the team in Division One when he finally got there, but for now the more physical approach would do just fine.

Strachan was beginning to work wonders within a well-functioning team. A perfect combination of brawn and brains saw the club reach the top before Christmas. Now they had to stay there. 'There was a tremendous amount of energy in that team,' says Wilkinson lovingly. 'A lot of that stemmed from Gordon. He was the perfect captain who led by example but could also discuss games sensibly and coherently. It began to work because Gordon got on his white horse and the other players got on theirs. They followed him, and he followed me. It was as simple as that.'

As the team galloped towards their peak, Strachan was playing with the blinkers off. He realised that he had been hampered by the pressure at Old Trafford where success would only be judged on how they did in the title race. Here, he had a freedom to express himself under less stifling conditions. Yes, there were pressures at Leeds but they were pressures he could thrive on rather than buckle under. As for the fans, they had taken him immediately to their hearts. He had arrived oblivious to the intense rivalry between Leeds and Manchester United but the average Leeds punter at last had something from Manchester they felt they could love.

The season passed into 1990 and the games were coming thick and fast, with incident, goals and tantrums never far apart. Wilkinson had recognised that his strike force needed more presence to get them through the coming months and so snapped up Lee Chapman for £400,000 from Nottingham Forest. Chris Kamara and Imre Varadi also arrived to bolster the squad; a lot had been put in to the challenge now, including funds from the chairman's own wallet. It had better not go wrong.

A fixture at Elland Road versus struggling Hull City should have been an easy three points, but, despite a cracking Vinnie Jones goal in the first half, they found themselves 3–2 down with the clock ticking away. Their Yorkshire rivals Sheffield United were their neighbours in more than geography as they swapped punches to see who could pull away at the top. This was no time to lose to visitors from Hull. Parity was restored through the experienced Varadi, and Strachan blew the roof off with a late, late winner.

The nerves shown that afternoon were a prelude to a run of four games without a win, and an advantage that once read a comfortable ten points was now reduced to goal difference. With only two clubs due to go up and a resurgent Newcastle also lurking in the wings, beads of sweat began to break out on the rooftops of Elland Road. They weren't too far away from the foreheads of the players either, especially the younger contingent. David Batty had impressed everyone with his dynamic midfield endeavours but was left panicking in March during an away game at Wolverhampton Wanderers. He had walked out for another pressurised ninety minutes when he started to feel a tightness in the stomach that suggested he needed a toilet rather than a midfield battle. It was too late, the game was about to kick off but his usual grimace on his face was for more pressing reasons than winning a football match. The pains continued as he half-heartedly made his way around the pitch dreading the worst. A lacklustre pass led to a Wolves goal and his team-mates were now wondering what was wrong with the player they had so come to rely on.

Batty couldn't go on; if he hadn't been the burly Yorkshireman that he was, tears would have rolled down his cheeks. Missing a vital penalty in the World Cup would have nothing on this. He couldn't do anything but relax, he had to do it to dispel the pain. Relief but only momentarily and then panic. In front of 23,000 fans there was only one thing for it and, without conferring with a player, the referee or a member of his coaching staff, he turned and ran for the dressing rooms, where he stood in embarrassed agony while the groundsman played with a set of keys that looked like they belonged to the Pentagon. 'What the fuck's going on?' screamed Alan Sutton, the physio sent to find out where their player had got to. 'What's up?'

'I've shit myself.'

Batty wasn't the only player to feel the tension. Even someone of Strachan's standing was going to let off steam, although in his case the shit hit the fan rather than the shorts. He'd played in European finals, World Cups and FA Cup finals but even to Strachan this was getting intense. So much so that even he, a testimony to the new, calmer and PR-conscious Leeds, was about to lose all control and kick up an old-school fuss.

Leeds were playing Bradford City at Elland Road. Again, Bradford were struggling (they would be relegated that season) but it seemed the weight on the players' shoulders was acting like a twelfth man for even the most mediocre of opponents. Gary Speed, a young and promising Welsh trainee, had given the team a 1–0 lead but as the final whistle drew near the referee gave the visitors a free kick. Strachan had been caught offside, having walked slowly back from a previous attack. It was a tactic. Bradford would have a free-kick but, never mind, it was deep in their own half and not a danger. However, they chose to and were allowed to take it quickly on the halfway line and while the Leeds captain was protesting his defenders had managed to give away a penalty, from which Bradford equalised.

There was stunned silence. Two points dropped right now was two too many. Strachan went mad. He chased the referee, a Mr John Martin, down the tunnel and let him know exactly what he thought of him. Lesley had come down and looked disbelieving at her husband. 'I've never seen you act like that,' she would tell him later, but for now there was more to come. The Leeds dressing room was flung open. A seething Strachan, his face matching his head of hair, marched in and having taken his anger out on the room's furniture turned on his own team-mates. Wilkinson looked on in disbelief as his captain and figurehead let everyone know just what he thought of an inept draw with relegation fodder.

'Sit down and shut up,' piped up Jim Beglin, the team's left-back. Beglin was met with an icy glare, but, with matching Celtic blood, the Irishman was unstirred. 'Shut up or I'll whack you in the fucking jaw. You're out of order!' With Beglin's soothing Irish lilt, the red mist that had enveloped their skipper receded. It was a mad moment, and one Strachan felt awful about. He was supposed to set an example not abuse those who looked up to him. It wouldn't be long though before he would make it up to his verbally battered colleagues.

Two more games passed without victory so a home fixture on the Easter Monday against a Sheffield United team still level with Leeds took on an even more clammy air of importance. In front of nearly 33,000 fans, the biggest gate of the season at Elland Road, Leeds were excellent and won 4–0 with Strachan scoring two. Apology accepted. This though wasn't going to be done the easy way. Barnsley arrived for the penultimate home fixture and left ecstatically with an unexpected 2–1 win. Leeds fans had grown accustomed to disappointment, and so feared the worst, especially as the minutes ticked down on their last home game against Leicester with the score tantalisingly stuck at 1–1. Another two points dropped and they might have to wave goodbye to promotion, let alone the Second Division Championship.

Their 'keeper, Mervyn Day, had prevented defeat as a future hero Gary McAllister threatened to derail a train that had looked for so long certain of reaching its destination on time. Strachan for one looked out of steam. He'd played over fifty games already, and it was a drained man who latched onto a loose ball in the dying moments and somehow pinged it into the roof of Leicester's net. Bedlam! It was his eighteenth goal of the season and as the Leeds players hoisted him above their heads, his frail face could only just about manage a smile. Promotion into the promised land was back on track.

With the final whistle there was an avalanche of noise, made even fiercer by a scoreboard bringing fantastic news. Newcastle had lost! Leeds had done it. They could go to Bournemouth knowing they had made the First Division. Vinnie Jones, by now every Leeds fans' idol, was taking bows before running into the dressing room with the good news. 'We're going fucking up!' he screamed. It was too much. Strachan and Day, the team's elder statesmen, burst into tears. All that effort, all that hard work ... Wait a minute, what's that? It turned out that the scoreboard at Elland Road was incorrect. Newcastle had *beaten* West Ham not lost; Leeds still had it all to do on England's south coast. Strachan was shattered. He looked for Vinnie Jones who, at that point, he would have gladly taken on without question. He wanted to play Bournemouth right there and then. His emotions were running away with him but instead he and Leeds would have to wait another week.

Leeds had to win to secure both the Championship and promotion but a loss against a Bournemouth team hoping to stave off relegation could mean another season in the Second Division. They were so close. A club that had been branded for years as nothing but trouble were banking on one result to help turn the corner and move them onto football's plush cul-de-sac. Someone, though, had forgotten to tell some of the remaining maniacs who dubbed themselves fans. Just a year after the Hillsborough disaster where 96 fans lost their lives due to the authorities' perception that they could treat football supporters like animals, a mob of Leeds fans swept like a crazed herd through Bournemouth's sunny streets.

The players, about to put nine months' worth of effort into ninety minutes, knew exactly what was happening. They had strived to change the image of the club but now, under a cloud of alcohol and mayhem, those members of the press would be proved right. As he sat in the dressing room, Strachan put the events outside to the back of his mind. They had put in too much to let anything distract them from their task. Leeds players walked out of the clouds that had been formed by a mindless few and into the May sunshine after a Lee Chapman goal secured a 1–0 victory. They were going up as Champions and, as the players' bus pulled away for the long drive north, Strachan sat content staring at a beautiful sunset. As he headed towards the dusk of his own playing career, this latest achievement seemed to bring a special sense of satisfaction. He had been asked to join Leeds with a specific job in hand. Wilkinson and his board had deliberately bought Strachan's services to help bring back some good times to a depleted club. That had happened and it was largely down to him. Even greater things were around the corner, but for Strachan this wouldn't be bettered.

It was a golden moment but, Strachan being Strachan, worries and doubt were not far away. They had done the important bit, that was all well and good, but this was the English First Division, one of the hardest in the world and a place that he knew well. Was this squad good enough to compete against the likes of Liverpool, Arsenal or Manchester United? Was it good enough to compete with the lesser clubs like Luton and Sunderland hoping to stay up, for that matter? Once the champagne had been drunk and the plaudits received, it wasn't a question he could answer with ease.

While his captain fretted, Wilkinson got to work. Strachan would later come to realise that the Second Division title was merely an *hors d'oeuvre* and his manager had some extra ingredients in mind that, when rustled together, would make for a fine main course. Gary McAllister, who had shone at Leicester against Leeds the previous season, and Arsenal's John Lukic came in at £1 million a piece, while Chris Whyte arrived from West Brom for £450,000. It was the sort of wild indulgence that Wilkinson's successors would try to emulate and that would bring the club to its knees, but for now it was a worthy necessity.

What it did mean, though, with a player of McAllister's undoubted ability in the squad, Vinnie Jones's position in the side's midfield was heavily under threat. Jones arrived back for pre-season as excited as anyone at the prospect of pitting his wits against the best in the country. He'd even had a tattoo marking Leeds' achievement the previous season done on his leg. He walked into the dressing room for training but hanging from his peg were McAllister's clothes, the Scotsman's name adjoined to the spot. That was a worry but he trained as fervently as ever, a man possessed.

The first game back in and Jones was not even on the bench and despite his efforts on the training pitch he couldn't break through. 'He'd left me out for the start,' Jones told me some time later. 'We were playing Luton away and I was going to stay in the area after the game and do some shooting, so I had my gun. I step onto the coach and there's Howard reading a magazine. I walk over and stick the two barrels up against his nose. He freezes and I go, "You'd better play me tomorrow or you're gonna get this!" There was silence and then mad laughter. I played the next day though.'

Despite the threat of firearms, that was to be his last game. His old boss at Wimbledon, Dave Bassett, was now in charge at Sheffield United and wanted him at Bramall Lane. Wilkinson told Jones he wanted him to stay, that he was important to the squad, but the damage had been done. Jones was off. 'That wasn't an easy decision,' admits Wilkinson. 'I didn't really want him to go. He would tell you today that his time at Leeds was his best time in football. He had a huge impact and could have developed further. I honestly think if he had stayed with me he would have probably gone on to be a football manager by now.'

Strachan was sad to see the back of his mate but completely understood Wilkinson's actions and the midfield his manager had settled on already looked a class act. Jones could have stayed and sat it out, taking the adulation, but Strachan recognised that his presence was too big, his cult status too powerful to be restricted to a bench. With Strachan, McAllister, Batty and Speed across the middle, Wilkinson now had made the step into the big league. 'It was a terrific midfield,' says Wilkinson gratefully. 'It had experience, youth, energy. It had good blend and great balance. Attacking and defensive qualities. We could only play if we had the ball and particularly if Gordon had the ball. His role therefore was simple. I'd start him on the right or the left depending on the game. He was neither a wide player nor a central midfield player; we played him where he could get the ball and cause damage.' Strachan was playing with a manager who was willing to play to his strengths and build so much of his team's game around him.

His enthusiasm, and a thirst for more knowledge, had seen him take his first steps into coaching that summer when he took his initial UEFA badges. For now though he wasn't even thinking about track-suits and whistles. There was his day job to think of. An hour into their first game at Everton, life back in the big time must have seemed more like a leisurely hobby than any day job. At 3–0 up and coasting, Strachan couldn't help but wonder what he had spent his summer months worrying about. Two goals from Everton reminded him but, thanks largely to John Lukic in goal, the newcomers hung on for a winning start.

It was to be a fantastic season for Strachan and the club. The outlay on quality talent had been helped by £3 million worth of season-ticket sales as the people of Leeds flocked to see a team that promised to be less physical but just as effective amid the big names of English football. Leeds were competitive, yet fluent, never outclassed and even made friends on the nation's back pages as they played their way to a commendable fourth place and a spot in the League Cup semi-finals. Lukic proved his class in goal; Whyte and Fairclough were a solid central-defensive pairing; the midfield was the oil in Wilkinson's engine and in Lee Chapman they had the top scorer in the division with 31 goals.

Strachan though was the catalyst to his side's good fortunes. He probed, he tackled, he tantalised, he scored (ten times). An energetic kid brother on the pitch, and a father figure off it, his form was rightly recognised by the football writers as he became the first and, to date, only man to win their Player of the Year awards both north and south of the border. Strachan cherished it, not only as personal recognition of his tireless game, but he also felt that a club that had very quickly found a place in his heart could also be liked and respected by outsiders in the game. 'I am so happy to pick this award up,' he said, this time dressed in the appropriate attire. 'I accept it as an award for the team, as well as for me personally. It gives me hope that the efforts we have all made to give Leeds United a better image are working.'

That image was about to get better. Strachan had sensed the same thing at Pittodrie all those years ago. Again he felt the players, the board, the fans and, of course, a pragmatic manager were all ready to take the club even further. 'I said to the squad that summer,' recalls Wilkinson, 'look we've done very well. We've finished fourth with 64 points. Our target for next year must be 65 points and if that puts us higher then so be it.'

Sensible words of course, but who needs sensible? The Rolls-Royce had been spruced up, polished and fine tuned. It was time to take it for a glorious spin around the country.

12. MARCHING ON TOGETHER

GORDON ON WAYNE ROONEY'S EMERGENCE IN THE ENGLISH GAME:
It's an incredible rise to stardom. At seventeen you're more likely to get a call from Michael Jackson than Sven-Göran Eriksson.

Thousands of fans flock to the Leeds City Art Gallery, making their way to an exhibition that has been eagerly anticipated for eighteen years. For so long, no one in the city had dared dream that such a fine array of both classic and modern talent would assemble again in a place once revered for its raw artistry, but whose recent work had been dubbed 'loutish' by an intransigent group of critics.

The proud curator, Howard Wilkinson, had taken a blank canvas and created a masterpiece, one of which the whole city could be proud. He looks on as his laughing cavalier and captain waits to step onto the gallery's balcony to show off the famous old Championship trophy that would again adorn the club's – for too long – dusty trophy cabinet. 'Ladies and gentleman,' bellows the day's compère as if announcing the start of a boxing bout in Vegas, 'please can you make some noise for our captain ... GOOOOORDON STRACHAN!' The crowd do just that as he walks out into the sunshine to deliver what every Leeds fan, depending on their age, must have thought they would either never see again, or would only ever hear about from countless and hearty renditions about the 'good old days under Revie' from their fathers and grandfathers.

As an open-top bus makes its way slowly around a city hell bent on honouring its idols, Strachan cuts a content figure. While the young stars such as Gary Speed and David Batty quite rightly soak up the adulation like heroic rookie cops, Strachan looks out onto the crowd with a retrospective glare. It was to be his last major honour as a player, but for now was simply the icing on the cake of what he had ever hoped to achieve with Leeds United Football Club. Winning the title was an incredible feat for him and the city, but didn't give him the same sense of fulfilment as winning promotion. This was a bonus; promotion was a necessity and that's where his satisfaction lay.

The previous summer, Strachan had wondered – Player of the Year, or not – if he would still be part of the club at all. Self-doubt and concern were staple ingredients to a Strachan summer. Like Wimbledon and washed-out barbeques, those long days and short nights wouldn't be complete without worries regarding his future in the game. The summer of 1991 was no different. He would be 35 halfway through the following season and his contract still had to be renewed. Would Wilkinson want to persevere with a man of his age? No matter that he had been voted the best in the country only weeks before, did the next step in his manager's plan involve a younger player operating on the right of that fine midfield? His concerns as ever were unfounded. Wilkinson sent him to see Leeds' general manager Bill Fotherby to thrash out a new two-year deal. He was going nowhere and that suited him just fine.

The club's season had been scheduled to start with a trip to Crystal Palace but due to unfinished building work that game would be postponed until the beginning of October and represent the club's first defeat after a scintillating start to the season. Wilkinson had been busy with his own building work that summer and worn his hard hat in a spending spree he hoped would allay fears that the previous year's success had been a simple case of overachieving.

The club, despite their unexpected high standing, had continued to lose money. However, the 20,000 season tickets sold convinced an ambitious board that their policy of trusting Wilkinson with the club's coffers was the right one and so he set about rectifying what he saw as his problem areas. The left-back position had long been an Achilles heel at the club and so Tony Dorigo signed for £1.3 million from Chelsea, hoping that the form that had already seen the Australian-born defender gain England recognition would improve even further. Steve Hodge arrived from Nottingham Forest for £900,000, having already played for Aston Villa, Tottenham and England. Hodge would be hampered both by injury and by Wilkinson's midfield spoils but proved worthy cover, often to Strachan, who began to be hindered by a troublesome back.

The biggest signing of the summer, and indeed Leeds' illustrious history, was that of striker Rod Wallace from Southampton. Wallace made the trip north with his younger brother Ray and, while the full-back would cost £100,000 and play only a handful of games, the elder brother cost a far more substantial £1.6 million and would offer the team far more mobility up front, proving a handy partner to the effective but cumbersome Lee Chapman.

These signings had underlined Wilkinson's and the club's ambition. He had had a clear vision of where he saw Leeds United going under his tenure and was not going to be content with just the faint whiff of success. 'I spent a bit of money that summer,' says Wilkinson. 'I was immediately pleased with what I had but I'd be a liar if I said that season didn't completely outdo my expectations.'

With the first game of a dreamlike campaign postponed, Leeds kicked off their campaign with a home fixture against the previous season's FA Cup finalists Nottingham Forest. A 1–0 win followed up by a home draw against Sheffield Wednesday, although constituting a solid start, hardly had the Leeds fans salivating at the thought of nine wondrous months.

The following game was, on paper, one of those early season matches where a team will hope to just consolidate its standing in a new season. Away to Southampton on a Tuesday night in August is not a barometer to how a season will go, but, to the cunning and quietly confident Wilkinson, he saw enough in his team's 4–0 win to suggest a quality worthy of silverware. 'That was the night I started to think we'd really come on a bit,' he says, unable to fully articulate the excitement he may have felt for his new team. 'Because it was mid-week, because it wasn't televised, because it was Southampton, because it was still August, it didn't receive as much attention as it could have done. On the bus, though, coming home I thought, 'What I've seen now, and what I've seen pre-season is what I now know we can do.'

Strachan scored two that night at The Dell, and despite only managing to double that over the course of the season, his overall game and inspiration was the driving force behind the club's ambitions. Just days after the Southampton victory, Strachan led his team out at Old Trafford. Under Alex Ferguson, it seemed that Manchester United were at last in a position to step out of the Championship doldrums. With Peter Schmeichel now in goal, Gary Pallister regimenting the defence and youngsters such as Ryan Giggs playing beyond their years, it looked likely that the previous year's success in the European Cup Winners' Cup would carry the club at last to where they wanted to be most. Leeds though played very well and were unfortunate to leave with only a 1–1 draw for their troubles.

Strachan had had to endure jeers from a section of the United fans but, just as he had in front of the baiting Old Firm fans while at

Aberdeen, he thrived on their displeasure. As ever, each boo was a sign of a player who, even at 34, was regarded a threat, while his club, promoted only eighteen months earlier, might turn out to be the pest that their lofty ambitions could well do without.

Leeds' form was quietly suggesting they could in fact be more than mere pests. Resolute in defence, yet smooth in midfield and attack, they had peeled off the label of long-ball specialists that had stuck with them from Division Two. The squad had strength, reliance, guile and balance and all were on show as they went ten games unbeaten and then a further 16 without defeat up to February. Tony Dorigo had brought much needed pace to the team. His partnership with the powerful Gary Speed on the left was an ideal foil to Strachan and Mel Sterland's more precise play on the right. Strachan, while delighted with Dorigo's contribution, felt there could and should have been that much more from a very talented footballer. His laid-back attitude must have stemmed from his Australian blood and, to the all-action Scotsman, ultimately cost him England caps.

Steve Hodge was unable to sustain a place in the starting eleven but managed to score seven goals that season, including the winner in an early 1–0 win over Liverpool at Elland Road. It was a victory that had followed the commendable draw at United and a 2–2 share of the spoils with the Champions Arsenal. Leeds could live with the country's best but, even after a 1–0 victory over Oldham that put them top towards the end of October, the country had little idea they may yet have to live with Leeds.

Strachan was being hampered by his sciatica and Wilkinson could only call upon his captain's talismanic services sporadically, denting the rhythm his team would need to find going into the vital Christmas period. Leeds with Strachan were all the richer for his incredible energy and enthusiasm and if they were going to peak then his presence was essential. That theory had been proved correct at Aston Villa at the end of November where Leeds put on their hitherto best performance not only of the season but arguably for some fifteen years.

Goals from Wallace, Sterland and a brace from Chapman carved the Villa defence open in front of their own, astonished fans. The game went across the country live and, although the pre-Premiership coverage on ITV's *The Match* lacked the razzmatazz of today's staple SKY offerings, the country on a dreary Sunday teatime was awoken to what

Leeds had to offer. Again and again, they opened Villa with all the ease of a waiter uncorking a bottle of claret on the Champs-Elysées.

Rod Wallace by now was demonstrating why Wilkinson had spent so much money on his talents. Like a cleaner fish on a basking shark, he stuck to Chapman, feeding off his presence before slipping away into freer and richer waters. With Leeds brilliant, so too of course was Strachan. His intelligence on a football field was there for all to see and savour, and if Leeds were finding it hard to get past a stubborn goalkeeper in open play then they could rely on his set-pieces to be delivered with almost military precision. 'We'd go over set-pieces a lot,' says his ex-Scottish coach Craig Brown. 'It was incredible, Gordon was like a machine. "Gordon, stick it on Gough's head near post", that's where it would go. "Back post", that's where it would go; "edge of the D", same again without fail.'

For Leeds' third goal that day, Strachan opted for a shorter corner and knocked it to Gary McAllister who back-heeled a cheeky return. Those unmistakable pigeon steps took him along the byline where he looked up, oblivious to the mayhem of jostling footballers in the Villa box, and delicately played the ball past Les Sealey in goal, for Chapman to receive the easiest of tap-ins. McAllister to Strachan and vice versa was never far from a commentator's lips. One was always the outlet for the other. Two pass masters with the brains of owls and right feet so sweet, they must have been dipped in honey at birth.

McAllister had arrived a known talent. He had turned down a move to Brian Clough's Nottingham Forest for Leeds, favouring Wilkinson's more down-to-earth approach to the Forest man's eccentricities. In Strachan he had come across a kinsman, not only in nationality but in the way he saw the game being played. In his early days at the club he had not found it as easy to get along with everyone to that same high degree and would often verbalise his frustrations with team-mates who hadn't read his more cerebral way of doing things. Now, though he, along with his Scottish captain, could direct the team's play and tempo. Like two puppet-masters they pulled the strings as their team strived to put on an award-winning show.

Without Strachan's steadying hand that show began to dwindle over what should have been a lucrative Christmas period. His back problems had flared up again and four consecutive yuletide draws meant that the initiative had been handed to Manchester United. The last of those stalemates had been a home encounter with their rivals, which finished 1–1 thanks to a late penalty from Mel Sterland. Even this early, the race for the Championship had come down to the two Uniteds, and by chance they would also be drawn against each other in the quarter-finals of the League Cup and in a mouth-watering FA Cup third-round clash, both to be played at Elland Road.

The trilogy of games was reminiscent of 27 years earlier when the two teams were both pushing for League and Cup success. Leeds would miss out on the 1965 League title on goal average thanks to a 1–0 defeat by Matt Busby's side at Elland Road. They were two very good, but very contrasting teams. Manchester United were close to peaking and becoming European Champions while Revie's Leeds were on a path to greatness but still had some way to travel. They were organised and efficient enough to outwit their adversaries and knock them out of the FA Cup semi-final that year, though, a game that riled many in red. 'That match was a disgrace,' bemoaned Manchester United's Pat Crerand some years later. 'I spoke to Les Cocker [Revie's assistant manager] who told me their players had been ordered to get close to Denis Law and myself early on and kick us so that we'd lose our tempers. It worked.

'At Old Trafford we considered ourselves to be the upholders of what was right in football. Under Don Revie, Leeds were hard, very hard. They'd kick you, yet if you went near them they'd do fourteen somersaults and collapse. We were always taught that the man's way was to get up straight away, to show you were not hurt but Leeds did the opposite. They dived; they pretended to be injured. They cheated.'

It is a rivalry that has gathered moss ever since and, going into 1992, had more reason than ever to fester. To many, the two clubs were as juxtaposed now as they had been under Messrs Busby and Revie. United, with their memory-evoking past, their square-jawed ex-England captain Bryan Robson and the flowing pubescent skills of Ryan Giggs, still had the purists drooling. Leeds were the spoilers, their productive football lost under a veil of negative punditry from both the past and the present.

That January, it seemed that the apparent idealism emanating from Old Trafford would have the upper hand. Leeds were knocked out of both cup competitions by United who, with two ferocious physiological blows, had their challengers punch-drunk on the ropes. Wilkinson though was a coach who in boxing terms was from the old school – red meat and a whistle over sequins and showbiz – and he knew that his players still had plenty of fight left in them. 'We all agreed,' he says. 'We may not have had the best players, but we could still be the best team if we worked hard.'

He was right: some of his players weren't the best. Chris Whyte, Chris Fairclough, Lee Chapman, Rod Wallace even; these guys hadn't been the cream of English football and nor would they ever be. Under Wilkinson's tutelage, however, they each reached the peak of their powers. Their tenacity, endeavour and bloody-mindedness, coupled with the ripe skills of Strachan and McAllister, created a force that would quite happily play the role of spoilsports if it meant reaching its goal.

In between their two Cup defeats, Leeds had travelled to Sheffield Wednesday and thrashed their Yorkshire adversaries 6–1, the club's biggest away win since 1930. Again the game had been transmitted live on the Sunday afternoon for the nation to marvel at the skills of a team supposedly there only to make up the numbers. As January came to an end, Wilkinson's team were still in touch with United, although Ferguson could count on games in hand. No matter, Wilkinson was just where he hoped to be. 'I said to my team,' he recalls, 'after Christmas we need to be close to where we want to finish. We were near the top and that is by now where we had set our sights of ending the season. "Now," I said, "just kick on for home."'

The Leeds manager's next move was to bring in someone who would, in time, become more famous for kick-offs than kicking on. Eric Cantona had been pondering a move to Sheffield Wednesday but, like Strachan, opted for the all-white of Leeds. The Wednesday manager Trevor Francis had been unsure about the maverick Frenchman who, amid his array of tricks, had a worrying penchant for trouble. He hardly seemed Wilkinson's (who wasn't nicknamed Sergeant Wilko for nothing) type. Wilkinson, ever the scholar, had kept Cantona in his memory banks having seen him play for France's under-21 side some years before. However, only months prior to his availability Cantona had been thrown out of his club Nimes for disciplinary reasons and had already antagonised his entire country's national team by branding the manager *un sac de merde* (or a bag of shite as his soon-to-be fans would say). He was a livewire all right.

Wilkinson was keen though. He called up those in the know – the French national manager Michel Platini, his assistant Gérard Houllier, Glenn Hoddle, who had just finished playing for Monaco – and they all came to the conclusion that Cantona's talents, while needing a firm hand, were worth the gamble. Wilkinson's decision making was hurried along by the fact that Lee Chapman had fractured his wrist against Manchester United in the FA Cup and would be out for over a month. His squad, hardly overflowing with cover, needed a boost. Cantona would sign on a loan deal until the end of the season.

In time of course, Cantona would ply his magic with Manchester United. The glorious goals, the magical touch, the melting glare, the upturned collar, all became the Premiership's and of course SKY television's major selling points as they went hand in hand into their inaugural decades. With those images of the Frenchman so ingrained in our national sport's psyche it would be easy to conclude that it was Cantona's arrival in Yorkshire with all his Gallic flair that simply wooed the League title back to Leeds. Reality suggests otherwise.

Cantona made his debut against Oldham in February where the team lost 2–0, only their second defeat of the season. His home debut was against Luton where he scored and immediately struck a chord with the Elland Road faithful. There was no doubt that his almost eerie talent was raising the bar in terms of ability at the club and Wilkinson admitted that his first training sessions were awash with 'devastating flicks, tricks and passes'. Was this enough though to steer the club through what was becoming a turbulent descent during the season?

'There's no doubt about it,' says Wilkinson without emotion. 'He was a very useful addition to the squad. In our Championship season he made only seven starts and scored three goals. Now history has a way of rewriting itself, so people think of that season as Cantona's Championship. That is very wrong. He was useful sure but only as a bit part. Chapman got another bagful of goals and was brilliantly aided by Wallace and Speed in that department.'

Strachan agrees and, although he didn't find the Frenchman aloof, was aware that Cantona wasn't a great mixer and although very talented didn't come on and clinch games or score vital goals.

Moving towards Easter and it seemed no one in white was going to clinch games. Leeds were thumped at Queen's Park Rangers 4–1, drew their next two games against Arsenal and West Ham, before losing 4–0 at Manchester City in a woeful and seemingly disastrous display at Maine Road. Wilkinson though sat down and concluded that his team still had one more chance. 'I got the team together and said, "We have five games left. If we can win four of them the pressure is still on Manchester United.'

Wilkinson had a point. Not only had United never been so close to the title since they last won it in 1967, the games in hand they had enjoyed had mounted and the strain on their squad both physically and mentally was about to constrict like a hungry python around Old Trafford's desperate midriff. Leeds won the first of their last five games 3–0 at home to Chelsea, the last of which was a wonder goal from Cantona. They then had to travel to Liverpool, the hardest-looking game of their remaining fixtures, where Wilkinson was willing to risk points to avoid defeat and sent his team out with the air of a side that if American would have had the cheerleaders screaming 'DE-FENCE, DE-FENCE'.

Strachan, feeling the effects of the long season, was to be sacrificed if his manager's hopes of a draw were to be realised. 'I pulled Gordon aside the week before the Anfield game for a chat,' says Wilkinson. 'I told him straight that I was going to leave him out.' The man for the big occasion? How did he take that? 'Very well. Gordon knew what I was trying to achieve. I told him that I wanted him fresh for the remaining games and that realistically I would be more than happy with a point at Anfield. That would have been fine because we felt the other games were very winnable.' Leeds got their goalless draw.

So what of Manchester's part in the equation? Going into Easter Monday they were two points clear with a game in hand. It was looking good for them but they were about to suffer a catastrophic bout of the heebie-jeebies. That Monday they lost 2–1 at home to Nottingham Forest, a team they had beaten at Wembley to win the League Cup just three weeks before. Leeds were kicking off later that afternoon and it was a very nervous Elland Road that prayed their side could take advantage of a Mancunian slip-up. It wasn't vintage stuff but Coventry City were beaten 2–0 and Leeds were back on top.

Manchester United though had that game in hand and went to bottom-of-the-table, and eventually relegated, West Ham hoping to put themselves back in the box seat. It wasn't to be. United lost 1–0 and it was now in Leeds' hands. For United it was an unmitigated disaster. In the world of the soap opera, it was as if *Coronation Street* had been beaten by *EastEnders* only for *Emmerdale* to top the TV listings.

The two clubs' penultimate games of the season were to be held back to back in order for ITV to screen them both live. It was to make for great and often surreal viewing. The maths were simple. If Leeds were to win at Sheffield United, then Manchester United would have to avoid defeat at their even fiercer rivals Liverpool to take the season into its final weekend still alive. Playing first suited Strachan but the game itself was a strange and messy local derby. Sheffield United got into their direct stride early on and battered the Leeds penalty area before that stalwart of the long-ball game Alan Cork gave the home side the lead. The blustery conditions were aiding the Sheffield side but it wasn't long before Leeds realised they were going to have to match their opponents' undeviating style of play if they were going to be victorious. The equaliser came but was hardly sublime. Moments before the half-time whistle Strachan had taken a clever (not in keeping for the day's events) free-kick which Wallace tried to get on the end of. In the mêlée that ensued, a Sheffield United clearance took a double ricochet off Gary Speed and Wallace before stopping in the goal like a lost pinball.

Strachan though was trying to play through the pain barrier. His back was in agony and it frankly wasn't the type of game that was going to benefit from his delicate skills. He was replaced at half-time and for the second half would have to join an anxious away crowd in watching a strange and nervous second period unfold. Leeds took the lead through their promising young defender Jon Newsome but were clawed back incredibly by an inadvertent Lee Chapman goal from one yard. Was it going to be one of those days? Their title aspirations cut to shreds by an effort from their main goal-scorer?

This game though was not finished and with all the grace of a bad children's party magician had another oddity up its sleeve. Cantona and Wallace had chased a bouncing ball onto the edge of the penalty area, before Sheffield's centre-half Brian Gayle sublimely controlled the ball on his knee and looped a fine header over his own 'keeper's head into an astonished net. Leeds had won and, to coin a phrase, their names looked on the trophy.

Manchester United would travel to a Kop even more fervent in their hopes of beating the old enemy. 'I'd rather Everton won it than United,' said Liverpool's keeper Bruce Grobbelaar mischievously. The Leeds players left Sheffield and spent the afternoon in varying ways. Lee Chapman invited David Batty, Eric Cantona and a television crew over to his place to watch proceedings while Wilkinson returned home pondering what had already been an odd Sunday. 'It was like a dream, that day,' muses Wilkinson with pride. 'I honestly thought United would at least get a draw so I went home and enjoyed the usual Sunday lunch with the television off.'

Strachan too chose to ignore proceedings on Merseyside and took Lesley and the kids swimming at the Holiday Inn in Leeds. While he was doing backstroke, Ian Rush had free-styled Liverpool into a lead before Mark Walters sealed it late in the second-half. Strachan's boys came running in from the bar. Wilkinson too heard it from his son. 'My boy was only a toddler back then,' he says. 'He was upstairs watching it and came down the stairs. "Daddy," he said, "I think we're Champions."'

Strachan drove home and dropped in on his chairman Leslie Silver's house for a celebratory cup of tea. A haughty smile from both said it all. Leeds were back at the pinnacle and Strachan had played no small part. The following Saturday at Elland Road, amid cheerleaders and pyrotechnics (an early sign of things to come), he lifted the trophy, unmoved by the hype. He'd seen too much for that; to call it an anti-climax would be harsh, but it had been won in a subdued manner, over seventy miles away and without a Leeds player kicking a ball in anger. No matter, Leeds were Champions and its football no longer constituted anger; as for Strachan, he had kicked enough balls to last a lifetime.

13. BANANAS, PORRIDGE AND SEAWEED

> RON ATKINSON: *There's no one fitter at his age, except maybe Raquel Welch.*

A hot July afternoon. The low thud of tennis ball on racket, the interspersed applause of an appreciative Centre Court and the distant clink of ice as another Pimm's is served at the All England Lawn Tennis Club. He sits at home, his feet up on the couch watching a sport he loves. He marvels at the players' athleticism, their ability to cover the court with such speed and such devotion. He wonders at their levels of concentration and how perfectly conditioned they seem. Ivan Lendl sits between games. His dark, menacing, Slovakian glare stares out onto nothing. What is he thinking? How does he keep himself focused and his body so in tune? Is there a secret? Yes there is, and Lendl is about to unravel it. It's a banana.

Strachan is immediately transfixed. Bananas, hey? They must be good for sportsmen; he'll try some of that. As Strachan moved well into his thirties and subsequently played arguably the best football of his career, talk surrounded his diet every bit as much as his clever passes, nimble runs and spellbinding goals. Bananas along with porridge and a staple diet of seaweed tablets were not your usual fare, especially for a footballer, but as his career's Indian summer turned into a heatwave everyone wanted to know how he did it. If his body was a temple it was taking on Taj Mahal proportions.

It wasn't always that way. As a young pro he had been led astray at Dundee and although unable to drink with the best gave it a good go. At Aberdeen in the early eighties, diets, stretches and physical well-being were more likely to be found on a Jane Fonda video than in a footballer's vocabulary. For all his raw talent it was only his natural enthusiasm for the game that suggested Strachan would play at the highest level until the age of forty. He was a young footballer after all and, like most, away from the training ground enjoyed his golf, a beer and fried food.

At Pittodrie, though, there was one player who seemed to be years ahead of the field. Stuart Kennedy was fitness mad and everyone knew it. 'I think I was one of those guys who used to bore their team-mates to death,' he says and laughs boisterously like a man who still looks out for himself. 'I would sit them down and offer diet tips and fitness regimes. They're all the rage of course these days but what I put into my body was off my own back and I was right.' The team would go out to eat and Kennedy would look down his nose at his comrades' choice of dinner. 'It was always steaks and chips,' he tuts. 'For me it was fish, lean chicken, pasta and definitely no alcohol. It all seems the norm in today's game but, the looks I got back then, you'd have thought I was a bit funny in the head.'

As it turned out not everyone thought so. 'I tried to rub off on them but most blanked me,' says Kennedy. 'The likes of Gordon and Alec [McLeish] though would ask about my habits. I think I bored them into submission to be honest. Can you imagine trying to chat to me and there I'd be stopping the conversation to check my pulse.'

Their full-back's 'different' approach didn't go unnoticed and both Strachan and McLeish went on to enjoy fruitful and long careers, but how much of that was due to those lectures from a colleague? 'Stuart was on and on at us about diets,' says McLeish, laughing. 'He would read American literature about how to fuel the body and go on about the benefits of pasta, the dangers of booze and how a player's body was to be cherished. Gordon and I would often just laugh as we were still into pork pies and a pint back then but gradually Stuart became a big influence on us.'

For all his keen interest, at Aberdeen Strachan was adamant that he would not be one of those players that went on and on until he dropped. Back then, playing into your mid-thirties was far from an attractive proposition to Strachan: that was the time to be on the golf course, your feet up with the odd appearance as a television pundit to keep your eye in. But those were also the days when the game of football in his native country had lost the gloss that he had always adored. Natural enthusiasm had begun to wane, replaced by a worrying boredom that he couldn't shake or hide. 'Gordon was a very restless character,' recalls his captain Willie Miller. 'He hated being injured, hated standing still but he always spoke to me about his desire to give up the game early. It sounds strange because of how long he went on to play but the week-in and week-out stuff at Aberdeen was tiring him out mentally and it affected him.'

So what happened? Why did a young man seemingly keen to get out of the game so early continue playing and putting himself through the physical chores of professional football until he was of an age where a run-out on a Saturday afternoon usually means accompanying the wife to IKEA? The first answer to that question doesn't lie in a porridge bowel or on a modern masseur's treatment table. The key to Strachan's staying power was that the game he saw himself leaving at a relatively young age was also the game he had cherished above anything else from a young age. Yes, his family came first now, but, as the years rolled by, the idea of life without the training, the camaraderie or match day seemed a strange and unfulfilling option.

It was that love for not only the game but also the everyday life that saw Strachan play for so long. While at Leeds it was his fitness that came under scrutiny, but his ability to compete against younger men wasn't something that occurred overnight. That had been born from his enthusiasm and the hard work he had put into his profession from a young age. At Dundee, Strachan would always approach training in the same way he would a Saturday afternoon. Looking back, that effort he put in during a session was not just a way of conditioning for what lay ahead the following weekend, but also a way of ensuring durability and long-term momentum.

'Gordon was a very good trainer,' recalls Kevin Moran, his teammate at Old Trafford. 'What makes you play and play so well into your thirties is your desire and the enjoyment you get out of it. He loved the Saturday afternoon, we all did. You can't beat match day but that isn't enough. Not if you want a long career. Gordon loved the training, the buzz of practising, working on things and getting them right on the pitch. It was that love of what he was doing that saw him play so well and so late into his thirties.'

Now as a manager, it's an enthusiasm he tries hard to instil in his younger players, young men whom he fears will be blinded by the commercial aspects of the game. When he first became a manager at Coventry it was watching the kids that reminded him of how much he had loved the game when growing up. 'We've said to the kids in our academy,' he said at the time, 'first of all they have to love the game. They can learn about winning later on in life, but early they have to love it. They have to fantasise about the game. I was always one to fantasise. When I was a kid no one told me to push up; nobody told me to play offside; nobody told me to pass it; nobody screamed at me when I had the ball at my feet. I didn't have one mum shouting at me to do this, one dad telling me to do that and a coach instructing me to do something completely different. I could do my own thing. I could play centre-half if I wanted; I could play right-wing; I could go in goal. When I got older, I knew the football pitch, all of it.'

Strachan's adamant that the enjoyment taken from the game from those young ages can only bear fruit when that same player reaches a certain mature age. But that enjoyment could only be realised in the right environment. 'People say kids now are getting too much football. That's not right. They're getting too little football, but what they are getting is too much pressurised football. They play with their schools and clubs and have adults screaming at them from the sidelines. They only play in front of coaches and parents and don't play on their own where they can learn from their own mistakes. If you're dribbling and get kicked on the shins you say to yourself it's about time I passed now, or your team-mates will say, "Oi, greedy guts, give us a pass." That's the way to learn.'

Strachan's prolonged playing days were as much down to hard work as they were to his raw love of the game. Strachan's career spanned the changing face of football. The diets, the training regimes, the preparation, it has all changed since his days on a train from Edinburgh to Dundee with coffee and a bacon roll. Strachan, though, seamlessly changed with the times and, by the time he was 34 and on the eve of Leeds' Championship win, fitness wise he was among the top four players at a club more conscious than most when it came to its players physical conditioning. Strachan was running the 800 metres and the 1,500 metres as fast as anyone and no different to when he was 28.

Strachan thoroughly understood that the modern footballer had to be an athlete. He and his colleagues could no longer return from their summer breaks, overweight, overfed and undermotivated. For twelve months a year a player had to think about his fitness and his game. Sacrifices have to be made. For years and even today footballers have – like a packet of crisps or a headache – been intransigently linked with booze. To Strachan, confining his drinking to a casual beer after a game was no big deal. To him the shaky hands, cold sweats and daily cravings were reserved for that other great passion of the Scots and footballers alike: golf.

Strachan's days at Aberdeen and Manchester United had been full of club outings to a local course. Players would unwind with what seemed a perfectly relaxing way to spend their time off the training pitch and to their manager's delight it didn't involve a bar or a book-makers. As Strachan started to think about his longevity and took steps to ensure his peak fitness was realised, he banned himself from the golf course, only allowing himself to indulge in his passion during the summer months.

Such was the intensity of his self-enforced conditioning that the energy spent traipsing from tee to tee was energy wasted. Energy better utilised in the skinning of opposition left-backs. Strachan had heard that his old Scottish captain Graeme Souness had enforced a ban when taking over at Rangers in 1986. It struck a chord. He had heard that many of the Rangers players had moaned about such regimental rules but, to the comprehensive Strachan, giving up a pastime to enhance a career was the most logical thing in the world.

Souness had learned and devised his methods from the two seasons he had spent with Sampdoria in Italy. What was odd to the British footballer was normal and accepted on the Continent and the same went for our players' eating habits. As Stuart Kennedy remarked and scoffed at, steaks, chips and fried food were the norm even as a pre-match meal. With his ex-team-mate's words ringing in his ears and by seeing how well tuned elder players were who had spent time abroad, Strachan changed his menu, and changed it for the better. Joe Jordan, Graeme Souness and Ray Wilkins, all of these guys had benefited from their Italian jobs.

As well as the bananas with porridge and the seaweed supplements, Strachan embraced the idea of pasta, fish and a lack of red meat. Even back in the early nineties, though, his methods were seen as novel. From the penalty area to the boardroom foreign influences are paramount in today's English game. With that influence has come a resurgence of older players, who have benefited from modern techniques, such as Teddy Sheringham, Les Ferdinand and Dion Dublin, all well into their thirties but all scoring goals last season.

When Strachan was approaching his mid-thirties, the foreign impact on British players meant finding a Pavarotti record strangely stirring. Back then players reaching that age were seen as spent. The word veteran would appear before their names in print; they'd receive knowing and patronising nods from pundits treating them like their grandfathers at Christmas. Strachan had noticed when playing against the likes of Beckenbauer in Europe that continental football judged only on merit and he hoped that his methods would help dispel the myth that being over thirty meant being over the hill.

He was ahead of the game, even bringing in his own foreign import to help. Harold Oyen was Strachan's own personal masseur from Norway who was an expert in the field of bio-kinetics. It may sound like something Saddam Hussein has kept well hidden from UN inspectors for years but Strachan swore by it.

He would argue to sceptical team-mates that bio-kinetics is the flow of energy through the body, which must be maintained and balanced at all times. If one part of the body is out of line then the overcompensating muscles suffer. This balance can be maintained using the fingertips and pressure applied to various points on the body. Acupuncture without the needles. With Oyen's help Strachan learned how to treat himself and would sit in the Elland Road dressing room prior to a game carrying out his ritual massages on his legs, forehead and other pressure points. He even managed to get Lee Chapman and Chris Fairclough involved.

Not everyone at Leeds was taken with the idea of gurus and energy lines. Strachan himself had been brought up on old-fashioned methods and would walk into the North Sea at midnight when at Aberdeen to cure most ailments. David Batty, for example, was going to take convincing. He has always been more Yorkshire Pudding than ancient healing and scoffed at such wacky ideas. One day at Leeds Strachan had Oyen come and give a session to the squad about the importance of a positive mental approach. Their striker Imre Varadi was asked to stand up and hold out his arms. As he held them up, Oyen remarked how disappointed Varadi must have been having not been well received by the club and its fans. He then pushed on his arms, which subsequently collapsed without resistance, due, according to Oyen, to the negative atmosphere he had created around him. He then made him hold them out again but this time spoke only of how brilliant a goalscorer Varadi was and how important to the cause he was. Again he pushed on the arms but this time they remained solid.

What was eye-opening to Strachan was mumbo-jumbo to the likes of Batty who later explained, 'I was happy to go out on the pitch after kicking a ball around the changing-room to release my nervous energy and downing a can of coke.' Batty has just been released by Leeds, aged 35, having started just twelve games in two seasons. Maybe Oyen had a point.

For all the modern lingo and new diets, Strachan stood by the simplest of methods to see him through to his football pension. It was the one thing he had found hard to do as a young pro but in time had discovered worked wonders for the modern footballer, and he needed no guru to help him find the inner peace to do it. It was rest. A nap here and forty winks there was something he could never do and envied the likes of Willie Miller and Kenny Dalglish on those long and often boring World Cups. But with age it had become far more natural.

Sleep, good food, hard work, a strange Norwegian and a simple love of the game kept Strachan going strong, and Wilkinson's dream alive. To his manager at Leeds, Strachan's age was a number on his passport while his vitality was a necessity to what he hoped to and eventually did achieve. 'I don't know why people go on about Gordon's age all the time,' said Wilkinson at the time. 'There is nothing in any book I've read that says God visits you one night in your thirties and you can't do it any more.'

If he did, he had forgotten to pass by the Strachans. Images of the game in the nineties are full of the lively redhead running with the ball, that quick step of his as nimble as ever. The smile is as broad as it ever was, the grimace towards a pertinent referee as fierce. At one point it seemed like it would never end. 'It's too good a game to give up,' he confessed. 'That's why I want to play as long as I can. I don't want to join the real world and get up at 7.30 am and go to work. I got a taste of that this morning and I didn't like it one bit.' He wasn't going to give up, not when he had a £100 bet with Bryan Robson on who would go on the longest. Let's hope he picked up his winnings.

The bottom line is Strachan was a great player up until the day he finally retired. Tony Cascarino, another player who managed to perform well into his thirties, once remarked that one of his proudest moments was knowing when to retire before he became a liability. Strachan's prowess on the field, even aged forty, was so great that it took a single-minded manager with guts and determination to finally let him know enough was enough. That manager's name? Gordon Strachan. After all, who else could have done it?

14. GOODBYE TO ALL THAT

REPORTER: *You don't take losing lightly, do you, Gordon?*
GORDON: *I don't take stupid questions lightly either.*

Just six months after lifting the English First Division title as captain of Leeds United, Gordon Strachan received a call from the Palace. Clearly he was in high demand but this was a far loftier request than a mere job offer from Selhurst Park. In the December 1992 New Year's Honours list Strachan was given the Order of the British Empire for his services to the sport. A small boy who had left Muirhouse in Edinburgh aged sixteen to go and play some football was now required by the Queen, and he was among exalted company. The actor Anthony Hopkins was given a knighthood for his services to cannibalism that year, while fellow Edinburgh hero and Scotland rugby captain David Sole was also named an OBE.

'Though it is a personal honour,' said a surprised Strachan, 'I regard it as one for the club and for the city of Leeds as well.' All very gracious but there were the usual jokes behind his new eminent standing. Even today, his long-term friend Mark McGhee laughs at the mention of his friend's gong. 'The funny thing about that,' he says with a chuckle 'is that he went to have the medal valued for insurance purposes and was told it was worth about £90. He thought the thing would be pure gold but they told him it was made out of something like nickel. He was very honoured, though, and his mum and dad, they were ecstatic as you can imagine. He doesn't take things like that lightly. He is very private about them but I know how much pleasure he gets from honours like that.'

That previous summer, the city of Leeds lay back to wallow in the clear and sparkling waters of the Championship. It was an occasion to float and gloat in their achievement, but at times they were drawn into murkier and rocky shores as fans, players and staff had to answer allegations that in fact Manchester United had lost the title rather than Leeds had won it. United had blown it again. 'I think you'll find,' said Strachan almost teasingly, 'the ones who say they lost it rather than us winning it are probably Manchester United fans.'

But did they have a point? Was Leeds' place back in the sun down to United's Championship jinx? 'How can I answer that?' says Wilkinson unapologetically. 'All I and the players and the fans, all any of us can do is accept your medal and feel content that the history books say otherwise.' Such trivial matters were not going to cloud Wilkinson's summer as he prepared for what would prove a far harder season than the glorious one just passed.

David Rocastle was brought to Elland Road for a club record £2 million from Arsenal. A right-sided attacking midfield player, he was a contender for Strachan's position but the captain was not about to do the expected and stand aside for the younger man. Rocastle for all his talent was going to find it difficult at Leeds where Strachan – who had had an operation that summer on his troublesome back – was as hungry as anyone to pit his wits again against European opposition. Like so many in the English game, he had sorely missed the European adventures during the clubs' ban from the Continent after the Heysel disaster of 1985, which would last until 1990. His game and his nature thrived on the challenge Europe brought and now, with as much experience as anyone could hope to have behind him, he relished another crack at it.

Champions, Strachan, new signings, Europe. These were all very well but most eyes, when turning towards Leeds United that late summer, were fixated on their new French superstar. Eric Cantona had signed a permanent deal that summer with Leeds paying Nimes £1 million for his services and his very presence demanded he become more than the bit-part player he had been during Leeds' Championship run-in.

The Charity Shield was won after a 4–3 victory over Liverpool at Wembley with Cantona bagging a hat-trick. Liverpool's third goal that trickled through Strachan's legs on the goal-line, ricocheting slowly off each ankle before stumbling over the line, and the good laugh he shared about it with David Batty, suggested the pressures associated with being Champions were far from burdening his playful spirit. Things though were soon going to get much harder for the club.

The League campaign started solidly enough with home wins over Wimbledon and Spurs, with a draw and a defeat at Aston Villa and Middlesbrough respectively. The Spurs game included a superb hat-trick from Cantona who by now had his own chant and a place in the fans' hearts. The First Division had just become the Premiership, its name a brand up in lights. In Cantona, Leeds seemed to have a player who encapsulated that brand but a manager more concerned with the old school, and finding it hard to build his club and his team around an individual of enigmatic talent.

The season's start became a splutter as draws and defeats meant the Champions were languishing at the bottom end of the table. The togetherness and spirit that had epitomised their victory only months before was missing and, to Wilkinson, the spotlight – that would befall him so often when wearing red – seemed to cast its light on Cantona. The Frenchman was dropped, something he simply wasn't going to take with a Gallic shrug of the shoulders. For Cantona it was an insult and his reaction was to slap in a transfer request stating he wanted to join only Liverpool, Arsenal or Manchester United. Wilkinson had started up some loose dialogue with Alex Ferguson regarding the availability of Denis Irwin and so, when it became clear that Cantona was available, the two again chatted and a deal was done.

Selling a man who had very quickly taken on iconic status amongst your fans for only £1.2 million to your biggest and most hated rivals was never going to be ideal business for Wilkinson, but Strachan understood his manager's motives. He realised that Wilkinson was not happy with Cantona's progress alongside Lee Chapman. Of course, now it looks preposterous that a talent such as Cantona's could be discarded due to his inability to gel with Chapman, but at the time and without the power of hindsight it was argued that that spark that had ignited the Championship had been dimmed by one man's flame.

Strachan joked that when Monsieur Cantona was good he was amazing, but when he was bad he was horrid. 'People have written a lot about it,' Strachan said having placed himself in the manager's corner. 'They try to analyse it but it's simple. Some people are selfish and Eric would get fed up if he felt things weren't right for him. He would terrorise those about him … Whatever Wilkinson would say, Eric would do the opposite. Howard had to do something.' Insolence, unpredictability and Howard Wilkinson do not make for comfy bedfellows and so Cantona was on his way to Old Trafford.

His penultimate game for Leeds was a European clash against Rangers at Elland Road. Cantona had scored that night but was far from at his best and, amid the hype of another 'Battle of Britain', Leeds crashed out to cap what was a dismal season. They were surprised to have made the second round at all. Having been drawn against

Stuttgart it seemed that, as ever, German opposition in Europe would hinder Strachan's aspirations. The Germans had won 3–0 in Stuttgart and, despite a gallant 4–1 win at Elland Road, Leeds were seemingly out on the away goal rule. There was, however, to be a twist.

The usually efficient Germans had fielded four foreign players in Leeds when only three were permitted by UEFA. Leeds United had every right to feel aggrieved with the governing body's decision to order a deciding game on neutral territory as the rules were clear that it was an offence punishable by disqualification. Instead the two would meet on a Friday night in Barcelona's grand Nou Camp. The tiny 7,500 crowd rattled conspicuously around the vast arena like two-pence coins in a Gucci wallet. The players tried hard to raise their games in such awkward surroundings and it was left to Strachan – a siren of quality amid the eerie silence – to get Leeds going. His old mate Steve Archibald was living in Barcelona having moved to the Catalan club from Spurs. He sat in awe at his old pal, trying hard to convince his Spanish friends that the small man with the red hair was 36 years old.

In the first half that small man took down a headed clearance, feinted to shoot, made the angle and sent the ball screaming into the net via the 'keeper's fingertip and the upright. Stuttgart managed to equalise but Leeds deservedly went through after Carl Shutt – and in such an oddly low-key match how appropriate it was one of their fringe players – had scored a late winner. It was to be Rangers next. The Old Firm revisited.

The hype surrounding the game was – even for a sport getting very used to the hard sell – incredible, and the atmosphere in Ibrox for the first leg, despite the banning of away fans for each fixture, was electric. Leeds may have had no support, but Strachan, while counting on a special reception for old times' sake from the Ibrox fans for an ex-Don, had sneaked in his own noisy reinforcements. For once, the match and the atmosphere lived up to its billing. Strachan got the 'friendly' greeting he had expected when he went to take a corner as early as the first minute and although his delivery was cleared it fell to Gary McAllister on the edge of the area who pinged a sweet volley back into the top corner. Deathly silence. Even the Leeds players wondered whether they should celebrate but then, out of nowhere, a piercing shrill, 'YEEEEESSSSSSS!' Strachan had got a ticket for his dad Jim, his son's biggest fan and of course an Edinburgh man, so there was no way he was keeping quiet while Glaswegians were suffering.

Under Walter Smith, Rangers had built their strongest team for years. They were four years into a nine-year Scottish Premier League winning streak with a nucleus of fine Scottish talent who would go on and reach the semi-final stages of that year's tournament and it wasn't long before Strachan senior was having to slide quietly back into his seat. A soft equaliser and a winner from Ally McCoist was enough to see Rangers travel to Leeds with a slender lead.

Leeds though had the away goal but three minutes into the second leg Mark Hateley smashed a fantastic half-volley past Lukic and the tie looked as good as over. 'Mark Hateley!' said Strachan with a laugh years later. 'God! That was the best goal he'll ever score!' Another McCoist effort meant Cantona's consolation counted for nothing, only disappointment for Leeds fans who had had such high hopes for the season. So why had it gone so wrong, so quickly?

David Batty regarded the slump in form and fortune testimony to how much the team had peaked the previous year. He commented on how many of the players had been approaching the end of their careers and, unlike Strachan, no longer had the legs for further struggles. Strachan himself cited the new back-pass law enforced that summer that decreed a 'keeper was no longer allowed to handle a pass back: Leeds' centre-halves, Chris Whyte and Chris Fairclough, were honest and strong but lacked the ability on the ball that was now required. Steve Bruce and Gary Pallister at Manchester United had that assurance and were building a partnership that didn't rely on slowing the game down.

Wilkinson remained philosophical and, although he compared the current apathy surrounding his team to a dose of ME, was proud of how far they had come, but mindful of how hard that could be to sustain. 'We had turned the club around very quickly,' he says. 'Our progress outstripped our capacity to genuinely keep pace with it. We went far too quickly and therefore were always trying to catch up in the resources stakes.' He was right: the place was staggeringly different to how he had found it and for Wilkinson now, despite the state the club find themselves in today, that is a source of pride. 'Finance, ground, training grounds, setting up the academy, car parks, everything; there was always someone with a brush in his hand or a trowel. Everything was changing and at a staggering pace. I look back on it and think we were like the German Army advancing into Russia in 1941. We did so too quickly and therefore carried weaknesses.

'It was successful no doubt but we had to consolidate as we had an outstanding crop of kids coming through. I gave debuts to Gary Kelly, Lee Bowyer and Harry Kewell. We had Woodgate there; Robinson was there and we knew Alan Smith was coming through; the future looked rosy and my big regret was not getting the chance to work further with those young men.'

Leeds finished a disappointing seventeenth in 1993 and, while they only lost one game at Elland Road, they managed to go the entire season without an away win. It is that sort of dismal record that counted most for their slump. Strachan though – and despite Rocastle's presence – was again brilliant, winning the fans' Player of the Year award. The team's fluency had suffered with changing personnel and injury but his form somehow remained a constant. He managed 37 starts that season and even rolled back the years with a hat-trick in April against Premiership new boys Blackburn Rovers. It was a timely victory that put to bed any lingering fears regarding relegation and achieved, due to injuries, using young and inexperienced cover.

In fact, it was the youth set-up that gave the club their only reason to cheer in 1993. They beat a talented Manchester United side over two legs that drew more than 60,000 fans. United boasted the likes of Gary and Phil Neville, Keith Gillespie, Paul Scholes, Robbie Savage and David Beckham but the Leeds players, less talented, but mirroring their seniors' efforts the year before in the Championship, came out on top. Strachan was starting to take notice and enjoyed putting his coaching badges into practice, although he remained adamant that he was still both player and captain at Elland Road.

The following season was an improvement with Leeds finishing a respectable fifth but the fans were finding it hard to meet their manager with the same enthusiasm of two summers earlier. Gary Kelly had broken into the team and behind Strachan was learning all the time. Brian Deane had come in and replaced Lee Chapman but to the fans' disgust David Batty, a local boy and hero, had been sold to Blackburn Rovers. People were now looking for reasons to pick holes in Wilkinson's management. The Championship team had broken up but Strachan again managed 37 games and again was a well of inspiration to players and fans thirsty for repeated success. David Rocastle had been replaced by Manchester City's David White but he too, as far as Strachan was concerned, was not going to be the bearer of a pipe and a pair of slippers, not just yet.

Like Billy Bremner at the end of his career at Leeds, Strachan was the lifeblood of the team. His very presence was inspirational and he shamed even the younger players in the side who looked unable to keep up with his admirable dynamism. The season ended with further discomfort amongst an only slightly replenished fan base. That summer Strachan, whose work with the youngsters was becoming more than just a distraction from his day job, decided to have one more season as a registered player. While not quite ready to hang those boots up, it was becoming clear that he'd better start hammering in the nail.

Going into the 1994/95 season Strachan knew his involvement on the pitch was going to be limited and therefore welcomed Gary McAllister being appointed captain. It didn't stop him being called 'Skip' by everyone at the club (including McAllister) and underlined he had taken on a certain air at the club: an air of authority that was almost managerial in its intensity, and offered those wanting a change the ideal replacement. That didn't sit well with Strachan. He had remained a firm advocate of all that Wilkinson had accomplished and was trying to still do at the club and the idea that it would be him that replaced him grated with the Scotsman.

As the season got going, Strachan the player was more than happy. His occasional run-outs for the first eleven, mixed with coaching and games for the reserves, were ideal; in this atmosphere, he saw himself at the club for a long time to come. Unfortunately that atmosphere didn't remain. On the pitch the team were as dogged as they had been in 1992 but lacked the spark and the guile necessary for success. Carlton Palmer, John Pemberton and Brian Deane did not offer the mobility that for three seasons had seen them sweep past defences in boundless waves. Fans saw Wilkinson as the man who had taken that team apart. Much of it was unfair as players had been injured and simply come to the end of their careers but he was soon going to suffer for his lack of quality replacements and the fact that a group of exceptional youngsters were just that bit too young.

In the reserves, things were better. Under Strachan the likes of Noel Whelan were blossoming and to Strachan the fun of playing the game he loved lay in seeing that improvement. With that in mind, he decided to bring forward his decision to retire at the end of the season and in January announced that he had played his last game. 'I have decided I no longer have sufficient influence on first-team football at

Leeds,' he said. 'I think, if you are a player with a club at any level, you must be an influence whether it be through playing ability or different qualities. If you are no longer an influence, it's time to move on.'

Move on maybe, but the persistent talk around the club was of him moving up and filling Wilkinson's beleaguered role. Ron Atkinson, who had remained Strachan's good friend despite the latter choosing Leeds over Sheffield, had recently taken over as manager at Coventry City. He chatted to Strachan and mentioned that he wanted a young man to come in, fill the role of assistant and eventually step in as team manager while Atkinson went upstairs. Ray Wilkins and Chris Waddle were mentioned but Gordon Strachan seemed to stand out to Atkinson. Would he be interested?

A similar partnership had never been offered at Leeds. Here, there were only rumours and counter-rumours. Coventry's offer had appealed to him but became even more attractive because of the Leeds hierarchy's seemingly lack of effort in keeping him. Rather than pulling out the stops they asked him to go and do some night work in the community. Not exactly highbrow coaching.

While he was mulling it over, the rumours regarding Wilkinson's position persisted and for Strachan enough was enough. 'Gordon came to me for a chat,' says Wilkinson. 'We talked it over. He said he wasn't comfortable with being seen as my successor. It was other people making him uncomfortable at the club. I told him it didn't bother me, but the offer he'd been made at Coventry was too good and so he took it.' At Coventry, the future was clear, mapped out. It was a future where Strachan's summer worries could be kept in the shade. After six years at Leeds he left.

As he had strolled out of Muirhouse to learn to be a player, he was now walking away from Elland Road to become a coach. In Yorkshire he had rediscovered those childhood days. Wilkinson, the club, its fans, they had all allowed him to play with the novel keenness of a child. Each goal he had scored had been celebrated like a boy on his local playground and each season had ended with a sigh; like a kid being called in for his tea, he had longed for the next day's action. That now seemed over. It was time to grow up and be the boss.

15. LEARNING THE SLIPPERY SLOPES

REPORTER: *Is this the best start to a season?*
GORDON: *Well, I've still got a job so it's far better than the Coventry one, that's for sure.*

'Dion, could I have a word?'

'Course you can, boss, what's up?' Dion Dublin walks into his manager's office like an innocent schoolboy racking his brain, trying to decipher what he may have done and how exactly he got caught.

'Could you close the door behind you?' says the serious-looking manager as he sits at his desk. 'I've got some news, Dion. I've just had Glenn Hoddle on the phone.' Dublin's mind starts to tick and guilt is replaced by nervous excitement. His manager's poker expression can take it no more and a proud grin cracks across his face. 'You've made the England squad. Well done, Dion, brilliant.'

That was the buzz. Those were the moments when it all made sense. 'He was ecstatic for me,' says a grateful Dion Dublin today. 'I think at one point he was even happier than myself. He was trying to be cool of course, but I could tell, I could see the emotion welling up inside.'

That emotion came from the satisfaction Strachan gleaned from seeing his players improve. He had sensed it when he played with the reserves and helped out with a talented group of youngsters at Leeds but this now was the real deal, the ultimate.

Dion Dublin, a good footballer. He had shined bright enough at Cambridge United for Manchester United to invest £1 million in him. He had been unfortunate at Old Trafford with injury and the talent he was up against, but arrived at Coventry's Highfield Road a talented, hard-working striker with a keen eye for goal. Almost four years later, and having been coached by Strachan for the vast majority of that time, he was getting international recognition. That was what being a coach was about, not a manager, not someone who wears a tie, gives press conferences and brokers deals with blood-sucking agents. This was real; this was the reward and he loved it.

Strachan spent over six years at Coventry. Those good times were of course balanced out with hardships which culminated in relegation and ultimately the sack; but he had arrived at the club to learn, and learn he would have to. For all the good results there was the booing from his own fans; for all the England caps there were the bad signings and fall-outs with disgruntled professionals. It was hard being the proprietor of a dug-out every Saturday but every now and then he got to call a player into his office and smile. It was a job worth doing.

Strachan arrived at Coventry in the April of 1995 as Ron Atkinson's assistant. It had been agreed that it was a role he would fill for two full seasons before taking over the reigns so Atkinson could step into that amorphous role of general manager. It was all finalised; dates, his job description, it was all settled. Elland Road had become a vague place: the exact same process was all set up at Leeds but no one took the firm step of making Strachan feel like it would ever happen. Strachan, his worries and his doubts never far from view, needed stability, and in the Midlands he could have just that.

Stability and Coventry City are not words that have, over the years, been commonly linked. Ron Atkinson had been appointed manager of the club in February 1995, with the threat of relegation, like an over-enthusiastic and unwanted admirer, as ever hovering irritatingly at its side. Phil Neal, the former captain of Liverpool and England, had been sacked, having lorded over the club for just over a year, after a run consisting of only one win in twelve matches going into 1995 convinced the chairman Bryan Richardson that not only was a new manager needed but it also had better be someone who could lift the gloom from a club becoming too used to downtrodden and hard times.

Cue Ron Atkinson. On such occasions it was as if there was an emergency hotline direct to the big man's house: CLUB IN CRISIS OF CONFIDENCE. NEEDS REVIVING AND NEW LIFE BREATHED IN. PLEASE HELP! Atkinson had not long before had his shoulder tapped and been asked to leave Aston Villa by their trigger-happy chairman Doug Ellis. It was a job Ron had thoroughly enjoyed and had been reasonably successful in. He lived locally and, while out of work, had been seen regularly at Highfield Road and had even trained with the squad on more than one occasion. He would often sit in the directors' box, a guest of the club, a good friend of Neal and a former boss of Neal's number two Mick Brown. It was embarrassing, then, with results going astray, when a fan shouted into the smart seats after another defeat, 'Oi, Richardson, why don't you give Ron the job and get rid of that Neal?' It was awkward, especially as Mrs Neal had been sitting next to the wanted man in question. Atkinson stayed away but Neal's time was soon up and, despite feeling for a sacked man, Atkinson was pleased to take the job and a new challenge.

Atkinson would be given the task of staving off relegation that season, manage the side for a further two seasons and then pass the baton on to a new, younger man specifically groomed. It was a comfortable arrangement and one the city could get behind and see a future in. With Atkinson's presence an extra 5,000 people turned up for his first game at home to West Ham, and a 2–0 win immediately had those punters relishing a glitzy future from a manager never one to play down his champagne and gold-plated bath taps lifestyle.

Immediately the club's kudos was heightened. Television cameras, packed press conferences, microphones at training, they all became the norm as Atkinson's presence lifted the profile and the spirits. It was going to take more than a nice suit and an expensive cigar to get Coventry out of trouble though. Away from his self-styled public persona, Atkinson was deadly serious about the job at hand. There was and is more to him than sometimes blinds the eye. The suits were all very nice but, as for the cigar, he hasn't smoked one in thirty years. It was the nitty-gritty that had him sign solid players, men both used to him and a good old dog-fight, and so Kevin Richardson arrived from Villa, while David Burrows came in from Everton.

'I'm sure Ron was like a breath of fresh air,' says Burrows in his broad Midlands twang. 'Coventry just weren't going to survive and he knew he had to get people in, and quickly who could give the place a lift. I think getting Gordon in at that time was his biggest coup. No one else could have brought him from Leeds to Coventry, and to a lesser extent the same goes for the likes of myself. I was at Everton, OK they were also struggling but I had a bloody good contract and was settled on Merseyside. Ron persuaded me though because of his presence and his manner. He was very old-fashioned, from the old school and it appealed to me.'

It appealed to most and results along with optimism noticeably improved. So Strachan arrived at a club with a clear and workable purpose, to avoid relegation. 'Strachs's time was up at Elland Road,' concludes Atkinson. 'I had chatted to him and he had been knocking about their reserves, helping out here and there, and so my definite offer meant he needed little ear bending. I had thought about possible others for the job but it was Gordon who seemed the ideal. He arrived as assistant manager and immediately set about learning and getting on with things.'

Strachan was the presence on the training pitch. He arrived brimming with ideas and an enthusiasm that had readily transferred itself from player to coach. Atkinson wasn't one to get muddy during the week anyway so the dynamics between the two were quickly defined and the players were in no doubt initially as to who was doing what. 'He arrived with a lot of new thoughts and ideas,' says Dublin. 'Training completely changed when Strachs arrived. It was very intense, very new and to be honest he upped the standards. He was allowed to get on with it by Ron, which helped.

'I think Gordon had come in and said, "OK, Ron, I'm here to coach so let me coach, let me get on with it on the training pitch my way." It was fine though. Ron may have had all the experience but Gordon was serious about learning and doing it his way.' Was it ever awkward? 'Not awkward, just precise and clear. They would have words but that is good. You don't want your management to be too cosy. You need an atmosphere, but we all knew what was happening. Ron was the boss, Gordon the coach.'

The coach makes his way out onto Coventry's training pitch at Ryton. He places down his cones and markers. Bags of footballs sit ready and waiting for their morning work-out. The players will benefit from his precision, attention to detail and another meticulously planned session. The manager trots out from the changing rooms. He's dropped an anti-inflammatory pill with his morning cuppa, oiled up those battle-scarred, leathery tanned legs and is ready to roll back the years. 'Forget all that, Strachs!' he barks, trotting, like Brian Glover in *Kes*, enthusiastically onto his battleground. 'We're playing five-a-side today.' A frustrated coach will have to put his plans on ice. It's time for the boss to show what he can do.

'Ron was very funny,' says Dublin, laughing. 'He'd be out there demanding the ball every week, running around with his brand new Adidas Predators on. "Give me the ball, I'm ready, I'm free," he'd shout, but the next day he could hardly fucking move.'

It was not Strachan's way of doing things but for now it would have to do. 'Gordon was very disciplined in the way he liked to do things,' says Steve Ogrizovic, the veteran 'keeper and today in charge of the club's youth academy. 'He wasn't complicated; he just got us working hard in order to get results. Ron would come in, have a laugh, a joke, try and take the pressure off and that sometimes frustrated Gordon.'

While Atkinson made every effort to roll back the years with small-sided games on a Friday, Strachan continued to shine in training every day. The players would arrive in the dressing room, worn out after training, but amid a sea of muddy kit and boots, and sit and deliberate over their coach's form. `Did you see Strachs's goal today? Bloody hell.'

'What about that pass from Strachs today, talk about pin-point.'

'I reckon he's fitter than you, mate.'

'I reckon he's fitter than most of us.'

'That would happen nearly every day,' says Dublin, admiration filling his calm and friendly manner. 'He'd talk us through how he saw a particular drill being done and then demonstrate, and each time that demonstration was spot on; first time, every time. He had amazing enthusiasm and could run around with us all day, no problem.'

Strachan's ability and fitness hadn't been lost on his boss, who had gone to cast an eye on the new boys in the reserves only to be left spellbound by an old-timer supposedly making up the numbers and working on his sharpness with a mid-week run-out. That 'engine' of his was purring very nicely indeed and Atkinson, having run the rule over his squad, knew he was looking at and working with a ready-made and nicely packaged improvement on it. 'I sat there that night and it slowly dawned on me,' says Atkinson, laughing. 'Here was a player who was still miles better than anything else I had at the club. By full-time I knew it was too soon for Gordon to resign. His fitness was too good, his expertise too necessary and his experience too valuable. He could help us to stay up and that's what he did.'

Strachan couldn't help himself. He agreed he would play in an emergency but had a taste for it and at Highfield Road, come May, emergencies are not usually far away. Anyway, the buzz from playing and competing simply wouldn't go away. For all his good intentions he needed the fix and in Atkinson he found a man more than happy to deal him his drug of choice. As he needed football, Coventry needed him. Under Atkinson they had shot off to a fantastic start, winning at Anfield in a run of six games unbeaten. Atkinson was named Manager of the Month for March and all was as shiny as the boss's cheeks going into the last third of the season.

This being Coventry City, though, meant drama and trepidation were likely and even expected visitors. For the following season the

Premiership was to see through its pledge of reducing the league from 22 teams to 20. That meant an extra club would be relegated, and that meant even more reason to sweat. Going into that all too familiar last furlong they looked a club intent on dismounting their ride and after five losses in six games all looked ominous, but their small trainer-cum-jockey was about to guide them calmly and intact into the survival enclosure. 'Without Gordon we would have gone down,' says Burrows without hesitation. 'Ron had brought in other players. Myself, Kevin [Richardson], Paul Williams, and we played a part, but Gordon's was a major role at the end when it looked bad.'

Coventry went to Spurs for their penultimate game knowing a loss would leave them in dire straits but set about their North London opponents like small wounded animals. Peter Ndlovu darted between defenders menacingly but it was another pocket-sized threat that really sank his teeth in that afternoon. Strachan was brilliant. Playing wide on the right he tormented Tottenham's Justin Edinburgh. He laid on the first and last goals for Ndlovu and Dublin respectively and persecuted their left-back sufficiently to win a penalty for the second. Coventry won 3–1 and were staying up. 'Strachs played out of his skin that night,' purrs Atkinson. 'He beat them almost single-handedly and I'm not exaggerating when I say that I rated that as one of the finest displays from a winger I've ever seen. Justin Edinburgh couldn't live with the little fella, and described him afterwards, twelve years his senior, as the most difficult opponent he had ever faced.'

Strachan was elated, not only with his performance on the pitch that continued to remind him and others of his ability (and even into his late thirties he needed that reassurance), but also because it meant that the following season he would be working at a Premiership club and he and Atkinson could go about using that gravitas to lure a better class of player to Highfield Road. On accepting the job, Atkinson had predicted great things for the club, if, and only if, they could stay up. They had, and so he went about using the cash rolling in off the Premiership gravy train to build what he saw as a new and exciting era.

Coventry's enthusiastic chairman Bryan Richardson was more than willing to oblige when it came to signing the cheques and felt that, by getting Atkinson to the club, he had presided over the most exciting event at the club since they won the FA Cup in 1987. That excitement meant new players, new hopes, but ultimately and surprisingly the same tensions. The squad Atkinson had inherited were honest and hard working but their chairman was the first to admit that they were a relegated side waiting to happen.

Ally Pickering, Sean Flynn, David Rennie, these were names and players lacking the buoyancy to remain afloat in an unforgiving Premiership ocean where waves of new money and expectancy meant clubs of Coventry's stature had to gamble on new blood or risk being dragged to a watery grave. The fans now, though, had reason to believe that the club's ambition matched that of their new management. Tempting offers were turned down for Peter Ndlovu and Dion Dublin and the arrivals gate at Highfield Road was far busier than that of the departures.

Isaias, a Brazilian midfielder, arrived from Benfica; John Salako came from Crystal Palace; Paul Telfer joined from Luton; Paul Williams from Derby and later Richard Shaw, also from Palace; Noel Whelan from Leeds (at £2 million the club's most expensive purchase) and Eion Jess from Aberdeen. The latter was a player Strachan had admired from afar for some time. A local boy, Jess had stood and marvelled at his heroes at Pittodrie as a kid and had gone on to fill Strachan's number seven jersey for club and country with distinction. His arrival was testament to Strachan's growing influence at the club and Atkinson's faith in the judgement of his right-hand man.

The role of assistant manager is a strange one. That man in the tracksuit. That fidgety man sitting in the shadow of a more suave, smart and demure manager. That overly aggressive man barking at the fourth official. Like Phil Neal in 1993, caught on camera infamously repeating every word that came from Graham Taylor's desperate mouth. That man.

That though is not the full story. Behind most great managers is a great assistant. Bill Shankly's charismatic bravado was perfectly complemented by the calming uncle-like Bob Paisley. Peter Taylor at Nottingham Forest was the *yin* to Brian Clough's madcap *yang* at the City Ground in the seventies and early eighties. Even today Pat Rice at Arsenal quietly goes about motivating an exceptional group of players while his manager Arsène Wenger cerebrally pulls the strings. There is no doubt, when done well, an assistant manager should be like a good stuntman, seamlessly creating the illusion that the Clint Eastwoods, Paul Newmans and Sir Alex Fergusons of this world have jumped from the high-speed train all on their own and saved the day.

Strachan found this task a hard one. The role of complementing Atkinson was tough. Here was a manager whose very methods meant he was a close ally to his players. His relaxed and motivational manner promoted his popularity within the squad and therefore an assistant needn't be that shoulder to cry on, the man to tell you the irate manager didn't mean it and everything was going to be OK. Instead Strachan was too impetuous, eager to improve both himself and his squad without distraction or indiscipline.

Coventry's Brazilian Isaias was a talented and popular part of the squad. The foreign player in the English game was still relatively novel then, especially a South American – or 'the Latins' as they were known in football circles – and Strachan struggled to come to terms with his laidback approach to the game and training. Archie Knox after all would never have tolerated a player strolling through a training session and neither would Strachan. The coach was horrified with the player's approach; the player couldn't understand the coach's intolerance and amid this clash of football cultures the two fell out and Isaias was on his way. 'Gordon is a typical Scot,' says Ogrizovic with a laugh. 'He has a fiery temper and would let people know when he wasn't happy. It was Ron who would defuse those situations but sometimes it just wasn't possible to answer Gordon back because, if you look at his career, he's been there, done that and bought the T-shirt.'

Despite a wealth of experience that could buy time and respect, Strachan had to learn about dealing professionally with a group of men. 'He was improving with time and his methods coming on,' says Burrows. 'Yes he was fiery and he wanted players to show the same enthusiasm as him but it slowly dawned on him that that just couldn't happen all the time. He had to deal with individuals too and he became prepared to be very open and learn.'

Strachan may have been learning, but the club, for all their reinforcements and optimism, was not. The road that Atkinson had hoped to take Coventry down instead had an all too familiar view and relegation again loomed menacingly on the horizon. A generous board, an extrovert and motivational manager and a hard-working and potentially successful coach, all of that was in place, but where it mattered most on that big green area (to steal a Strachanism), it just wasn't working.

By Easter, that weekend where so many triumphs and failures are played out, Coventry were in the middle of a catastrophic run that usually coincides with the big drop. One win in twelve were the locks and chains around the box, but somehow this Houdini-like club would again pick its way out of trouble and breathe top-flight air once more. Not to say that the suffocating atmosphere wasn't getting to them. Atkinson was a manager apt at taking the pressure off his players; those broad shoulders were made for the task, but, after a narrow and uninspiring defeat at Southampton, even his thick skin showed signs of flaking.

Richard Keys (SKY presenter and an avid Coventry fan): Bottom line, Ron, you are below the drop zone, how are you going to get out of it. Where do you go from here?

Atkinson: Tottenham, Saturday, that's next *(underlining that charming but efficient optimism).*

Keys: But surely, Ron, you have to show more than you did tonight?

Atkinson: You may say that. We don't think so you know, Richard. I'm sorry, you can sit there and play with all your silly machines as much as you like. I'm a manager of a football team. An experienced manager. If the boys haven't done enough, I'll whip 'em, but I ain't whipping them for that tonight. Who won the Man of the Match award?

Keys: Dave Beasant *(Southampton's 'keeper).*

Atkinson: We must not have played that bad then. Thanks very much, lads, see you later *(Ron throws off his earphones at a technician).*

Strachan must have observed just how to play the camera and entertain the watching public from Atkinson, but more importantly the manager had stood his ground. He had backed his players publicly, that was essential, and it was now time for them to back him. They did. Strachan himself managed fifteen appearances that season and helped out as title-chasing Liverpool were beaten at Highfield Road, as were Queen's Park Rangers. A win at Wimbledon meant it was in their own hands going into the last game of the season and as ever the locks were picked, the chains removed and a 0–0 draw with Leeds enough to secure survival at Manchester City's expense. Richardson and Atkinson were strangely applauded from the pitch. Optimism reigned but why had the season again been such a struggle? 'It's hard to say,' says Burrows. 'There was a lot of movement amongst the playing staff. Ron had gone about spending the few bob that was available and that affected the team. Ron wanted to move players on and change things around quickly. That can upset the mechanisms of a squad and so it was slow to become a settled place of work.'

The season was again all about getting by, keeping heads above water and taking harsh lessons and realities on board. Even Atkinson had felt the strain. His father, to whom he was very close, had been taken ill and, going into the summer of 1996, those around him could tell just how hard he was finding it. Bryan Richardson for one saw a change in the man and thoughts began slowly to shift regarding what was best for the club.

Atkinson had one year left on his contract. One more season left before Strachan took charge, and so for all his personal problems set about again trying to make additions to the squad and bringing in faces he hoped would change it and his fortunes. He had hoped to sign Carlton Palmer from Leeds, a player who, for all his critics, he hoped would bring stability to Coventry's midfield. He agreed a £2 million fee but his enthusiasm was not matched by a usually overenthusiastic board. Things might be changing.

Strachan himself was unsure about Palmer. 'Carlton is a good player,' he told Atkinson. 'Having said that, I don't think I could handle him. You must remember, Ron, you are finishing at the end of the season and I'll be left with the task of handling Palmer.' Instead Gary McAllister was audaciously signed for £3 million, a decision that had little to do with Atkinson and more to do with his assistant's relationship with the Scotland captain and a former Leeds team-mate. Atkinson felt aggrieved. He was no longer in sole control.

He didn't think that the move for McAllister was the wise one. As much as he rated him, he felt his ability on the ball wasn't what the side needed. They required a grafter not a playmaker, especially when that playmaker was an old friend of the assistant manager, especially when that playmaker was earning a reputed £20,000 a week. That sort of money was being trumped up by more than mere television and increased gate receipts. Geoffrey Robinson MP, a member of Tony Blair's New Labour movement, had been acting as a benefactor for the club he supported and that meant further trouble for Atkinson.

As did a disastrous start to the new season. The writing had been on the wall in the pre-season and a 7–2 defeat by an ordinary Benfica side spelled trouble. McAllister had been left 'feeling numb for a month' by that result and one win in their first six games hardly had the spectre of relegation looking for new corridors to haunt.

Richardson was under pressure from Robinson and would have to approach his manager. Both were aware that the players at the club were better than other struggling teams but something wasn't working. Richardson had chaired a board meeting where Robinson had proved the least comfortable with proceedings and as the 'Money Man' his voice was loud and clear. The MP had already pulled Strachan aside after an uninspiring goalless draw with Sheffield Wednesday. 'I want you to run the show from this point on,' he said. Strachan didn't like the cloak and dagger way of doing things. This wasn't the shadowy corridors of Parliament where careers were ended in its dark nooks and policies agreed in its cobwebbed crannies. This was a friend after all, but this too was football and the club were in trouble. Big trouble.

For all that, the ever-sanguine Atkinson was pointing out the positives. Fewer goals were being conceded; draws were replacing defeats and solidity had replaced fallibility. It wasn't enough. With a fixture at Everton scheduled for the Monday, Atkinson was called in to see the chairman on the Sunday. The call had come from above and was a call so succinct not even Richardson had a say. 'Ron,' he said calmly. 'Things aren't going well, why not hand the day-to-day stuff to Gordon, as we agreed he would do at the end of the season, only bringing it forward?' Richardson has stood by the fact that he simply put it to Atkinson. He did not fire him and that if he had said no he would have allowed him to carry on.

Atkinson sees it differently. 'Quite bluntly,' he recalls, 'he told me the decision had been reached three days earlier, among the ivory tower people, that I should stand down from the manager's post.' To make matters worse, the story was leaked to the *Daily Mirror* and ran on the morning of the Everton match, his last game in charge, and therefore preventing him even arguing his case and changing matters. While most papers had it as Atkinson stepping down, the *Mirror* story reported a sacking, completely undermining Atkinson's future role as Director of Football. Somebody wanted him out and suspicious eyes were on the offices of Geoffrey Robinson. Nothing was proven and all Atkinson muttered was, 'Suffice it to say that I won't be voting Labour again at the next election.'

Atkinson though would fill the role of Director until his contract ran out and he quietly left at the end of another traumatic season. It was hard to step into his shoes but, while he knew what was happening, it was all over his head. Later Atkinson would be asked whether he thought Strachan had helped turn him over, perhaps been instrumental in his downfall. The two men remain friends and Atkinson emphatically answered 'No'. What had troubled Atkinson, however, was that, when it had come to meeting Strachan and the chairman, there had been a lack of firm support. Instead his assistant had seemed unsurprised at the turnabout of events. 'I feel he should have stood by me with more conviction when it came to crunch time. But that, as far as I am concerned, is the end of the matter.'

Strachan was in an awkward situation. Something had to be done at the club and that meant someone's fingers and ego getting stepped on. To quote Atkinson when he himself received the job following Phil Neal's sacking, 'That's football and there is no time for crocodile tears. We all understand the rules.'

What was harder to understand was the boundaries defining Strachan's and Atkinson's roles. What is a Director of Football and what sway does he have over the manager? They are ambiguous questions and ones made far from clear when broached with the chairman. 'I'll leave that to you two to sort out,' said Richardson. That wasn't good enough for a now confused 'Director'.

'There was nothing defined and that made it very difficult to work,' Atkinson told me. 'The chairman hadn't really thought it through. You can't do that; these things have to be mapped out and roles distinguished. It was hard and got to the point that I thought it was pointless being here.'

Amid the confusion, Strachan wanted clarity. He was a manager now and had to set out his stall. Atkinson approached him to ask where he felt his predecessor should be on the Saturday of an early home game. 'I would expect you to be away from here,' came the reply from the new boss. 'Scouting probably.' It was harsh but necessary. Bob Paisley and Wilf McGuiness had struggled with Bill Shankly and Matt Busby being seen at Liverpool and Manchester United having retired. This was smaller scale, sure, but to Strachan it was the biggest job in the world, and Atkinson's presence was bound to only confuse the playing staff.

Amongst that staff and on the terraces there had been murmurings that the wrong man had been asked to step aside. Atkinson's relaxed approach to the game and the players would be missed, while Strachan's more pragmatic style might just hinder their survival hopes. That though proved to be the concern of an unheard few, and most were impressed with how easily he took to the job. 'There was no problem as far as I was concerned,' says Dublin. 'No problem at all, in fact, it was done very smoothly. He was the gaffer immediately and that came from the respect we all had for him from playing and training with him. What you must remember is that we had all grown up watching him, mostly all played against him and had now worked under him as a coach. It was hard not to have time for him.'

Strangely, Strachan's first task as manager had been to arrange a farewell party for Atkinson in a local pub. As much as he wanted to do this alone, he was still a friend and knew how much Atkinson liked this sort of goodbye bash from his days at Manchester United. It was, as ever, a raucous affair. Boys being well-off boys, the drink flowed and as a PR exercise it wasn't an overwhelming success. A brawl and Noel Whelan being breathalysed on his way home wasn't ideal but at least the players saw a side of the new man that suggested he wasn't the strict disciplinarian that some had feared. 'Oh yeah, that was a crazy night,' says Ogrizovic with a knowing snigger. 'Gordon won't thank me for saying but he got hammered. None of us had ever seen him have more than one drink let alone get so pissed but that night he had to be carried out. Of course, he was adamant that someone had spiked his drinks. Noel Whelan got the blame I recall.'

Strachan awoke the next day with a banging hangover. His team were in a similar state. Red eyed, furry tongued and with its queasy looking head right over the Premiership's porcelain, they needed a cure and Strachan had only months to let his medicine do the trick. Things looked terminal after his first game in charge: a League Cup defeat at home to Gillingham was far from what he had hoped for or expected. 'If players listen and play to the standards I require then they should be all right,' he said purposefully in the press conference. 'If not there will be changes. It's up to the players.'

It seemed the players weren't listening as their League form continued to falter and they remained in the bottom two come December. It was then that Strachan made his first positive move and appointed an assistant. Alex Miller, a fellow Scot, had been working with the national team, overlooked many of the sessions taken by Strachan in earning his coaching badges and had played with Alex Ferguson at Rangers. That was the thin extent of their acquaintance but Strachan was sure he had the right man for the job.

'We met in Birmingham to discuss the offer,' says the chirpy Miller sitting at his desk at Liverpool's training ground as their chief scout.

'We'd played against each other so weren't complete strangers but I had to ask, "Why me, Gordon? Why have you asked me?" He told me that he'd seen a lot of me during Euro '96 in England coaching the Scottish side. McAllister had said good things about me too and so he felt I was the best choice.'

Atkinson had had his doubts about the appointment. He wondered whether he possessed the right amount of experience of the Premiership and its players. 'What's more,' he said in his autobiography *Big Ron*, 'he's never exactly been the colourful, bouncy, expansive sort of bloke to rouse a dressing room full of suicidal footballers.'

Results over Christmas though were fantastic, Strachan was named Manager of the Month but the New Year meant old problems and one win in twelve again meant they were stalled at the bottom of the table with seemingly no way back. Strachan feared the worst; action would have to be taken because those suicidal players needed an agony uncle and that is where Atkinson came in.

Strachan was battling hard. His fighting spirit and determination meant he couldn't give up, but he was not too proud to accept an offer from Atkinson to join in training for a week to lift spirits before an impossible-looking trip to Anfield in April. 'Why don't you let me get among the lads for a few days for a jolly-up?' said Atkinson. 'Let me get their chins off the floor and I'll go up for the game with you at the weekend. If you don't like the idea forget I mentioned it.'

Strachan, to a degree, did like the idea. Atkinson had a great record managing clubs against Liverpool and the players could respond to his own brand of inspiration. To an outsider, Ron's presence must have looked like the band still playing as the *Titanic* went down but there was more to it than that. 'Ron had massive respect for Liverpool and used that record of his against them to gee us up,' recalls Burrows. 'He lifted us psychologically and told us that we *could* win the game.'

Spirits were raised but Strachan was aware he needed to keep a check on Atkinson. He didn't want people thinking this was a last act from a desperate man. Atkinson would come to Anfield but sit in the directors' box, not the dug-out. And after that game it would be business as normal. 'If Gordon was put out, he didn't show it,' ponders Burrows. 'At that point people weren't concerned with moods and egos anyway. What needed to be done needed to be done. If he was feeling put upon then tough. He got on with the hands-on stuff that day and we won, brilliant. We were ecstatic.'

It was an incredible win at Liverpool but, despite being followed by a win over Chelsea (inspired by Strachan in his last ever start in pro football) and draws with Southampton and Arsenal, a woeful defeat at home to Derby in the penultimate game of the season left the team up a familiar creek without a paddle. To secure safety Coventry would have to win and both Middlesbrough and Sunderland lose, and so it was a trip to Spurs for what would surely constitute their last game in the top flight for thirty years.

For so long now a Fat Lady in sky blue had been priming her vocal cords, ready to serenade the club from the upper echelons of the English game. Only Arsenal, Everton and Liverpool had been among the top flight longer but now all seemed doomed as she practised her scales and prepared for an almighty swansong. Incredibly she would again be disappointed. A supreme effort and crescendo from Strachan's orchestra instead drowned out her eager tones, which were replaced by a sweet, dulcet calling from the club's disbelieving, but harmonious support: 'STAYING UP, WE'RE STAYING UP, WE'RE STAYING, CITY'S STAYING UP!'

It had been an amazing day, one not matched since Wembley in 1987 when the club's opponents had again been Tottenham Hotspur. As the club's coach slowly made its way into North London though, it was unsure whether Strachan's side would find a way through the London traffic, let alone Spurs' defence. 'We're going to have to ask for a half-hour delay to kick-off,' rasped Strachan over his mobile to an unyielding Premiership official. 'No, no, fifteen minutes isn't enough ... we need thirty minutes ... OK ... OK ... If that's the best you can do for me then so be it, fifteen minutes ... OK bye then ... Prick!'

It wasn't the first time this had happened to the club. In 1977, Coventry were playing Bristol City in the last game of the season knowing they had to better Sunderland's result to stay up. Legend has it that Jimmy Hill had managed to get the game delayed and, with Sunderland having lost at Everton, his side played out a 2–2 draw and were safe. Twenty years later their fans again had those same transistor radios at the ready as their side somehow took a 2–0 lead but were clawed back by a Spurs goal and had to endure the most tense of second halves. Thirty minutes in, and with the final whistles bringing an end to Premiership seasons around the country, Coventry's fans, staff and players heard the news: Sunderland and Middlesbrough had both lost. Hold on and stay up!

'We knew all right,' says Dublin catching his breath just thinking about the day. 'Fans were telling us; the coaches were telling us and of course Gordon was up screaming blue murder at us. For the last ten minutes we played a new system. A stroke of genius from Strachs. We played the ten formation and it was all hands to the decks.'

Strachan paced like an orange tiger cub about his technical area. 'I wanted to get him on,' says Miller. 'He had the experience and I felt that would be ideal, but he suggested that with all the preparation he hadn't trained enough that week. We stood there arguing with mayhem all around us but eventually agreed to disagree.'

Strachan was the powerless manager now. A slalom-like run or infiltrating pass wasn't possible, so he could only stand, bark and hope like a fan that his players kept their concentration. Spurs winger Ruel Fox has the ball and has slipped his man. He's in the box and a hush descends on the ground as the Coventry fans behind the goal stop; their still, sky-blue tops look like a spring afternoon while a cloud of relegation threatens their party. He gets his shot away and it's goal bound but an Ogrizovic leg, the leg of a legend, blocks the ball and a collective sigh gushes from an agonised away end. 'CITY'S STAYING UP!'

Strachan ran straight to McAllister and embraced a man who he had shared triumphs with in the past. They had won nothing this time but here was an outpouring of emotion that bettered anything that he had shown in Gothenburg in 1983, Hampden on countless occasions, Wembley in 1985 or Elland Road in 1992. 'That was relief,' says Miller. 'He was ecstatic to have kept us up but that wouldn't last long. He celebrated with the fans and we had a good knees-up but I think Gordon knew, now the hard work had to really start.'

As the celebrations died down, Strachan knew it wasn't enough. It wasn't enough that a club able to spend £17 million on players was clinging on to its Premiership survival by the skin of its teeth, or rather the skin of Steve Ogrizovic's shins. It had to be addressed. Where did the club go from here, just how good a manager was Gordon Strachan going to be and how would the players respond to the raising of standards? 'We had a good night after the Spurs game, sure,' says Dublin. 'The thing was, though, we hadn't won anything or achieved anything and the Gaffer knew that. It's strange, because you're pleased you're staying up but you didn't want to be too happy with simply avoiding relegation and Strachs drummed that into us. You could see that by how much we improved the following season.'

Coventry City had become a byword for failure. Their success was measured by how many points they had avoided the drop by and it had affected their standing in a game obsessed with achievement and unwilling to focus on the delight on those fans' faces that afternoon as they made their way out of North London. Instead the club had become a cliché for the near miss. It was nothing new; two years earlier, Jasper Rees wrote the following in the *Daily Telegraph*:

> *What, ultimately is the point of Coventry City? ... In 28 seasons they have failed to imprint themselves in the nation's consciousness, let alone its affections ... No one even notices them for most of the calendar, but by an odd coincidence, you vaguely begin to notice them around Valentine's Day, when they begin their annual worm-like wriggle away from danger.*

The Football Factory, a novel about football hooligans begins: 'Coventry City are fuck all. They've got a shit team and shit support. Hitler had the right idea when he flattened the place. The only good thing to come out of the place is The Specials and that was years ago.' OK, so it's a book about the strange mechanisms of the football lout but you catch the drift. The reputation was set in stone and Strachan was intent on addressing it. 'Over the following pre-season we worked the players harder than ever,' says Miller, by now a popular and hard-working assistant. 'We continually put it to them that avoiding relegation wasn't enough and definitely wasn't success. "How far can we go this season?" Gordon would ask them, and it worked.'

The whole club and its manager grew in confidence and proved there was more to it than its Robinson Crusoe-like dedication to survival. The football was good, the plaudits positive and the manager a success. It was as if a plane had spotted the fire on the desert island and the club had returned to competitive civilisation. Strachan's persona as a manger grew. He was on his own, in charge; to use footballer speech, he was the boss, the gaffer. Alex Miller had worked with and observed some of Europe's great managers and was impressed with how professional everything was done by such a young man. 'He was spot on with his methods as a coach,' he says fondly. 'He changed how the club thought about itself and he did it quickly. He wanted to improve fitness, psychology, scouting, he wanted to change it all and he did. The players responded because they knew he was new to all this and got a buzz from his own enthusiasm.'

Strachan was a keen student. 'I think I am getting more and more of it,' he said shortly into his first full season. 'It was a help serving under Big Ron for a time, watching and learning, but you have to do it for yourself.' It seemed he had been watching and learning throughout his career. Coventry beat Chelsea on the opening day of the season and Strachan got his tactics spot on. Gianfranco Zola was man-marked for obvious reasons but to many people's surprise so was their centre-half Frank Leboeuf. Strachan had concluded that much of Chelsea's play was dictated by the expansive defender and by keeping him quiet you could nullify much of their threat. Ron Atkinson had attempted just that when facing Liverpool. Kenny Dalglish was marked and so was Alan Hansen for the same reasons.

Working on theories, putting them into practice, seeing them come off on a Saturday afternoon – it was a job, but a special one. 'You could see how much he was enjoying it,' says Dublin. 'He loved being out on the training pitch, he loved it. He loved to pass on information and loved to see it being taken on board. That's how he got his kicks at work.' That enjoyment transferred itself onto the pitch and Coventry came a marvellous eleventh, securing famous wins over Manchester United, rivals Aston Villa and reaching the quarter-finals of the FA Cup. Amazingly they could enjoy the run-in without the usual sweat on. The final game instead was a stroll at Goodison Park where Everton needed a result to stay up and secured their survival after a draw. For Coventry, like porn stars at a peep-show, it must have been a curious afternoon as they bore witness to the raw emotion that to them for so long had been the norm.

It was a great season. Strachan had moved confidently into the transfer market signing the Swede Magnus Hedman as a replacement for the iconic Ogrizovic, Roland Nielsson, George Boetang and an unknown Romanian striker Viorel Moldovan. All four were a success and in Bryan Richardson Strachan knew he had a man supporting him, still willing to sign those cheques. It was a policy that would eventually cause the club near financial melt-down but in those heady days who was to know? 'He is almost too helpful,' said Strachan at the time. 'All you have to do is mention that so-and-so's not a bad player and he's off to Bucharest or somewhere, and you get a call, "Hi, Gordon, I've just got him for you ... Viorel Moldovan." And I'm trying to shout down the phone, "I only said he wasnae bad!"'

For all the success on the pitch Strachan had to deal with change off it. Alex Miller accepted the manager's job at Aberdeen and would be sorely missed. His presence and input had been invaluable to the new manager and, despite Atkinson's misgivings regarding his experience and personality, he was a hit with the players. 'That pre-season with Miller was instrumental to what we achieved and was the best I'd ever had,' admits Burrows. 'The sessions weren't too long; it was intense but didn't drag. That set up our season nicely and I think it was a body blow to Gordon when he left.'

Miller was eventually replaced by the reserve-team manager Garry Pendrey, but it was a hard transition. Miller had been the perfect foil to Strachan's strive for perfection. A training session would end but the boss would be intent on staying out: 'No way, Alex, we're doing more.' Miller though had the authority and the wherewithal to say no, enough, this is where we end today. 'Alex was very much his own man,' says Burrows. 'Gordon needed that and benefited from Miller's presence and experience. In Alex, Gordon had a man and a coach he could leave to do a session alone, go and let off steam on the golf course and clear his head, knowing all was well with the lads.'

Pendrey was and is a close ally to Strachan. He was his right-hand man as the club moved into the new millennium, comfortable in its new lofty lower- to mid-table surroundings and remained with him at Southampton. To some at Coventry and its fans, though, the concern was he was 'a bibs, balls and cones man', unable to influence the manager when he was going wrong – a yes man. It was harsh criticism as things were usually going right but Strachan was, by now, coming to terms with the fact that his chosen profession was indeed a tough one. Away from the pleasures of the training pitch, away from the camaraderie of the dressing room and away from the intensity of the dug-out, things were not so enjoyable and reality started to bite.

With Coventry avoiding their nail-biting finishes to the season, Strachan had to deal with expectations of himself and his football team. He knew what the limits were; he knew that despite a generous board he was never going to compete for silverware. 'What we have to do is make life as enjoyable as possible for Coventry City fans,' he said after the merriment of the 1998 season. 'It's been great fun this year and that is success for us. When people knock on the door and say I enjoyed that, that was fun, I enjoyed watching you playing. That's our glory.'

Strachan though wouldn't tolerate being the little manager of a fun little football club. His very nature wouldn't stand for that. At Coventry he could be the competitor; competitors don't have to win to succeed but he expected the same from his players. 'If all my players were hungry, I could go to my bed on a Friday night quite content,' he said. 'It doesn't bother me if a player cannot do the same things as Juninho; the thing I cannot handle is someone not giving everything.'

That was Strachan. That was the image we all had and have of him. The full-blooded little player, the archetypal manager and Scot, prowling the touchline with the intensity of a small tornado. A man obsessed, a man who goes home to bed wearing football-covered pyjamas and snoring to the tune of *Match of the Day*. It was an image that worked. In the post-Nick Hornby and lad-mag era when it was cool for football fans to be fanatics somehow guided through life by their love of the 'beautiful game', Strachan's screaming face was one that highlighted the point. SKY TV used exactly that to sell its coverage but to Strachan it was an unfair assumption.

Sure he hadn't mellowed with age; in fact, he had been sent off playing for Coventry's reserves in 1996, was reprimanded for walking onto the Stamford Bridge pitch as assistant in condemnation of a dodgy goal and at the same ground two seasons later was sent off as manager after a scuffle with Chelsea's coaching staff: 'Nothing happened, but they pick out the small ginger-haired guy who wasn't about.'

He would prove later by quitting Southampton just how much his family meant to him and he resents the public persona of him as the mad football professor. 'I've not got an obsession for the game,' he argues. 'I know a lot of people who do and that's fine, but if you have an obsession I think you can blank out everything around you that's good, be it your family, your social life, a bit of entertainment for yourself and your family ... Obsession can do silly things to you and, if you don't get to where you want to be, you become a basket case. I've seen loads of them.'

At home Strachan is able to switch off, be Gordon, but there is no doubt that here is a man who remains in love and lust with the game; so devoted that even what he whistles suggests what he is thinking: Cher's 'If I Could Turn Back Time', when being asked about his playing days; 'The Jackson Sisters' 'I Believe in Miracles' when musing over Coventry's plight. They are reminders that the game is never far from his mind, but doesn't that add to the pressures put upon himself?

'There has to be pressure, has to be,' he said. 'You just cannot get away from it. I find it much harder now than I ever did as a player. I say I'm not obsessed and I'm not but I have respect for the job, you have to, otherwise it will make a laughing stock of you and eventually kick you out. It's a great game, great for the fans but sometimes you realise, as a person in it, that you are just a product for those fans, the pub gossip, that can sometimes be too much.'

To Strachan the pressure, the real pressure was having to get the best out of his team. The buck stopped with him and, while as a player he would often hear from team-mates before the game, 'Wee man, you can get us going today', as manager it was a case of an inner voice urging 'Wee man, you *must* get them going today.'

The volatile Strachan, when dealing with the stresses of modern management, could blow that short fuse at crude gestures, that at other times he would simply laugh off. For example, he and Lesley were stuck in a traffic jam in the Midlands during his time as manager at Coventry. We've all been there, stuck behind the school bus, the boys from out of the back window gesticulating in a less than polite fashion as we smile through gritted teeth. Strachan though shot out of the car, boarded the bus and gave the boys the shock of their lives by royally ticking them off. It was a strange release valve when often there isn't one to be found.

Chastising naughty schoolboys was not exclusive to the local roads. Strachan loved nothing more than joining in games with the youth players. He would stay behind late, turn up early, just to see them play and improve but, if they stepped out of line, then he felt was the time to get at them, make sure they knew the score. Strachan is playing a small-sided game with some of the trainees and the staff. He is as enthusiastic and as competitive as ever. The game in fact won't end until his team has won. A young hopeful collects the ball and is challenged by the boss. The kid slips the ball though Strachan's legs. 'Nuts,' he shouts, as the on-looking senior pros can only wince in horror at the boy's fatal error. 'We all just stopped,' says Burrows, laughing. 'We knew what was coming. Gordon laid into the kid, letting him know his place in the grand scheme of things. I don't know if the boy made it but if he did he must have had amazing mental strength.'

Cheeky schoolboys, insolent trainees, they had a harsh Scottish tongue-lashing coming their way, but unfortunately so too did some senior pros. Strachan had been brought up by the old school and soon realised that the players under him at Coventry were not all the same as the ones who had played alongside him. The Stuart Kennedys, the Drew Jarvies, they were hard-working professionals, but today's game meant often dealing with well-paid celebrities and Strachan had to adjust. It wasn't easy though. To Strachan the new generation came with accessories. The car, the phones, the model girlfriend, a pushy agent, all were necessary if you were going to fit into the dressing room's hierarchy. 'When I was a young player, managers never had these problems,' he bemoaned two years into his managerial career. 'Now players are bigger than the club and you can't just wield a big stick like Alex Ferguson did at Aberdeen, where he put the fear of God into everybody.'

Maybe not a big stick but he certainly managed to bruise a few egos with an icy glare or a granite turn of phrase. When Strachan was finally sacked in 2001, a few of the players commented how nice it was to be treated again like adults and respected by the new man Roland Nilsson. Central defender Gary Breen for one had not liked Strachan's manner from the start and felt put upon by the feisty manager but that's football – men don't have to be and so often aren't bosom buddies. If it was the new breed of player that upset Strachan, it is a shame that one of his players that he fell out with was one of the old guard, a solid and dependable professional, David Burrows. Burrows invests in houses rather than Ferraris, has moved to France rather than the Costa del Sol, but left the club and its manager with a sour taste in his mouth.

By the Christmas of 1999 the Midlander had been waiting on a new contract that was not forthcoming. Strachan had told him that he didn't know what the club would be able to offer him, but Burrows at least wanted to hear that they would talk come the New Year. 'He wasn't being honest with me,' says Burrows, still clearly upset by the events of almost five years ago. 'He couldn't be straight and that hurt. He could have said, "Listen, David, play for me for the rest of the year and then I will help you get a good move." He didn't.

'Ironically the team were suffering and he needed me towards the end of that season. He came to me and said here is a two-year contract. I was suspicious but said OK and left it at that. Nothing was ever said about it again. It was a lie, there was no contract, and he only said it to keep me sweet so I'd play hard for him. That I felt was disrespectful. I lost a lot of respect for him through that. I was devastated. I'd always got on so well with Strachan. We played golf at each other's clubs and I had a lot of time for him. We haven't spoken since. Some players are arseholes, I'll admit that, but I had played for him for five years and played properly. He was a young manager and was learning. I hope he learned from that.'

Much of the ill feeling between manager and player these days concerns contracts and even Dion Dublin left for Aston Villa under a cloud, when the club were unwilling to pay him £20,000 a week. It was part of the job, though, part of the modern game, and Strachan had to deal with it. The same went for the press. The public today know him of course by his antics in front of the cameras and microphones but to him that is him at his least natural. It is another part of the job he could do without. Not quite as stomach churning as dealing with agents granted, but still an annoyance at best.

'I just find that it is a game we play,' he has admitted. 'Reporters versus managers – and it's not a game I enjoy to be honest. You try and get information out of me and hopefully somewhere along the line I'll say something sensational, which makes the headlines. The game I play is I'll try and give you answers but without giving you that quote.' Strachan has become a champion of that game. 'You keep chucking 'em at me and I'll keep batting them away.' That's exactly what he does. As a manager, Strachan could revert back to his boyhood days, use a joke as a shield against those bigger, intimidating boys out to get him, and then move on unscathed.

There was so much to learn. Let's recap. Expectations, his own obsession, the pressures of management, the modern player, the press, it was tough but that was nothing compared to the lesson he, like all managers, has had to learn: just when you think you've got it sussed it can all go wrong. Coventry had finished fifteenth and then fourteenth in 1999 and 2000; players had come and gone; he had an improved contract and had attracted attention, as one of the countries most celebrated young coaches, from a host of bigger clubs.

Robbie Keane had been bought in for £6 million; Moroccan World Cup stars Mustapha Hadji and Youssef Chippo arrived for £5 million; McAllister was pulling the strings; even Strachan's oldest boy Gavin was a first-team player, and there on merit. That though meant no special treatment. 'Bloody hell, no,' says Burrows, laughing. 'There was no cotton wool around Gavin; in fact, he was on the end of some mad bollockings I can tell you. It was business as usual, kids or no kids. Craig, his other son, was on the books too, but had had injury problems. They are smashing boys; all his kids are a credit to him and Lesley.'

The team had done well; they were nicknamed 'the entertainers' by the local press and Strachan's stock was up but it was about to all go wrong. In 2001, after 34 years in the top flight, Strachan was about to enjoy the infamy of being the man who finally took Coventry City down. But why now? Why when everything had looked so secure? 'I had gone by then,' says Burrows flatly. 'I could see that things were not right as I left though. Gordon had done a lot in the transfer market and brought in lots of foreign players. It didn't work. We had become an attractive team to play for and at that point had hoped to push on from mid-table. It should have gone on from strength to strength but it didn't.'

McAllister left for Liverpool, Robbie Keane was sold to Inter Milan for a huge profit and that, rather than success, was now the objective for clubs like Coventry. His replacement Craig Bellamy showed none of the exciting form that he has since shown at Newcastle and time began to run out.

As did the cash. Coventry City, like so many others, were about to pay for chasing the dream. The team lacked cohesion. Like the condemned prisoner who, for so long had waited on Death Row, sensing a reprieve over his last two years, only to have to finally make that walk to the chair, Coventry disappeared from Premiership sight. It was McAllister who scored the goals that effectively sent them down and for all Strachan's dogged resistance there was nothing he could do about it.

Throughout the tribulations of 2001, Bryan Richardson had been a solid ally to Strachan, whose popularity had dwindled on his own terraces, as relegation got ever closer. The two had bravely attended a supporters' club dinner. 'I hope the bread rolls aren't hard,' the manager said, leaning over to his chairman nervously. 'Because I reckon a lot of them will be heading in our direction.'

Strachan was eager to carry on and get on with the job of bringing the club back up as quickly as possible. He had moved into the transfer market and signed West Bromwich Albion's Lee Hughes and hoped that with Richardson's support and the fans' patience things could get back on track. He got neither and soon it was more than a stale bread roll threatening the manager. They had won their first game at Stockport but failed to win any of their next four games including a final 1–0 loss at home to Grimsby. That was enough to see the fans' frustrations literally spill onto the pitch and aimed viciously at Strachan.

Hatred and abuse rained down on the manager and his staff that afternoon as Strachan made his way from the pitch to the dressing room for what would be the last time. Reports stated that he went straight to the board that evening and resigned, but those who know the man were adamant that he was not one to walk away because of a bit of terrace scorn. 'He called me at about 7.30 that night,' recalls Mark McGhee, who had witnessed his friend thriving on similar abuse from fans while at Aberdeen. 'He sounded very disappointed but, as always, very mature. He'd have taken as much aggro as anybody was able to throw at him in order to turn it around. I don't think he's ever been a quitter and that's why he played as long as he did and in the way he did. He has this inner belief, this determination, and he'd have stayed there as long as he could.'

That thick skin had been pierced but he could live with a mere flesh wound as long as the board could. He went home with a League Cup tie at Peterborough that week on his mind as much as the rantings of some angry fans. He had his parents down from Edinburgh to stay and attend the christening of his first grandchild. As ever, Gordon's father was riveted by his boy's progress and so joined him at training that Monday. With Gavin there, too, three generations of Strachans were in attendance but when the manager noticed his chairman's car he knew it was going to be far from a day to celebrate the family name.

Strachan and Richardson chatted amicably for hours. The latter spelled out that it was agreed that his manager's presence at the club, given the fans' grievances, was a hindrance and that the players' concentration levels were being fatally undermined. There was no scene, no fuss. Strachan was proud of what he had done, proud of how he had handled his first, challenging job. He took Lesley, or should that be Lesley took him, back to Edinburgh that night to escape the rigmarole that surrounds a sacked manager. There it is, that word, sacked. It had happened and was another vital ingredient of any football manager's syllabus. Now, back where it had all begun in Edinburgh, he was left to ponder where it would all go next.

16. SAINTS ALIVE

> GORDON: *I've got more important things to think about. I've got a yoghurt to finish by today, the expiry date is today. That can be my priority rather than Agustin Delgado.*

'Help of the helpless, Lord ... Abide ... With ... Me.' As the Cup final hymn comes to an end he looks over at the opposition: Robert Pires, Patrick Viera, Thierry Henry; he may need some of that help. A mammoth roar and what looks like a million yellow and blue balloons go up towards the ... hold on, not the sky – the Millennium Stadium's retractable roof is today covering the May sunshine. That is not the only strange thing about the occasion. Here he stands, not limbering up, not worrying only about his own performance but instead that of maybe fourteen others. Instead of kit, a tracksuit and a nervous smile, he wears the club's well-cut FA Cup final suit. The pink shirt and tie match his sun-touched cheeks as the guest of honour Sir Bobby Robson shakes his hand and offers a few words of luck and advice. Here he stands, the biggest game of his managerial adventure to date. He's won them in Scotland; he's won them in England, and now as the boss he is about to watch his team in Wales.

He had learned the hard way that, just when you are expecting a gentle kiss, football can kick you in the backside. Still bruised, the game was about to rekindle her affections for him only weeks after he was sent *from* Coventry. He had left Highfield Road proud but hurt. Just as he had doubted himself when playing in Scotland, when joining Manchester United and Leeds, and when accepting the manager's job at Coventry, uncertainty and question marks about his own character dogged his sleep. He'd get up and watch a film rather than the ceiling, with a feeling that, for all he had achieved, it wasn't enough. 'It almost made me feel like a bad person, let alone a bad manager.' For all his confidence on the pitch, it had taken him until he was forty, and having finally retired, to appreciate how good a player he was. Now he could hardly rid himself of that angst that in some form had always been there, but would also drive him onwards.

But then came a job offer, a job offer with a purpose. As Leeds had asked him as a player to bring them back to life, Southampton Football Club were now imploring him to help before a fatality could occur. To some Southampton fans – still perhaps aggrieved that as Coventry manager Strachan had had words with a few of them during a game at the Dell the previous season – that decision needed to be explained. It was a mixed reaction and those unsure aired their views on various phone-in shows, concerned that here was a man who had only just taken a club of similar standing to their own into the First Division, becoming far from popular in the city on the way.

Having lost Glenn Hoddle to his native Tottenham at the end of March that same year, Stuart Gray had been given the post of managing the club. Many locals thought then that the club had missed the boat when it came to appointing the new man. The experience of Harry Redknapp had been available; the promise of David Moyes had shown an interest and come close to the getting the job, but it was Gray who finally got the nod from a board willing to give him a chance. Although not for long.

Gray's record of only four wins in seventeen matches as the full-time boss (he had come in as caretaker) meant the club, come October – and as Strachan was making his way from Coventry – were second from bottom of the Premiership, which, like Coventry, was not exactly pastures new but it wasn't acceptable to a club who had just moved into a pristine new stadium capable of entertaining 32,000 fans.

Southampton had lost again at West Ham on the Saturday and so on Sunday Gray was asked to leave. Southampton's chairman Rupert Lowe had been a long-time fan of Strachan, having enjoyed his company whenever his team had faced Coventry. He was a friend of Bryan Richardson and with his club's struggles in mind approached the resting manager the Tuesday before Gray's sacking. 'It wasn't a long-term plan carried out behind Stuart's back,' argues Lowe. 'It was a club preparing itself for a change that was by now pretty inevitable.

'We had appointed Stuart in good faith. I feel that, in football, it is important that there is a supply of up and coming young managers and that isn't possible unless they are given the chance. The downside to that is, if they get the chance and it doesn't work out, then they have a problem. We all know the rules and Stuart knew he had eight games into the new season and the bottom line was it wasn't working. I therefore approached Gordon. He was scarred after what had happened at Coventry but he wanted another go and I gave him that chance. We chatted and I basically liked the cut of his jib.'

Strachan's jib was back in the game. He and Lesley had taken in some football at home and abroad simply as fans; he'd helped around the house for the first time in years, and both were ready for more than the eventual six weeks he had off between jobs. Lesley for one thought he was mad even thinking about the job so soon after Highfield Road. The situations were too similar, the risk too great. If he took Southampton down as well, think of the consequences. Strachan secretly felt the same but this was a job, a big one and how did he know a similar chance would arise again?

Strachan felt sorry for Gray, he knew more than anyone how he felt, but that's life. Now was the time to prove to the doubters (and in some small way that meant himself) that he could do the job. Having started in the town of Discovery, like Captain Scott, he seemed drawn south. 'My next job will be Marseille,' he joked, but he was serious about how he wanted to see his team play and perform. The club had lost key players such as Dean Richards and Hassan Kachloul, but he had been promised some of that money to spend and set about trying to convince the doubters that he would – having been a punter himself for six weeks – bring a style and flair to the place that hadn't been enjoyed since Kevin Keegan's perm was all the rage. 'I feel this club,' he said purposefully during his first press conference, 'should be challenging for a European spot.'

Garry Pendrey joined him as his assistant and Paul Williams also followed from Coventry to replace Richards at centre-half. The squad and the club were suffering the same old problems, but now they had a brand new stadium, a brand new manager and soon a brand new meaning to the words 'fitness training'. Strachan had said all the right words about how pleasing on the eye he hoped to make Southampton, but, when it came to work at their Staplewood training ground, it was going to have to be hard, hard graft.

To Strachan, it was all about starting with the basics. A player has to walk before he can run, and for now he would have to run before he could play. 'Character running,' as Strachan so sweetly called it was a shock. It's running, and then running some more and then running again, until you're nearly sick. It was hard, but, after their players' pale, off-green faces got used to it, the rewards were reaped and vital games won. It wasn't going to happen overnight though.

Sceptical fans had reason to feel smug when, after four games, they had only won one point under the new man. The club were yet to win a game at St Mary's and things got so bad that they even called in a witch to exorcise any unwanted lodgers. 'I didn't know the witch had been there,' said Strachan with a laugh when he heard. 'But she can take training for the next two weeks if she wants so I can practise my golf.' At the end of November with a heady mix of sweat, hard work and black magic, Southampton won their first game at St Mary's, beating Charlton 1–0, and to Strachan that was all the voodoo his team needed.

The Londoners had hit the post in the last minute and with that his side's luck changed. Strachan saw that as the catalyst, the turning point and they slowly with increased fitness and rejuvenated self-belief climbed out of trouble. Strachan had silenced those disbelievers and could sleep without having to watch another John Wayne or Humphrey Bogart flick. Not that he would get comfortable; his objectives, having spent enough time in a manager's overcoat, were simple and clear. He still felt a novice and therefore was adamant that his aim must be to survive; have a job in the modern game and you must be doing well. He saw an increasing blame-culture had taken a stranglehold on those trying to get by and learn their trade. If he could still be in a job this time next year, that represented success; the rest would be a bonus.

Strachan's impact, authority and raised level of professionalism hauled Southampton to a respectable eleventh that season. He had brought the best out of his players and used a canny knowledge to help get results. His was an honest squad, but a small one where the only thing likely to rotate was the players' stomachs after another bout of 'character running'. Its size dictated that those good players he had at his disposal would have to be utilised properly and that is where he came in.

Wayne Bridge had been a good left-back, a popular local player but hardly setting the world alight. Strachan saw something in him, saw that he wasn't getting involved enough in games and wasn't getting forward. He had Chris Marsden, a central midfielder, move from the centre of midfield to the left with instructions to remain narrow so as to allow Bridge to overlap. It worked a treat and the two forged a partnership that went a long way to explaining the success the club enjoyed as well as why Chelsea were prepared to splash out £7 million on the left-back in question.

Bridge and Marsden weren't the only success stories. James Beattie went from being a struggling forward likely to be sold to an England forward likely to score goals, and that summer Finland's goalkeeper Antti Niemi arrived from Hearts. Strachan had been a fan of the peroxide blond keeper for a number of years and had tried to sign him at Coventry in 1997. Niemi and his agent had arrived in the city to sign the contracts but were first enjoying breakfast when the agent's mobile rang. It was Glasgow Rangers wondering if he'd signed yet. 'He hasn't. That's great,' said the excited voice down the phone. 'Tell him not to because we want him.' That was that, Niemi was on his way to Scotland. Not that Strachan didn't pursue the man.

'Antti,' he said over the phone having heard the news, 'don't sign for them. I'm in Spain playing golf and you've ruined my round but I'm getting a flight home now.' It was too late but, five years later, Niemi was eager to play Premiership football, and Strachan hoped this time he'd get his Finn.

'I think he understood my reasons for not joining back then,' says Niemi, whose enthusiasm when approached by me to chat about Strachan underlined his fondness for the man. 'A choice between Rangers and Coventry had been pretty straightforward but he was still keen. I thought about Southampton's offer and, as well as the Premiership now selling itself to me, I was touched that he must have really seen something in me to come back after I had said no, all those years ago.'

Niemi was impressed with the set-up, the ground, the ambitions, but most of all the manager. 'He told me how confident he was in the squad, how he felt it could really compete in the Premiership and even take honours. He had a great way about him, very funny, but I wasn't laughing when I got to the training pitch.' Welcome to the south coast. 'Every day he had us working hard, but do you know what, no one worked harder than Gordon Strachan. He was the first one on and the last one off the training pitch. As a player you respect that; you instinctively follow that example.'

Popular and admirable maybe, but Strachan had lost none of his authority and would rule as ever with an iron fist or tongue if need be. He arrived at the club and, along with the basics in fitness, he assured his players that he would not tolerate unprofessional behaviour. He made himself known to a local night-spot, The Lizard Lounge, in order to keep tabs on stray pros and when one player, who hadn't taken his manager's words seriously enough, arrived at training smelling of booze he was immediately fined two weeks' wages. The rule, henceforth, was strictly observed. 'When you have thirty young men in a working environment there are going to be rows,' admits Niemi, with a strange Scandinavian-cum-cockney accent. 'He could be very hard on us when we were playing badly but no one ever questioned his authority and that is something you have or you don't.'

There were reports about the odd rift but they were just the everyday goings-on of a football club. Just as you would have disagreements on the shop floor or around the Cabinet, these were working disagreements. He had learned from the problems he had faced at Coventry regarding some players and was more prepared to curb his desire to scream at those who stepped out of line. During the memorable 2002/03 season, there had been reports suggesting a few of the players weren't happy with the way things were going. They weren't happy with being left out and that was fine by Strachan. That was real; even he could recall that emotion. Andrei Kanchelskis had arrived on a free transfer from Rangers in the summer of 2002 but was unable to get into the team, and wasn't happy about it. 'Well, play better, and be fit,' came the curt reply from the manager.

Andres Svensson, Fabrice Fernandes, Kevin Davies, they may also have been upset about Cup final places and substitutions but, when push came to shove, Strachan was their boss not their enemy. This was highlighted towards the end of Strachan's tenure when Fernandes was involved in a car accident on a Hampshire road. Shook up, the first person he called and the first person on the scene was his manager.

Not so much the ogre any more but he had remained the jack-in-the-box when it came to watching his team. That trait came with the territory he found himself working in. 'The managers who can sit there and relax are the ones with great players,' he argues when questioned about his touchline antics. 'The ones who get all excitable are usually at the wrong end of the table, with not so great players. If you have great players you can just sit back, light the big Jack cigar, and say, on you go, boys, entertain me. If I was the manager of Brazil or Juventus I'd be the most relaxed man in the world.' Success, winning games, seeing players win international caps, that might relax him but that wasn't always possible, and, while it is hard to imagine him in the lotus position or saluting-the-sun, he's content with his feet up at home and *Countdown* on the television.

If a winning manager is a calmer manager, Strachan was a far more content man during the second half of the season. His team were winning; Europe was tentatively being mentioned (although the closest thing to Europe he would allow himself to talk about was his annual golfing trip to La Manga in Spain) and he, Lesley and his now teenage daughter Gemma had settled nicely into their Hampshire home. The sweet villages strewn with cattle-grids, wild ponies comfortably walking the fields and pavements alike – it's hard not to fall in love with the place, and now with survival and competitive football assured, the feeling was more than reciprocated. Southampton's own version of the Tartan Army had appeared, with red wigs and tartan hats a feature on the terraces. His journey from sinner to McSaint was complete and about to get better.

As the snow melted from the New Forest's beautiful woodland, and winter turned to spring, Southampton found themselves in the semi-final of the FA Cup for the first time since 1986. Back in January an in-form Tottenham team were taken apart at St Mary's in front of the live television cameras. The club were in and out of the top seven in the Premiership and First Division opposition were forming a winnable path to Cardiff. 'We were brilliant against Spurs,' recalls Niemi. 'Then some people said we had it easy, not having to play against Premiership opponents again on our run but they forget that we were seconds away from going out against Millwall in the fourth round before Kevin Davies scored and we won the replay.'

Of course, Strachan would, like a resolute Scottish schoolmaster, argue that it was the League form that was all-important, as that was how a team would be judged, but even he couldn't help but throw off the mortarboard and drop the cane as the Cup run took flight. 'Of course, we were constantly reminded about League form,' says Niemi, laughing. 'However, you could see he was enjoying the experience. I think he relaxed as we rode our luck and got closer and closer. It was great.'

Norwich and Wolves were dispatched in later rounds and so it was on to Villa Park for a semi-final with Watford. Strachan was no longer in charge of the underdog – the pressures that came with that were different – but he enjoyed sending out a team who could look each other in the eye and, along with an excitable group of fans, expect to win. Watford were seen off 2–1 and to many the joy of getting to the Cup final was better than the final itself. The FA Cup can be a vilified old lady in today's Champions' League-obsessed environment, but as the final whistle went in Birmingham, as if marking the start of a momentous party, it was a throwback to the days when it meant a team had won the right to be part of the greatest of days. Strachan immediately turned and caught the eye of Lesley who today was accompanied by a toddler loving every minute of his first game and seeing his granddad's smiling face.

So on to Cardiff. Southampton's last final had been in 1976. Strachan was a nineteen-year-old footballer with recently relegated Dundee when Bobby Stokes slipped through to score the winning goal for the Second Division side against Manchester United. This time it would be the holders Arsenal. They had just thrown their Championship away but represented the harshest of tests. 'They are the best team in the country now,' says Niemi, 'and to me they were the best team then. They were clear favourites but we went intent on doing well and giving them more than just a good game.'

Southampton had already beaten Arsenal back in November and, despite losing heavily to them only ten days before Cardiff, their manager, in his own unmistakable way, remained upbeat. 'Despite that result,' he quipped on the eve of the final, 'we had twelve goal attempts and scored one; they had thirteen and scored six.' With such easy logic, gulfs in class can be minimised and the players went to the final confident and excited.

'As a young boy even dreaming about it you don't realise how fantastic an occasion it really is,' says Niemi with all the enthusiasm that epitomises so many foreign players who take part in our showpiece event. 'The actual game flies by but the days leading up to it will stay with me. I did a press conference on the Thursday with Beats [James Beattie] and I sat there looking at all the press and the microphones and realised they were all marked with media associations from around the world: Canada, Peru, Africa. I turned to Beats and said, "Fuckin' hell, this *must* be big."'

Strachan stood above his players in the dressing room and waited to address the team. He had had a hard morning having to go to individual rooms first thing to tell men they wouldn't be starting or even playing. He had been left out in 1978 by Billy McNeill and knew how it felt but he was the manager now. He wasn't here to enjoy the big occasions like players; he was there to make sure they were run efficiently. For all the joy of seeing the fans, their colour, his family and his players play the biggest game of their lives, it was those faces of professionals he had to tell would not be involved that was an abiding memory.

'When you come back here having finished the match I want you to promise me one thing,' he said to an expectant team. 'Promise me you'll be able to look each other in the eye without regret. I want no guilt in this room.' With that the bell sounded and it was time to walk the team out onto the pitch and the wall of noise and colour generated by 75,000 fans. As Strachan walked out a proud man, he was struck by the mass of yellow. The shirts, the flags, the scarves, the balloons swayed like sunflowers as he waved to Lesley, his parents, his children and theirs.

'It was just a great day for Southampton Football Club,' purrs Lowe. 'I stood there ever so proud of what Gordon had done and what the club had achieved. To see everyone's families there, it was special. A seminal moment in one's life if you like. The only sadness was that we didn't win, but judging by our fans you would have thought we had.'

Southampton's supporters cheered the team on but there was to be no repeat of 27 years earlier. It was close though. A Pires goal in the first half separated the two teams but David Seaman had to make a sharp save from Beattie to prevent extra-time, in which Strachan was confident that his fit side would have prevailed. It wasn't to be. Having reached the final, Southampton had qualified for Europe but that was all to come. The players and Strachan took the plaudits and savoured the applause. He had come a long way since leaving Coventry and was adamant that he would enjoy this. Not that he wanted to go overboard, that wouldn't do. There would be no consolation parade in an open-top bus around the town. 'Gordon and I felt it was inappropriate to celebrate losing,' explains Lowe. A sure sign just how far the club had developed under their manager.

Strachan left the players and fans to it. That was enough of the spotlight and it was time to find Lesley, have a drink with his mum and dad and start thinking about the following season. As he walked away from the pitch, the laughter lines around his sparkling eyes told a tale about his career to date. The day was now just another set of blurred memories. As great as finals and medals are, it was the less glitzy occasions that would stay with Gordon Strachan. 'If you ask me about picking up a medal, I can't remember. But if you ask me about sitting in the bath at Dundee after a hard day's training and singing with the boys when I was fifteen or sixteen, I can remember that. I cannae remember much about picking up the trophies. But if you ask me about jokes and incidents with people, I can remember that, things that make you laugh, sometimes make you cry.'

BIBLIOGRAPHY

Big Ron: A Different Ball Game (Andre Deutsch 1998) by Ron Atkinson

The Official Manchester United Illustrated History (Carlton Books 2001) by Justyn Barnes, Adam Bostock, Cliff Butler, Aubrey Ganguly, Graham McColl and Mark Wylie

David Batty: The Autobiography (Headline 2001) by David Batty

Looking for Eric: In Search of the Leeds Greats (Mainstream Publishing 2000) by Rick Broadbent

Coventry City: The Elite Era, a Complete Record (Desert Island Books 1998) by Jim Brown

More than a Match: A Player's Story (Stanley Paul 1992) by Lee Chapman

The Boss (Simon and Schuster 2002) by Michael Crick

Manchester United: The Quest for Glory 1966–1991 (Sidgwick and Jackson 1991) by Tommy Docherty

Managing My Life: My Autobiography (Hodder and Stoughton 1999) by Alex Ferguson with Hugh McIlvanney

Staying Up: A Fan Behind the Scenes in the Premiership (Little Brown and Company 1998) by Rick Gekoski

The Story of the World Cup (Faber and Faber 2002) by Brian Glanville

The Leeds United Story (Breedon Books 2002) by Martin Jarred and Malcolm Macdonald

Vinnie: The Autobiography (Headline 1999) by Vinnie Jones

Scotland: The Complete International Football Record (Breedon Books 2001) by Richard Keir

Bob Paisley: Manager of the Millennium (Robson Books 2001) by John Keith

The Essential History of Leeds United (Headline 2000) by Andrew Mourant

The Official Manchester United Illustrated Encyclopaedia (Manchester United Books 1998) by Jillian Somerscales, Deborah Murrell and Louise Pritchard (editors)

Aberdeen, A Centenary History 1903–2003 (Desert Island Books 2002) by Kevin Stirling

Strachan Style (Mainstream Publishing 1991) by Gordon Strachan, with Ken Gallacher

Gordon Strachan, An Autobiography (Stanley Paul 1984) by Gordon Strachan, with Jack Webster

The First 100 Years of the Dons: The Official History of Aberdeen Football Club 1903–2003 (Hodder and Stoughton 2002) by Jack Webster

Cantona (Virgin Books 2002) by Rob Wightman

INDEX

Aberdeen 9, 17, 21, 27, 28, 33–99, 107, 109, 116, 117, 118, 119, 120–2, 123, 125, 132, 134, 135, 144, 146, 150, 152, 154–9, 166, 182, 190, 191, 193, 222, 223, 229
Adams, Tony 160–1
Aitken, Roy 133, 154, 158, 159
Aitken, Tom 9, 14, 19, 62, 140, 141, 143
Aizlewood, Mark 170
Albiston, Arthur 14, 15, 18, 104, 113, 159
Anderson, Ian 122
Archibald, Steve 36, 38, 51, 52, 54, 56–7, 59, 120, 133, 134, 200
Arnott, Tom 19
Arsenal 25–6, 33, 100, 161, 186, 211, 237
Aston Villa 182, 227
Atkinson, Ron ix, 98, 100, 101, 102, 103, 104–5, 107, 108, 110, 111, 114, 115, 123, 128, 129, 160, 161, 163, 165, 166, 190, 204, 206, 207, 208–9, 210, 211, 212, 213, 214, 215–16, 217, 218, 222, 223
Augenthaler, Klaus 87
Auld, Bertie 28, 44

Bailey, Gary 116
Baird, Ian 170
Ball, Alan 25, 26, 167
Barcelona 124
Barnes, John 126
Barros, Omar 145
Bassett, Dave 176
Batista, Jose 145
Batty, David 172–3, 177, 179, 188, 195, 198, 201, 202
Bayern Munich 66, 82–7, 95
Beasant, Dave 213
Beattie, James 1, 4, 130, 234, 237, 238
Beckenbauer, Franz 78–9, 83, 143, 194–5
Beckett, Alex 37
Beckham, David 103, 117, 125, 202
Beglin, Jim 173–4
Bell, Dougie 67, 85
Bellamy, Craig 228
Best, George 18, 111
Big Ron 114, 218
Black, Eric 49, 67, 79, 87, 90, 92, 158
Boetang, George 222
Bould, Steve 161
Bowyer, Lee 202
Bradford City 173
Brazil, Alan 77, 78, 102, 104, 131, 133, 136, 137, 138
Brazil 64, 144
Breen, Gary 226
Breitner, Paul 83, 84, 85, 88
Bremner, Billy 26, 131, 164, 167, 170, 203
Bridge, Wayne 233, 234
Brown, Craig 142, 144, 147, 183
Brown, Mick 206
Bruce, Steve 125, 201
Buchan, Martin 56, 98, 104
Buchanan, Archie 17
Burley, George 77, 133
Burns, Tommy 153
Burrows, David 207, 212, 218, 223, 225, 226, 228
Busby, Sir Matt 102, 104, 114, 127, 167, 184, 216

Caldwell, Alec 22, 23, 24, 25, 29, 32, 33, 151
Cantona, Eric 185–6, 187, 188, 198, 199, 201
Capello, Fabio 162
Cascarino, Tony 196
Celtic 23, 27, 29, 33, 34, 36, 37, 38, 42, 43, 49, 51, 52–3, 54, 55, 58, 62, 65–7, 70, 71, 74, 91, 120, 125, 132, 141, 152–3, 155, 157–8, 173
Chapman, Lee 172, 175, 177, 181, 182, 183, 185, 186, 188, 195, 202
Charlton, Sir Bobby 105, 111, 114, 123
Chelsea 187, 219, 222, 224, 233
Chippo, Youssef 227
Clark, Bobby 36, 48, 49, 54, 55, 75
Clark, John 39
Clarke, Allan 164

Clemence, Ray 76
Clough, Brian 183, 211
Cocker, Les 184
Collins, Bobby 167
Cologne 100, 117
Connery, Sean 11, 137
Cooke, Charlie 9
Cooper, Davie 63, 133, 140, 141
Cooper, Neal 49, 64, 67, 85, 90
Cooper, Paul 78
Cooper, Terry 167
Cork, Alan 188
Coventry City 2, 160, 161, 187, 192, 204, 205–29, 230, 224, 225, 230, 231–2, 234, 235, 238
Craigroysten school 9–10, 12, 13, 14, 15, 16, 17–18, 19, 27, 53, 105
Crerand, Paddy 104, 184
Cropley, Alec 25

Dalglish, Kenny 12, 42, 43, 76, 107–8, 129, 131, 133, 134, 137, 142, 148, 150, 196, 222
Davenport, Peter 114, 126
Davidson, Duncan 47
Davies, Kevin 235
Davison, Bobby 170
Day, Mervyn 174
Deane, Brian 202, 203
Denmark 142–3, 144
di Stefano, Alfredo 91
Dickson, John 10, 12, 13, 19, 20
Docherty, Tommy 102, 127
Dodd, Jason 4
Donald, Dick 43, 44, 45, 51, 63, 122
Donnelly, Dick 33–4
Dorigo, Tony 180, 182
Dublin, Dion 194, 205, 208, 209, 210, 211, 216–17, 219–20, 222, 227
Duncan, John 21
Dundee 17–20, 21–39, 56, 102, 108, 114, 151, 152, 166, 190, 192, 193, 237, 238
Dundee United 14, 27, 28, 37, 46, 49, 50, 53, 57, 59, 65, 66, 106, 112
Durban, Alan 64
Drybrough Cup 25
1980/81 57–8

Edinburgh Schools Select 14
Edinburgh Thistle 9, 13–14, 16, 17, 62
Edinburgh, Justin 210
Edwards, Martin 99–100
Eintracht Frankfurt 91
Ellis, Doug 206
Elvis 11, 154
England, Mike 140
England, Sir Patrick 60
English Division One:
1985/6 111–12, 125
1986/7 114–15
1988/9 126–9, 168–9
1989/90 168–9, 170–6
1991/2 180–9
1992/3 198–202
1993/4 202
1994/5 203–4
English League Cup:
1991/2 184
English Premiership:
1995/6 205–14
1996/7 214–22
2000/1 228–9
2002/3 235–6
2003/4 3–5
European Championships:
1980 132–3
1984 139–40
1988 148, 150
1996 218
European Cup:
1960 58, 91
1975 167, 170–1
1980 58–9, 77–9, 107, 222
European Cup Winners Cup:
1966/7 73–4
1982/3 62, 65, 66, 67–8, 72–5, 80–95, 95, 97, 119–20
1983/4 97–8
European Super Cup:
1983 95
Eusebio 139
Evans, Allan 14–15
Everton 107, 109, 110, 111, 177, 188, 215

FA Cup:
1984/5 106–11, 116
1985/6 236
1986/7 210
1988/9 127–8
1991/2 184
1996/7 222
2002/3 1, 236–8
Fairclough, Chris 168, 185, 195, 201
Ferdinand, Les 194

Ferguson, Alex ix, 44–7, 50, 51, 53, 54, 55, 57, 58–60, 61, 62–3, 65, 66–7, 69, 70, 75, 76, 78, 79, 80–1, 83, 84, 85, 86, 88, 90, 91, 92, 93, 95, 97, 98–9, 102, 103, 104, 113, 116–28, 131, 140, 141, 142, 144, 145, 146, 152, 163, 181, 199, 211, 217, 222, 226
Fernandes, Fabrice 235
Finland 150
First 100 Years of the Dons, The (Webster) 73
Fitzpatrick, Tony 45, 151
Flynn, Sean 211
Football Association 163
Football Factory, The 221
Ford, Bobby 22
Forsyth, Tom 156
Forsythe, Roddy 162
Fotherby, Bill 180
Fox, Ruel 220
France 101
France Football 158
Francis, Trevor 185

Galvin, Tony 59
Garner, Willie 74
Gayle, Brian 188
Gemmell, Tommy 28, 29–31, 33
Gemmill, Archie 133, 135
Gibbons, Glenn 48
Gibson, Terry 114, 126
Giggs, Ryan 181, 184
Giles, Johnny 167
Gilzean, Alan 19
Glover, Brian 208
Graham, Arthur 38, 39–40, 104
Graham, George 42
Gray, Andy 133
Gray, Eddie 164
Gray, Frankie 133
Gray, Stuart 231, 232
Greaves, Jimmy 19
Greig, John 42, 56, 69
Grobbelaar, Bruce 188

Hadji, Mustapha 227
Hamburg 78–80, 95, 119–20
Hamilton, Billy 134
Hansen, Alan 59, 76, 107, 108, 133, 138, 142, 222
Harper, Joe 36, 45, 49
Hart, Tom 17
Hateley, Mark 201
Hay, David 158
Heart of Midlothian 17, 21, 22, 50
Hedman, Magnus 222
Hendrie, John 168
Henry, Tom 23
Hewitt, John 49, 62, 77, 78, 88, 89, 90, 93–4, 121
Hibernian 7, 8, 10, 11, 15, 16–17, 18, 21, 25, 40, 47, 53, 56, 57, 73
Hoddle, Glenn 4, 185, 205, 231
Hodge, Steve 180, 182
Hoeness, Uli 82–3, 84
Hogg, Graeme 104
Holt, John 14
Houllier, Gérard 185
Hughes, Lee 228
Hughes, Mark 4, 105, 107, 111, 114, 124, 140
Hunter, Norman 164, 167

Ipswich Town 77, 101
Irwin, Denis 199
Isaias 212
ITV 187–8

Jackson, Colin 48, 156
Jackson, Mike 37
Jarvie, Drew 51, 52, 54, 76, 226
Johnstone, Derek 48
Johnstone, Jimmy 29, 31, 114
Jones, Vinnie 160, 168, 169, 170, 172, 174, 176–7
Jordan, Joe 132, 138, 194

Kachloul, Hassan 232
Kamara, Chris 172
Kanchelskis, Andrei 235
Keane, Robbie 227, 228
Keegan, Kevin 60–1, 78–9, 232
Kelly, Gary 202
Kendall, Howard 107
Kennedy, Stuart 34, 35–6, 38, 45, 51, 52, 55, 61, 64, 74, 79, 81, 87, 88, 90–1, 92, 94, 95,
118, 122, 154, 190–1, 194, 226
Kewell, Harry 202
Keys, Richard 213
Kilmarnock 157
Knox, Archie 57, 84, 89, 104, 123, 125, 212

Law, Denis 43, 104, 111, 131, 150, 161, 184

Lawrenson, Mark 159
Lech Poznan 82
Leeds United ix, 42, 132, 147, 149, 150, 160, 163–89, 193, 195, 196, 197–204, 214, 230–1
Leighton, Jim 49, 76, 79, 87, 92, 124, 140, 144
Lens 126–7
Littbarski, Pierre 143
Liverpool 11, 58–9, 74, 75, 77, 100, 107, 109, 112, 113, 125, 126, 129, 133, 151, 159, 182, 187, 188, 189, 198, 213, 216, 217, 218, 222
Lowe, Rupert 2, 3, 4, 6, 231, 238
Lukic, John 176, 177
Luton Town 186

MacAskill, Ken 12, 15, 18, 105
MacDonald, Alex 156
MacLeod, Ally 34, 35, 38, 42, 131
Mackie, George 22, 24, 32, 39
Magath, Felix 119–20
Managing My Life (Ferguson) 45, 93
Manchester United ix, 14, 18, 58, 60, 74, 98–129, 141, 146, 147, 151–2, 159–61, 163, 167, 171, 181, 183–4, 187, 188, 193, 197, 201, 202, 205, 216, 217, 230, 237
Maradona, Diego 139
Marek Dimitrov 74
Marinello, Peter 33
Marsden, Chris 233, 234
Martin, Lee 125
Match of the Day 224
Matthaus, Lothar 143
McAllister, Gary 174, 176, 177, 183, 185, 200, 203, 214, 218, 220, 227, 228
McClair, Brian 125
McCloy, Peter 47
McCoist, Ally 64, 201
McDonald, Alex 48
McDonald, John 63
McDoughall, Allan 9, 11
McFarlane, Bill 26
McGarvey, Frank 45
McGhee, Mark 49, 50, 52, 54, 56, 60, 64, 69, 70–1, 76, 77, 82, 89, 93, 94, 97, 100, 118, 155, 157, 158, 159, 197, 229
McGrain, Danny 56, 133, 150
McGrath, Paul 114, 126, 159
McGuiness, Wilf 216
McLean, Jim 29, 46, 48, 49, 66, 113
McLean, Tommy 44
McLeish, Alex 38, 49, 54, 56, 57, 63, 66, 76, 77, 83, 87, 90, 92, 94, 100, 121, 130, 133, 134, 142, 154, 155, 191
McMaster, John 38, 39–40, 74, 87, 133
McMenemy, Lawrie 3, 60–1, 114
McNeill, Billy 33, 35, 36–7, 38, 39, 40–1, 42–4, 49, 52, 56, 62, 74, 97, 132, 155, 237
McPhail, John 14
McQueen, Gordon 104, 113
McStay, Paul 147
Mee, Bertie 26
Memphis Austria 75
Miller, Alex 217, 220, 221, 223
Miller, Jean 55
Miller, Willie 36, 40, 44, 46, 49, 51, 55, 61, 65, 69, 72, 74, 76, 77, 81, 83, 85, 86–7, 88, 92, 96, 120, 121, 134, 137, 138, 142, 144, 150, 153, 191, 196
Mills, Mick 78
Milne, Ralph 127
Moldovan, Viorel 222
Moran, Kevin 109–10, 124, 125, 192
Moses, Remi 102
Muhren, Arnold 102

Narey, David 14, 66, 137, 138
Ndlovu, Peter 210, 211
Neal, Phil 206, 207, 211, 216
Newsome, Jon 188
Nicholas, Charlie 67
Nicholas, Peter 141
Nielsson, Roland 222, 226
Niemi, Antti 1, 4, 6, 234, 235, 237
Nottingham Forest 181, 183, 187

O'Hara, Alex 15
Ogrizovic, Steve 208, 212, 217, 220, 222
Olsen, Jesper 102, 105
Ormond, Willie 35
Oyen, Harold 195

Pahars, Marion 21
Paisley, Bob 58, 59, 84, 211, 216
Pallister, Gary 181, 201
Palmer, Carlton 203, 214
Payne, Graham 14, 48
Pemberton, John 203
Pendrey, Garry 223, 232
Pflugler, Hans 87
Phillip, Iain 24, 59

Pickering, Ally 211
Pitesti, Arges 78, 118
Platini, Michel 185
Porto 98
Prentice, John 19, 22, 29

Quiniou, Joel 145

Radio Tay 34
Rangers 15, 34, 36, 38, 40, 41, 42, 47, 48, 62, 63–4, 65, 66, 67, 69, 123, 129, 152, 155–7, 158, 194, 199, 200–1, 217, 234, 235
Rausch, Friedal 75
Real Madrid 67, 72, 88–9, 91, 92, 94, 95, 109
Reaney, Paul 167
Redknapp. Harry 231
Reid, Peter 109, 110
Rennie, David 211
Revie, Don ix, 132, 164, 167, 168, 184
Rice, Pat 211
Richards, Dean 232
Richardson, Bryan 206, 213, 214, 215, 216, 222, 228, 229, 231
Richardson, Kevin 207, 210
Ritchie, Steve 36
Robertson, Hugh 33, 151
Robertson, John 133
Robins, Mark 125
Robinson, Bobby 22
Robinson, Geoffrey 214–15
Robinson, Paul 202
Robson, Bryan 102, 105, 108, 112, 113, 114, 115, 116, 144, 184, 196, 210
Robson, Sir Bobby 77, 101, 144, 230
Rocastle, David 198, 202
Rooney, Wayne 179
Rough, Alan 138
Rougvie, Doug 48, 63, 80, 92–3, 118–19, 153–4, 157, 159
Roxburgh, Andy 6, 146, 147, 148, 149, 150
Rummenigge, Karl Heinz 83, 85, 88
Rush, Ian 140, 189

Scanlon, Ian 36, 38, 52, 54, 151
Schmeichel, Peter 181
Scotland *see also* World Cup *and* European Championships 14, 30, 56, 117, 130–50
Scott, Jocky 27
Scott, Lesley 25, 32
Scott, Ron 26, 133
Scott, Teddy 38–9, 46, 119
Scottish Cup:
  1969/70 17
  1977/8 40–1, 48, 49
  1980/81 62–4
  1982/83 66–7, 70, 121
  1983/84 158
Scottish Football Association (SFA) 11, 35, 158
Scottish Football Writers' Player of the Year 131
Scottish League Cup:
  1978/9 47–51, 53
  1982/3 65–6
Scottish Premier League (SPL)
  1975/6 25–8
  1977/8 30–1, 32–41
  1978/9 42–7
  1979/80 50–6, 152–5
  1980/1 57–64
  1981/2 65
  1982/3 65–6, 70
Sealey, Les 183
Shankley, Bill 11, 75, 211, 216
Sharpe, Lee 125
Sheffield United 172, 174, 176, 188
Sheffield Wednesday ix, 112, 128–9, 163, 164, 166, 181, 185, 215
Sheilds, Lex 7
Sheridan, John 170
Sheringham, Teddy 194
Shirra, Jim 33
Shutt, Carl 165, 200
Silver, Leslie 164, 189
Silverknowes primary school 9
Simpson, Neil 49, 82, 87, 90, 154–5, 157
Sky TV 182–3, 186, 224
Smith, Alan 202
Smith, Walter 46, 144, 201
Somerville, Alex 18
Souness, Graeme 76, 77, 107, 129, 133, 134, 138, 140, 144, 145, 148, 150, 194
Southall, Neville 110–11, 140
Southampton 1–2, 3, 4, 5, 42, 60–1, 128, 152, 180, 181, 213, 223, 224, 231–8
Speed, Gary 173, 177, 179, 182, 186, 188
St Mirren 45, 47, 49, 53, 61, 62, 69, 124
Stanton, Pat 46, 56, 57, 75, 120
Stapleton, Frank 102–3, 105–6, 107, 108, 110, 113, 114, 124, 128
Stark, Billy 69

Stein, Jock 35, 42, 43, 59, 91, 123, 132, 133, 134, 135, 136, 137, 140, 141–2
Sterland, Mel 168, 182, 184
Steven, Trevor 126
Stewart, George 22, 33
Stewart, Rod x, 137–8
Stielike, Ulrich 91
Strachan, Catherine (mother) 7, 8, 16, 56
Strachan, Craig (son) 62, 101
Strachan, Gavin (son) 50, 56, 101, 227–8, 229
Strachan, Gemma (daughter) 111
Strachan, Jim (father) 7, 8, 16, 18, 56
Strachan, Laura (sister) 8
Strachan, Lesley (wife) 2, 5, 29, 38, 41, 50, 56, 62, 101, 111, 121–2, 146, 154, 157, 173, 189, 225, 228, 229, 232, 236, 237, 238
Stuart, Alex 35
Sullivan, Dom 34, 38
Sunday Standard 85–6
Sutton, Alan 173
Svensson, Andres 235
Swan, Harry 73

Taylor, Graham 211
Taylor, Peter 211
Thatcher, Margaret 89, 133
Thomas, Mickey 141
Thys, Guy 139
Todd, Willie 44, 47
Tottenham Hotspur 19, 57, 59, 219
Trappatoni, Giovanni 132, 162
Turnball, Eddie 17

UEFA 5, 72–3, 74, 75–7, 177, 200
UEFA Cup:
  1979/80 74–7
  1980/1 118
  1985/6 106, 112–13
Ure, Ian 19
Uruguay 142, 144–5

Valentine, Bob 158, 159
Varadi, Imre 172, 195
Voeller, Rudi 143, 144
Vogts, Bertie 143

Waddle, Chris 204
Wales 140–1
Walker, Jack 85–6, 88, 95
Wallace, Gordon 21, 23, 24, 26, 33
Wallace, Jock 36, 40, 42, 156
Wallace, Ray 180
Wallace, Rod 180, 182, 183, 185, 186, 188
Walsh, Paul 108
Walters, Mark 189
Wark, John 77, 78, 133
Waterschei 88
Watson, Andy 54, 79
Webster, Jack 55, 73
Weir, Peter 61, 67, 70, 78, 82, 89, 93, 118, 133
Welsh, Irvine 10, 17
Wenger, Arsène 58, 91, 162, 211
West Germany 142, 144
West Ham United 60, 106, 148, 174, 186, 187
Whelan, Noel 203, 217
White, Davie 23, 24, 27, 28, 29
Whiteside, Norman 107, 110–11, 114, 115, 126, 159
Whyte, Chris 176, 177, 185, 201
Wilkins, Ray 15, 144, 194, 204
Wilkinson, Howard ix–x, 160, 163–8, 170, 171, 173, 175, 176, 177, 178, 179, 180, 181, 182, 183, 184–9, 196, 198, 199, 201, 202, 203, 204
Williams, Paul 210, 232
Willis, Peter 110
Wimbledon 180
Woodgate, Jonathan 202
World Cup:
  1958 90
  1974 131
  1978 35, 131–2
  1982 64, 65, 130, 134–9
  1986 14, 114, 122–3, 139–47
  1990 147

Zola, Gianfranco 222